Prisoners of Culture

A volume in the series
Communications, Media, and Culture
George F. Custen, series editor

Prisoners of Culture

Representing the Vietnam POW

Elliott Gruner

Rutgers University Press
New Brunswick, New Jersey

The views expressed in this book are those of the author and do not reflect the official policy or position of the Department of Defense or the U.S. Government.

Library of Congress Cataloging-in-Publication Data

Gruner, E. G. (Elliott G.)
    Prisoners of culture : representing the Vietnam POW / by E. G. Gruner.
        p.   cm. — (Communications, media, and culture)
    Includes bibliographical references and index.
    ISBN 0-8135-1930-6 (cloth) — ISBN 0-8135-1931-4 (pbk.)
    1. Vietnamese Conflict, 1961–1975, in mass media—United States.
    2. Prisoners of war in mass media—United States.   3. Prisoners of
    war—United States.   4. Prisoners of war—Vietnam.   I. Title.
    II. Series.
    P96.V46G78   1993
    303.6'6—dc20   92-30903
                                                                              CIP

British Cataloging-in-Publication information available

Contents

Illustrations

Acknowledgments

This book would have been impossible without the help of a few key people. First, I want to thank Colonel Peter L. Stromberg for giving me the opportunity to change my life. His subtle encouragement made it all possible. Second, I must thank my friends at the University of Washington. I would never have been able to do such work without the help of the faculty at that wonderful place. In particular I would like to thank John Griffith, Susan Jeffords, Paul Brass, and Evan Watkins for their thoughtful counsel. I also want to mention two people who may be unaware of their influence: Carolyn Allen and Ross Posnock. Their teaching and quiet example continue to be an inspiration. I have to thank H. Bruce Franklin for his help in publishing this book. His support provided a catalyst for my efforts. Finally, I must thank Leslie Mitchner for her patient, attentive editing.

Many have helped me access debates and materials on the POW issue. Among them are John Baky, who has collected an excellent archive of Vietnam War reference material at Lasalle; Eric Sundquist, who provided key commentary at a crucial stage in my writing; Jean-Jacques Malo, who answered all of my questions concerning Vietnam films; and John S. Lawrence, who encouraged and illuminated various aspects of my work late in the process.

At this point, it would be customary to thank my wife or mention my children and their help in and/or tolerance of my writing. They certainly deserve such praise, but they also played an even more important role: the joy in their lives has made the sheer lunacy of the POW drama quite obvious. They, more than anyone else, have made me certain that we must do without the superstructures of honor and glory I have found so often in my work on this book. They convince me that we can find hope in the humanity all around us rather than in the mythologies that destroy us.

I would be remiss not to mention my students at West Point. It is, after all, some of them who are likely to be our next POW heroes. It is to them and such dubious futures that I dedicate this book.

Prisoners of Culture

Introduction

It would be hard to look back to the Vietnam War and how we have come to know that war without taking into account the image of the American POW. We can find this image just about anywhere we might look: in magazine advertisements, news stories, movies, books, and video games, on flags, T-shirts, television, and audio tapes. When the television image of Navy Lieutenant Jeffrey Zaun and his fellow captives in Iraq appeared in American living rooms in January of 1991, the news media jumped to the phones looking for someone to explain what was going on. The Vietnam POW returned to our television screens to explain what it all meant.

But what does it mean to be a POW? When Americans think of the POW do they remember the autobiographical accounts of James Stockdale, Fred Cherry, or John Dramesi? Do they see a handsome Colonel Hogan facing a bumbling Colonel Klink in "Hogan's Heroes"? Do they see John Rambo tied to an electrified bed frame telling the Russians nothing they want to know in *Rambo: First Blood Part II*? Do they see Robert DeNiro sweating in the barbed wire river cage under that filthy hut in *The Deer Hunter*? Or do they see Monika Schwinn wasting away in the Hoa Lo Prison? This book is about how we make sense of competing images in American culture. More specifically, it is about how America has come to know the POW.

Malcolm Cowley advised that "the first of [the critic's] functions is to select works of art . . . that are new, not much discussed, or widely misunderstood." If we accept this as a valid starting point for the critic, then perhaps no collection of texts is more appropriate for my examination than the ensemble of representations surrounding the

American POW experience of the Vietnam War. These texts are "new" not only in the sense that new texts emerge almost daily, but also in the sense that existing texts remain wholly unexamined. What's more, these texts are, to my mind, "widely misunderstood": few critics have taken the time to examine them. Yet, as I look out into my classroom at West Point, I see young men and women who find heroes in these same texts.

The POW is a persistent image in America. This book attempts to capture the sense we make of one type of lived experience in the context of American culture. I attempt to follow one subject through an array of representations by providing readings that show how a lived experience has become part of American consciousness. I hop from autobiography to television and from film to magazine ad in much the same way I might surf the channels on television. I do this to study the "totality of this process of production, signification, and consumption" in our society.[1] In doing this I hope to answer both the theoretical and practical questions that surround the image of captivity in 1992. I seek to write a "history of the present" that will explain the productions of our experience.

In *Prisoners of Culture* I will describe how the language of news, autobiography, film, and advertising makes or unmakes the POW experience. This study is also very much about how the language of magazine advertising or popular film appropriates lived experience. It is about the authority these languages have in the context of American culture. I begin by discussing the image of the POW before and during the Vietnam War. This introduction and chapter 1 explain how and why the POW gained consistent public attention during the sixties and seventies. Chapter 2 describes the POW myth and attempts to show how closely Vietnam POW stories mirror earlier captivity stories that date back to the Indian captivity narratives of Puritan America. In chapters 3, 4, and 5 I give examples of how the language of autobiography, film, and advertising address the POW experience. These chapters reach beyond the problematic facticity of experience and concentrate on the "fabulative character" of the text. In doing this I hope to leave the POW story open to negotiation so we might learn from POW discourse without being drawn into its essential rhetoric.[2] Chapter 6 shows how the POWs reconcile their precaptivity expectations with their actual prison experience. In chapters 7, 8, and 9 I discuss how assumptions about gender and culture have become part of the POW story. In these chapters I read some of the marginalized stories to make clear how particular understandings and versions of the POW experience differ. These chapters attempt to show how myth deals with difference and excludes troubling but important aspects of experience. Chapter 10 examines the belief systems found in POW narratives and their relation to POW mythology. Chapter 11 outlines some of the consequences of POW myth. My final chapter discusses how the image of the Vietnam POW informed the POW experiences of the Gulf War.

I seek to break up what I see as a monologue, a dominant myth of the POW experience in American culture. I want to show the polyphony that lurks beneath the surface of popular culture. I juxtapose the representations and productions to make their contradictions visible and to soften the hard objective truths that feed POW myth. I do this not so much to oppose the texts but to embrace the differences. I want to show that the array of representations I examine has rehistoricized the American POW experience in ways that channel us into certain roles and patterns of action.

It may seem that I would like to exclude the POW experience from popular culture, or to privilege certain forms of representation over others. This is, however, exactly the kind of cannonization or silence that I would reject. Instead, I would have us look at a broader range of experiences and ideas in order to make visible the assumptions behind the representations themselves. The POW story seems to hide out in the self-confirming authority of autobiography or late-night paid TV programming. Such presentations, if taken by themselves, leave us with the deceptive, simplistic closure of narrative rather than the more complex implications of human experience. The challenge is to engage all the stories. Such an approach makes both the contradictions and the convergences of the POW story obvious.

A misconception I must head off at this point is the notion that I am somehow critiquing the POW him- or herself. I want to make it clear that I am concerned with public texts and images. Nowhere in this study do I reach for transcripts of official and still classified interviews conducted by either side. More important, I am not dismissing the painful experiences these people suffered. On the contrary, by examining these texts I hope to move the negotiation of this history from emotional appeal to the realm of examined knowledge.

═══════════════

James Bond Stockdale, one of the few surviving POWs to receive the Congressional Medal of Honor and the coauthor of a POW chronicle entitled *In Love and War,* wrote the foreword to John McGrath's account of his POW experience. Stockdale reminds us that war was different for the POW.

> For Americans who became POWs in North Vietnam, capture meant not that they had been neutralized on the war's sidelines, but that for them a different kind of war had begun—the war of propaganda. The enemy admitted to us that propaganda was their main weapon against the United States. The POWs were to have top billing in that theatrical production.[3]

Stockdale implies that the "theatrical production" ended when the POWs returned to the United States. But it is just at that point, when the POWs returned to America, that the "theatrical production" really began. The former POWs became all manner of performers in the play of popular culture. They were featured in endless popular articles, wrote their own autobiographies, and collaborated with other writers to record events that had eluded the camera eye of America's "television war."

Their notoriety would not fade as it had for prisoners of previous wars, however. The POWs truly received "top billing"; they were instantly famous. Many used that fame to help rebuild their lives after captivity by seeking political office, pursuing business opportunities, or continuing their military careers. The POWs became icons on the cultural landscape, endorsing products in magazine advertisements, appearing on television self-help programs, and providing the stuff of major motion pictures.

A year before the North Vietnamese captured their first American soldier, Albert Biderman attempted to deal with the captivity experience of the Korean War in his study, *March to Calumny*. Biderman attempted to reach beyond the empirical conclusions of psychosocial analysis to examine how the Korean War experience appeared in American culture, "to say that the major reflections on the soundness of American institutions and character reside not so much in the behavior of the POWs as in the reaction of officials, press, and much of the public to the prisoner-of-war story." Biderman summed up reactions to the POW experience of the Korean War as "an overreadiness to damn one's compatriots and one's own institutions, a victimization by a Communist-fostered propaganda version of events, and an instance of the difficulty in gaining public attention for responsible, scholarly studies of public issues in competition with sensationalistic and tendentious portrayals."4 The "sensationalistic and tendentious portrayals" Biderman refers to made the Korean POW infamous. Biderman concluded that the Korean POW was a double victim—of harsh imprisonment abroad and undeserved ridicule at home: "The prisoners became the subject of another type of propaganda—propaganda by Americans, about Americans, directed to Americans."

The American POW story of the Vietnam War, however, became the obverse of its predecessor. The POWs became instant heroes. They went on extensive speaking tours; they were instant authorities on religion, culture, politics, leadership, marriage, and the self. The POW "theater" actually happened not in Vietnam, but in the United States. It was almost as if Americans had consciously wrested the POW image from the North Vietnamese and put the theater in motion themselves to show how it really should be done.

This book is not intended as a historical comparison of POW experiences or representations so much as one reading of how these representations come to populate our televisions, movie screens, and supermarket checkout stands. It is the story of how a lived experience moves through our culture.

Finally, I must confess an omission in my work that troubles me. I have, for what I keep telling myself are a number of good reasons, consciously ignored the overwhelming majority of the captivity experiences of the Vietnam War. This study, however completely it may address American narratives of the war, does little or nothing to tell the story of the majority of the POWs of the Vietnam War: the Viet-namese themselves. The enduring hostile relations between Vietnam and the United States prohibited much credible research in this area. I cannot fail to point out the irony of my dilemma: the barriers to my research exist primarily as a result of the issue under discussion. My study might appear, although unintentionally, to divert our attention from examining accounts of the "tiger cages" on Con Son Island in South Vietnam or the Vietnamese interned in hundreds of nameless reeducation centers, the Vietnamese gulag. That part of the story remains to be told. The rest of the story about the POW myth in American culture involves the lore surrounding those missing in ac-tion, the MIA, whom H. Bruce Franklin has studied in his *M.I.A. or Mythmaking in America.*

This book may cut deep into old wounds opened many times during the past twenty years. But I think the reincision and pain are necessary in the context of what we see and hear today. I don't think that we want the armed-avenger image of John Rambo to take the place of a more informed sense of memory. I want to expand the possibilities and choices Americans have for dealing with a very difficult period in their history. This study explores the "theatrical production" that has kept the POW experiences of the Vietnam War actively in the minds of Americans. I examine the texts of American culture to find out what happened to some of the few recognized heroes of the Vietnam War. I want to examine closely the authority we claim for them. How did the story get told, who told it, and what does all this say about American culture? Have we taken lived experiences and learned from them, or are we more interested in entertaining ourselves with myths?

1
A History of the POW Image

When the North Vietnamese released a French POW in 1964, ten years after the end of the war between France and the North, few Americans took any notice. The *Newsweek* cameo that mentioned the event called Yves Le Bray "Fortune's Scapegoat." The plight of the captured Frenchman seemed remote from anything an American might endure.

The North Vietnamese captured Le Bray in December 1953. Unlike most French POWs, however, Le Bray remained in North Vietnam after his fellow POWs went home in 1954. The French authorities had lost any trace of him. In May 1954 the French added his name to a memorial in his hometown. According to *Newsweek*, Le Bray was held in a labor camp near the Chinese border: a forgotten MIA. Contrary to what we might expect today, no one was waiting for Le Bray when he arrived back in France. However authentic Le Bray's MIA experience might have been, stories of living MIAs would eventually become a staple of American lore.

If Le Bray had been an American POW and returned to America ten years after the fall of Saigon, he would have had a different reception. His arrival would have coincided with the release of POW/MIA films like *Uncommon Valor* (1983) and *Rambo: First Blood Part II* (1985). His appearance would have sparked a groundswell of popular concern that would dwarf the front-page stories sparked by the bogus photos of American MIAs circulated in the American press as late as August 1991, or a number of more recent stories concerning Soviet interrogations of American POWs in the former Soviet Union.

If you subscribe to conspiracy theories surrounding the MIA issue, an American Le Bray would have been secreted back to the United States and detained until he signed some nondisclosure agreement similar to POW come-home-lately stories played out in films like *Welcome Home* (1989) or *The Forgotten* (1989).

But in 1964 Americans barely noticed Le Bray. He wandered off the newswire into obscurity. Such stories from the French experience would eventually fuel MIA speculation in America, but this early in the war he seemed an oddity, a scapegoat of fortune. No one seemed to think much more of the whole affair. Certainly America could not, at that time, see much interesting in the homecoming of some missing POW ten years after a lost war.

Americans had no stomach for such things in January of 1965. In fact, many Americans were just tuning in to "Hogan's Heroes." The images of the well-fed, forever joking, imminently free clan of Allied POWs of World War II made America happy. Seeing those ingenious good guys constantly outwit the bumbling, almost harmless evil of their Nazi captors was infinitely comforting. The face of captivity seemed to be a handsome Bob Crane always ready with a new scheme to foil whatever the Germans had planned. The face of the enemy was either the hopelessly incompetent Klink or the blameless Sergeant Schultz.

When Le Bray's story appeared in *Newsweek* and "Hogan's Heroes" first aired, Everett Alvarez, the first American POW held in North Vietnam, had already endured four months of captivity. It would be years before the American media featured the POW story. It would take even longer for the POW issue to become a major, if not the major, issue between North Vietnam and the United States. It would take yet another decade for the POW to become an icon of American film and media during the Vietnam Renaissance of the eighties.

In 1965 the American public was content to watch "Hogan's Heroes," or perhaps alternately *The Great Escape* (1963), both fictions that recovered the POW experience of World War II in some sensible and comforting way. No one wanted to remember much about the Korean war, at least for entertainment.

A year before the first Americans became captives in Vietnam, *The Great Escape* became one of the "ten best" movies in America. Al-

A prisoner is shot while trying to escape in *The Great Escape*. POW films have continued to romanticize the escape theme despite the escape record of real POWs in Korea, Vietnam, and the Gulf War. *Courtesy of the Museum of Modern Art/Film Stills Archive.* (1963, United Artists)

though it is not surprising to find escape themes in heroic lore, it is interesting to highlight here what the movie leaves as a footnote: the actual "Great Escape" of seventy-six Allied POWs resulted in tragedy. Seventy-three POWs were recaptured. Fifty of these were executed. The escape did little or nothing to harm the German war effort. The escape set three prisoners free at the cost of fifty lives and harsher conditions for thousands of remaining POWs. The escape was not so "great" after all. But it was infinitely more satisfying to watch the intrepid heroes in the movie than to face the realities of the POW experience in books from the Korean War like *March to Calumny, In Every War But One,* and *The Captives of Korea.*

The popular success of *The Great Escape* spawned a host of clones that romanced the escape motif of World War II lore instead and in spite of the POW experience of the Korean War, where there were no escapes, and where almost 40 percent of Americans captured died in captivity.¹ Of course, this high mortality rate compared somewhat favorably to the 63 percent mortality rate of soldiers involved in the "great escape." But no one was counting then.

The POW experience of the Korean War came closest to foreshadowing the POW experience of Vietnam. The images from the Korean POW experience were troubling, however. America had treated its last group of POWs with an understanding double standard. Although Americans rejected prosecutions of misconduct among POWs, they nevertheless accepted that the Korean POW had somehow "caved in" during captivity. And although most observers agreed that the overarching lesson from the Korean and World War II POW experience seemed to be that no individual could ever be sure of resisting interrogations, President Dwight D. Eisenhower saw fit to institute a Code of Conduct for the Armed Forces to ensure that POWs made just this impossible commitment.

One of the few texts that attempt to recover the POW experience of the Korean War is a film called *Prisoner of War* (1954), starring none other than Ronald Reagan. This film attempts to provide some explanation for the "failure" of American POWs of the Korean War. The moral of the film is that it would be wrong to judge the actions of a POW, however complicit with the enemy he may appear.

In *Prisoner of War,* the protagonist, Web Sloane (Ronald Reagan), cooperates with the enemy and eventually refuses repatriation. He appears to be a collaborator; unbeknownst to his fellow POWs, however, he parachuted into North Korea and became a POW on purpose. He is an intelligence agent specifically assigned to report on conditions in the POW camps.

This was the extent to which Hollywood and America would go in 1954 to explain the failed performance of Americans in captivity. A decade later American POWs in North Vietnam could not figure out how their captors got some screwy idea about Americans deliberately entering captivity to spy on the enemy. Larry Guarino, a POW held in North Vietnam for eight years, remembers an episode when his interrogator alleged that he was "an intelligence officer" sent "to spy" on the North Vietnamese. Guarino was dumbfounded by such a prepos-

Paul Newman plays a Korean War officer, Captain Edward Hall, convicted of misconduct as a POW in *The Rack*. Korean War POWs were roundly accused of "caving in" during captivity. Public images of the Korean POW played heavily on this theme. *Courtesy of the Museum of Modern Art/Film Stills Archive.* (1956, MGM)

terous claim: "It was an incredible accusation, I jumped up, too: 'Are you serious? Could you actually think that I flew up here and bailed out of a multimillion-dollar airplane just to check on what you guys are doing? Really!' "[2] Apparently Guarino hadn't seen *First Yank into Tokyo* (1945), *Prisoner of War,* or *The Bamboo Prison* (1954), all of which tried to sell just such a scenario to Americans who desperately needed heroes in POW camps otherwise populated by "collaborators" and the dead. Ronald Reagan himself testified to the "documentary accuracy" of his starring role in *Prisoners of War.*[3]

Few wanted to see *Prisoner of War,* however. The story of the Korean POW was not what America needed. Despite lavish promotion, the film failed miserably at the box office. It failed for many of the same reasons that representations of the Vietnam War would fail to capture audiences in the 1970s: no one wanted a reminder of recent experience—especially failure. It was fine to examine and even entertain with an experience from World War II, à war that had clear winners and losers. Experiences in Korea and Vietnam provided no such comforting conclusions.

In 1965 little had changed regarding popular perception of the Korean POW. World War II films and "Hogan's Heroes" implied that resistance was probable, if not easy, in captivity. It is no coincidence that the underlying assumption of *Prisoner of War* is played out for comedy in the television sitcom: the POW is such a hero that, although able to escape, he remains in captivity to dupe his captors and continue the war effort from the very site of captivity. Such is the dream of military doctrine: the POW who continues to fight for his country even after capture, to be, as one biography title openly declares, the *Prisoner at War. Prisoner of War,* like the more popular "Hogan's Heroes" and *The Great Escape,* shares and makes plausible such dreams.

But the reality of the Korean War was, unfortunately for the studios and mythmakers, quite different. There were no great escapes. POWs at established camps found it impossible to attempt escape, let alone work some subterfuge against their captors to aid the American war effort. The *Pueblo* incident in 1968 forced Americans to face the reality of the Korean POWs. The *Pueblo* crew suffered a debilitating and divisive experience. Their release was a humiliation: they were a humiliation. They had disappointed Americans against the backdrop of phantasms from Web Sloane (Ronald Reagan) to Colonel Hogan (Bob Crane). The *Pueblo* experience, like countless captivity experiences before, should have put the myths to rest. But the dream of resistance that motivated Eisenhower to write the Code of Conduct and fueled fantastic expectations would not die. Rambo grew from

In *The Bamboo Prison* Sergeant Bill Rand (Robert Francis) appears to be one of many collaborators in a Korean POW camp, but his friends know he is really an intelligence agent posing as a turncoat to spy on the North Koreans. North Vietnamese interrogators suggested such a scenario to American POWs in Vietnam: American POWs saw this claim, which had been played out in at least three American feature films, as another sign of their captors' peculiar Vietnamese imagination. *Courtesy of the Museum of Modern Art/Film Stills Archive.* (1954, Columbia)

these resistance and escape themes, which had occurred in earlier POW films.

In the 1960s, America had no Rambos. But there was a small group of soldier-heroes carefully presented to and recognized by the American public. They were the POWs of the Vietnam War, who became the focus of American peace efforts. Their plight proved to be one of the few issues that might solidify American sentiment about the Vietnam War. It was the political appeal of the American POWs, not their inner strength of character, not their triumphant resistance, not any debt owed to them for their immense suffering, that made them heroes. They became the focus of a political administration that struggled for some scrap of credibility. Their plight had a metonymic quality: their suffering stood for the suffering of a nation through an uncertain war guided by unreliable and frustrating forces Americans did not understand. In contrast, the POW problem was simple: get them back!

The returning POWs came to represent the United States emerging from the darkness of struggle and uncertainty. When Americans watched the returning POWs walk off sleek military aircraft at air bases all over the country, the nation saw itself emerging from a nightmare. The lavish public honors accorded the POWs in 1973 enabled American culture to reassert its boundaries: by welcoming the POWs home the country signaled the limit of its commitment to South Vietnam. America joined a lying President Nixon to welcome home and knight the surviving POWs as the "threshold bearers"[4] of America, the few who might be accepted as heroes.

The Vietnam POWs received more attention than any previous American POWs. This is remarkable not only in the sense that the experience as a whole seems to persist as a subject of representation, but in terms of scale. There were fewer than 800 American POWs in the Vietnam War. The number of Americans captured during the Korean War was 7,140; there were 130,201 during World War II; 4,120 during World War I; and over 400,000 American prisoners from both sides during the American Civil War. Although each captivity had received some attention, no previous POW experience was so persistently represented in the United States. From a number of perspectives, it is remarkable that the Vietnam POWs received such disproportionate attention.

———

D espite their later fame and the popularity of the World War II POW image, Vietnam POWs were not front-page news during the early years of the war. From 1964 until early 1968 it was difficult for POW wives and supporters to interest the news media at all. The public was most interested in escapes. A few intrepid soldiers like Dieter Dengler, Walter Eckes, James Dodson, and Nick Rowe were able to escape from jungle camps in Laos and South Vietnam. Their stories made the papers; they could catch a headline in a society that was watching movies like *The Bridge on the River Kwai* (1957), *The Great Escape* (1963), *The McKenzie Break* (1970), *Von Ryan's Express* (1965), *The Secret War of Harry Frigg* (1968), or *Stalag 17* (1953). But the other POWs, the ones still in captivity, rarely sparked national interest. The only people who could seem to make the media respond were the North Vietnamese.

The former POWs testify to their captors' attempts, beginning in 1965, to use their predicament for media attention. POWs were routinely asked, then coerced, tortured, and blackmailed into writing autobiographical statements, making fictitious audio tapes, and cooperating with foreign visitors for photo and film opportunities. These efforts eventually produced some dubious but nevertheless widely publicized images. The first and most widely covered event of the POW experience was the "Hanoi March," during which many POWs were forced to march through the streets of Hanoi. Their route was lined with angry North Vietnamese citizens who jeered and physically abused the Americans. The North Vietnamese released the film of this sordid affair to the world press. They captioned the film with the threat of criminal trials for POWs in Hanoi.[5] Although this event seemed to backfire for the North Vietnamese politically, it made one positive point to them: the government in Hanoi could capture the attention of the American press. Other propaganda proved successful in this small way and, at least in part, fueled North Vietnamese efforts to extract material for such events from their helpless captives.

A little over a year later the North Vietnamese paraded another POW, Lieutenant Commander Richard Stratton, before a group of visiting journalists. In this widely publicized sequence Stratton walked through a curtain and mechanically bowed to his captors. This unusual act by the tall and serious American naval officer prompted *Newsweek* to begin its story, "It seemed like Korea all over again," implying that America would experience yet another painful cycle of POW failures. It made little difference whether Stratton had been coerced: if he had been "brainwashed," he had "broken"—if he had collaborated willingly, he was a traitor. Both possibilities played the same way on the screen: another failure for the American character. Stratton survived the remainder of captivity in the shadow of his public appearance.

Saying that it was like Korea all over again did nothing to explain what might be happening to the POWs. Americans knew little about the Korean POW experience. Stratton's wife, Dorothy, certainly had no idea. By her own account she had no conception of the poor treatment and torture her husband may have been subjected to. She had little to go on besides what she might have seen in movies or gleaned from captivity lore in the military community. It was almost three years before Dorothy Stratton realized that her husband had been tortured and starved into making appearances like the one covered by *Newsweek*. She finally learned the truth when Douglas Hegdahl, one of Stratton's cellmates, was released in August 1970. Dorothy Stratton talked to Hegdahl and learned that her husband had been systematically tortured while she had waited at home hoping for the best. After talking to Hegdahl, her world changed. She had been deceived by what the American imagination had offered her.[6]

Dorothy Stratton's plight was not unusual. Her vocabulary did not include the things that Douglas Hegdahl had told her. Nothing she had seen could tell her about the Korean War experience, and nothing the American press or the American government released prior to Hegdahl's talk would add much more.

The POW story remained minor news unless the North Vietnamese made it otherwise. This changed in 1968 when Sybil Stockdale began to question the status quo. According to her own account, she had worked hard to support the government's secretive policy regarding the POWs. She collaborated with intelligence officials who wanted to communicate with her husband in a clandestine code. Such dangerous liaisons were necessary to get at the truth concerning POW treatment in Hanoi. The code worked, but the confirmation of POW torture in Hanoi that she and her husband had worked so hard to reveal was not released. Such information could only have embarrassed the Johnson administration, making the lame-duck President seem even more impotent, unable as he was with all of America's military might to keep a few good Americans from being tortured in North Vietnam. Disclosure could only have increased the pressure on the crumbling Democratic administration. Frustrated with the government and the press, Sybil Stockdale began to tell her own story.

Unlike Dorothy Stratton, Stockdale had a good idea of what might be happening to her husband in the summer of 1968. By her own account, "Long into the endless hot, humid sleepless nights, I pored over *The Prisoners of Korea* [sic], *The Road to Calumny* [sic], *In Every War But One, In the Presence of Mine Enemies,* and many more books and articles of a similar nature."[7] From these books, she learned about the harrowing experiences of Korean War POWs. She could not have missed Albert Biderman's sobering conclusions about how American "propaganda" had given those POWs an overwhelmingly negative image.[8] Stockdale knew what she had to do. She was determined to make the Vietnam POWs' image the obverse of its predecessor.

She helped found an organization for wives and families of POWs and MIAs of the Vietnam War: the National League of Families of American Prisoners and Missing in Southeast Asia.[9] According to Stockdale, the issue of POW treatment did not receive adequate recognition until the grass-roots campaign organized by the National League of Families took hold. The League would eventually play a crucial role in making the POW issue a national concern.

When, in January 1968, the North Vietnamese captured the *Pueblo* and its crew, the action itself attracted unprecedented media attention. Although it might have seemed that such publicity would encourage the League, quite the opposite was the case. To Stockdale, "the tremendous amount of attention the incident received in the press doubled my frustration and agony over our guidelines for silence about our men in North Vietnam."[10] The wife of the *Pueblo*'s Captain Bucher publicly admonished the U.S. government for its handling of the incident. Although this infuriated Vietnam POW wives, it seemed to show the League what was possible. The wives ostracized Mrs. Bucher for her apparent lack of loyalty but nevertheless moved their own campaign further toward the radically vocal stance she had taken.

Throughout 1968 Stockdale attempted to find someone willing and able to move on the POW issue. At one point she wore a "hidden tape recorder" to a meeting with government officials.[11] She had to figure out how to get the administration moving. The summer of

1968 was a turning point for the Vietnam POW image-making process. On 20 July 1968, Stockdale began a letter campaign to her "friends" in the League. In the letter she asked them "to write their elected representatives requesting that everything possible be done to effect humane treatment to all prisoners in Hanoi."[12]

After writing to a variety of senior officials in the Johnson administration and receiving unencouraging responses, Stockdale went public. On 27 October 1968, the *San Diego Union Tribune* published her story on what the Defense Department knew. This move was strategic: the 1968 presidential election was only days away. As Stockdale watched the election returns, she clung to the hope that Richard Nixon would transform the government's position on the POW issue.

But she could not rest on idle confidence. Determined to solicit help directly from the President-elect, Stockdale tried to get in touch with her governor in California, who would soon attend the 1968 governors' conferences hosted by the President-elect.

At first she was unsuccessful, but her persistence paid off. She "was puzzled and fascinated by the marvelous resonance of the masculine voice asking to speak to Mrs. Stockdale," when she answered the phone one evening.[13] Ronald Reagan made a deep impression on Mrs. Stockdale. He promised to bring the issue to the attention of President-elect Nixon. If we accept Michael Rogin's compelling conclusions about the convergences between Reagan's political life and his film roles, Reagan felt intimately connected with the POW experience because he had seen himself as a POW on the screen. His activism and assumptions sprang from his behind-the-lines movie roles in *Desperate Journey* (1942) and *Prisoner of War* (1953). But however Reagan might have felt, he made a limited impression on Nixon. It wasn't until 19 May 1969 that Secretary of Defense Melvin Laird publicly charged the North Vietnamese with mistreating American POWs.

A month later *Look* magazine invited Sybil Stockdale for an interview. The meeting prompted Stockdale to expand her organization. In Stockdale's own words, "Never was a national organization launched more efficiently."[14] Popular support for the organization and the POW issue grew quickly.

When Stockdale approached the *New York Times*, hoping for publicity, an assistant editor, not wanting to be used, intelligently asked "if somehow the government were responsible" for the organization. Stockdale vehemently denied that it was.[15] To her, the League of Families was working against government inertia and forcing the new revelations about POW mistreatment. However, the administration aired its concerns about the issue just when American war crimes began to receive national attention. The League of Families became a political tool. Administration disclosures were politically strategic: satisfied groups like Stockdale's justified a hard line in what was left of the war and invited scrutiny of the North Vietnamese instead of the U.S. war effort. The release of three American POWs (including Navy Seaman Douglas Hegdahl, who had talked to Dorothy Stratton) on 3 August 1969, only provided the occasion to implement a new policy dedicated to making the Vietnam POWs national heroes.[16] Support for the POWs was now one of the central issues of the Vietnam War.

After 1969 the POW issue was absolutely essential to any discussion about the Vietnam War at the national level. President Nixon continually referred to the issue in interviews and at press conferences. National news media followed the POW issue with increasing interest. The POWs began their rise to hero status in the eyes of the public. In the age of the astronaut, here were potential astronauts and other military leaders being held hostage, robbing America of people with "the right stuff." The POWs were victims, brutally mistreated by an inimical Asian enemy. The humanitarian dimension of the issue could erase partisan divisions in the Congress (although radicals like Jane Fonda and Tom Hayden resisted allegations that the POWs were mistreated). Publicity about POW mistreatment in North Vietnam eclipsed alleged war crimes perpetrated by American soldiers in South Vietnam. Evil versus evil was not a satisfying plot for Americans.[17]

The POW was a powerful symbol, one that could prove that the North Vietnamese were sadistic and evil, deserving of the renewed military campaigns Nixon supported, of which the most prominent examples were incursions into Laos and Cambodia and the bombing and mining of Hanoi and Haiphong. The POWs were physically and emotionally appealing evidence that the War in Vietnam was justified. Their image became critical as a pretext for forcing a peace. Their cause became a source of agreement for a divided America.

In the summer of 1970 President Nixon sanctioned the operation that would become known as the Son Tay raid. A task force of special operations soldiers executed this rather small-scale (by Vietnam standards) yet extremely significant military operation on 20 November 1970. For the POW/MIA support movement, the raid proved that the administration was finally actively working on the issue. At last military families had action they could understand.[18] The raid prompted the North Vietnamese to crowd most American prisoners into Hoa Lo Prison (the Hanoi Hilton).[19] The resulting change improved conditions for the POWs who had been kept in solitary confinement for years: they were allowed contact with fellow prisoners; torture came less often.

These positive effects were the opposite of what the administration had expected, however. They had expected reprisals directed against the POWs rather than improvements in POW treatment. The only significant positive effect the raid was expected to have was a boost in POW morale. It had achieved that, but the Son Tay raid was still technically a failure. Prisoners had left the camp raided by Colonel Simon's elite task force in August, four months before Americans executed the dangerous rescue.

Although architects of the raid consistently claim that poor intelligence caused the failure, there is a possibility that the United States knowingly raided an empty camp.[20] Such claims, however preposterous they might seem in fact, captured the American imagination ten years later when audiences watched an unprecedented cycle of POW/MIA rescue scenarios played out in movies like *Uncommon Valor* (1983), *Missing in Action* (1984), and *Rambo: First Blood Part II* (1985). An essential plot element of such films would become not only the planning and successful execution of a POW/MIA rescue, but the double-crossing of the rescuing hero by some government agent. This becomes explicit in *Rambo,* where the protagonist is sent on an elaborately planned mission to what his handlers know is an empty POW camp. But however the government betrayed the hero, those fictions had successful conclusions. Americans would endlessly try to rewrite Son Tay as a success. This should not be surprising considering that the administration and the Pentagon turned the Son Tay raid into a political success ten years before John Rambo appeared on the screen.

Gene Hackman as a retired marine colonel and MIA father
rescues POWs in *Uncommon Valor.* The image of Vietnam
POWs haunted Americans for over two decades in a cycle of
over fifty POW/MIA films. *Courtesy of the Museum of Modern Art/
Film Stills Archive.* (1983, Paramount Pictures Corporation)

Regardless of the raid's intention, Son Tay signaled a continuing
awareness that the POW issue was all-important both in America and
North Vietnam.

The aftermath, measured in terms of the broader context of the
war, was not so comforting. Benjamin Schemmer measured the value

of the POW to the Pentagon and the Nixon administration in concrete terms in his book on the Son Tay raid: "From early 1969 . . . until early 1973, when 566 American POWs were finally released . . . there was only one purpose left in the war. America spent 20,683 lives and over $62 billion in those five years to achieve what a small party of brave men tried to do at Son Tay—bring those prisoners home."[21] An oversimplification to be sure, but nonetheless Schemmer underscores the emerging importance of the POW to America. The real-life Rambos had failed to rescue the POWs.[22] The failed rescue had amplified the importance of the POWs in the eyes of the American public. The task force's failure ensured hero status for the POW while confirming, however justly, the impotence of America's military.

At the Paris peace talks the POWs became a critical issue. The delicate negotiations made extensive and specific provisions for the safe conduct and return of all American POWs. In the words of one POW, Nixon had made the POWs "the primary focus, the hinge on which the door to peace would swing open."[23] The negotiations eventually succeeded to a degree. Meanwhile, a troubled President Nixon began preparing a homecoming unprecedented in the history of POW repatriation. Whereas POWs of the Korean War found themselves sequestered in the holds of returning ships and faced with headlines questioning their performance and integrity, the Vietnam POWs were flown from Hanoi to the United States with lavish welcomes at each stop on their way. "Operation Homecoming," originally planned by the Pentagon, would be carefully supervised by the White House. The Vietnam POWs would become heroes, no matter what.

The return of Vietnam POWs was just about the only tangible benefit the Nixon administration might claim for all its efforts at the peace table. The POWs were a portable artifact, a symbol of success: no matter what else might happen, Nixon had gotten the POWs home. Plans for the homecoming escalated. Some media expert in the administration realized that the POWs' return would be the last and possibly only event that could even remotely resemble success for America in Vietnam. The press followed POW events with daily headlines. Fold-out maps of their return trips were popular; well-wishers mobbed arrival airports; and hundreds of organizations offered gifts to the returning men. The Pentagon provided the returning POWs with their "own coterie of attendants—doctors, public relations people, even junior officers as chauffeurs."[24] The POWs were among the few popularly recognized heroes of the Vietnam War.

The POWs were not spontaneous heroes, however, but men who stepped into a carefully prepared costume of fame. They had been lost to captivity in a failed war effort. They had suffered some of the worst treatment experienced by any American captives in the twentieth century. They returned home emaciated, many years older, and traumatized by a horrible experience—but triumphant, in a homecoming designed not so much to compensate them for their years of captivity as to sell an American President.

Nothing made this clearer than the "homecoming" other Vietnam veterans received. Whereas most of the POWs were welcomed with an elaborate and carefully managed sequence of medical treatment, press attention, and military honors, other veterans got much less. Veterans' programs were unpopular; soldiers were unpopular. A cartoon in the *New York Post* captured the irony. It showed two tattered veterans standing alone in a desolate foreground while, in the background, POWs stepped off planes to the cheers of supportive crowds. The press footnoted Operation Homecoming by calling attention to others who had fought in South Vietnam: there were, after all, hundreds of thousands of Vietnam veterans and almost fifty thousand war dead. But the irony of lavishly welcoming a few hundred soldiers while doing little for the rest was lost on a White House and Pentagon that otherwise had a hard time selling any American soldier from Vietnam as a hero. Over a decade later *Newsweek* would resurrect the failed metaphor in a feature article on veterans entitled "We're Still Prisoners of War."[25]

However other veterans might have been treated, the POWs became heroes. The POWs became spokesman for the lost American self: they restored continuity with a pre–Vietnam War America many ached to recover. Americans listened closely, featured them in endless magazine cameos, read their autobiographies and wore their bracelets. They watched the obligatory television movie of Jeremiah Denton's POW experience, *When Hell Was in Session*. The POWs cashed in on America's guilt. They were elected to public office (Denton and John McCain were elected to the Senate), sent on sabbatical, carefully placed back into public life with all the praise and sympathy America could not seem to give the other veterans.

The story could not hold an audience for long, however. The POWs were heroes, but their stories had little to tell America. They reminded Americans too much of their suffering, their own helplessness in a war that recast "victory" so many times that it came to mean—and was—defeat. Most of the stories wanted to demonize the enemy, sell an essential American self, or bring back religion: few Americans found this appealing at the time. So America left the story behind. In the late seventies Americans virtually forgot about the Vietnam War and the POWs. The movie contracts stopped coming; the autobiographies went out of print. Then something strange happened.

In the decade following the Korean War, the United States had no trouble finding its new demons in a new Communist neighbor and the specter of a distant but technologically superior Soviet enemy. And then, of course, came the Vietnam War. But in the decade after Vietnam it was difficult to find a new cause. The hostage crisis in Iran galvanized American sentiment for a time, but its utility was short-lived. Ronald Reagan attempted to dust off the Soviet threat, and got some pretty good mileage out of it. But the other persistent image that captured American attention was the horror of captivity. The plight of captives in Lebanon gave the issue real time, but the hostage situations in the Middle East ultimately proved too difficult to solve until the politics of the Gulf War changed the U.S. relationship with Israel. In place of solving then-current hostage crises, America accomplished a miraculous recovery: it resurrected the POW as hero and the MIA as the pretext to play out vengeful fantasies. The POW/MIA dyad was and remains a powerful combination. The list of films, television movies, books, and other works that appropriate the POW as the subject of or pretext for dramatic plots (most often involving Ramboesque revenge/violence) is staggering, and we have not even begun to stop producing and consuming them.[26] The POW was already a hero-veteran. The story of the POW fueled the forces that would rehabilitate all Vietnam veterans and romanticize the Vietnam War.

Geoffrey Norman ends his recent account of the POW experience, *Bouncing Back,* with "some interesting, even startling facts." He cites Robert Mitchell's fifteen-year study of POW health after the Vietnam War. Norman explains how the ex-POWs have turned "all the dire predictions upside-down" in the wake of their captivity. Pentagon medical authorities and other experts had feared the worst about the physical and psychological condition of returning POWs. Other Vietnam veterans became famous not for their service to the nation but for their various ailments, particularly psychological ones now generally labeled post-traumatic stress disorder. Physically disabled veterans became stock characters in popular films like *The P.O.W.* (1973, a documentary-style film about a disabled veteran that attempted, in its title, to draw attention to the plight of disabled veterans by foregrounding a dubious metaphor), *The Deer Hunter* (1978), and *Born on the Fourth of July* (1989). Norman works against the prevailing image of the veteran by again trying to distance the POWs from other Vietnam veterans. Norman's evidence also runs contrary to claims made by former POWs of other wars.[27] But however accurate Norman and the medical study he cites may be, the image of the former POWs looks quite different in American fiction and film.

Rolling Thunder (1977) began a long list of movies that would appropriate the POW story and dramatically play out America's "dire predictions." The protagonist in *Rolling Thunder,* Charles Rane, is an ex-POW who returns home to a glorious welcome. But everything else seems to go wrong for Rane. After a group of criminals attacks his estranged family, Rane takes revenge in a string of murders. The cool, complex character at the beginning of the film becomes a killing machine who seems to inhabit "the closet in the back of his soul" just as his ex-POW friend says. Even the original writer and director of *Rolling Thunder,* Paul Schrader, ended up calling his film a "racist movie" that "stripped away my social arguments and left only the violence itself."

The Hanoi Hilton (1987), probably the most thorough film on the POW experience of the Vietnam War, specifically failed to address the aftermath of captivity. The film ends with a shot of the POWs on their way home at the airfield in Hanoi. *The Hanoi Hilton* for some reason scrupulously avoids the impact of Operation Homecoming or anything after. This aftermath became perhaps the most troubling aspect of the entire experience. It was left to the POWs themselves, MIA myth-makers, and "action market" film productions. The POWs ended up losing control of their image, an image already prefigured in American culture by captivity myths dating back to the Puritans. What little the Vietnam POWs could add to existing lore once they returned would be appropriated for magazine ads, paid-TV programming, and other profit-making media, which would strategically alter and recast their story for the American mass market. The same biographical information they fought so hard to withhold from North Vietnamese propaganda would become American propaganda. The POWs would confess their most disturbing experiences for the enjoyment and titillation of the American public. They helped make the war entertainment.

During captivity, POWs like James Stockdale, John Dramesi, Dieter Dengler, and Nick Rowe dreamed of the feature movies that would someday capture their POW experiences. Those movies came to the screen in greater numbers than they could ever have imagined, but their experiences would show up more in B movies and violent action-exploitation videos than in feature presentations. In the end the honest, God-fearing, morally upright POW heroes modeled by Stockdale and his fellow POWs would become flat, shadowy specters in the minds of sadistic movie heroes perpetrating violence that would have given the most brutal of Stockdale's captors pause. Far more Americans have heard of John Rambo than of even the better-known actual POWs: John McCain, Jeremiah Denton, James Stockdale, Robinson Risner, or Everett Alvarez. More Americans watched *Rolling Thunder* than the award-winning documentary of Richard Stratton's captivity, *2251 Days* (1974).

No matter how healthy the real ex-POWs may have been, American culture was busy transforming them into something far less salubrious. The actual POWs and their message, however important it was, faded into the corners of used bookstores, while their simulacrum took center stage. The POWs' fame took on a life of its own; the POW image was flattened to a decal. The real "heroes," the ones Americans paid the most to see, the ones who became rich and famous, were the ones who embodied what Americans needed to see rather than what was; the ones who fed their audience imaginary resolutions that created the optical illusion of a just, honest war with healthy, if not entirely happy, veterans. The Vietnam POW had become a prisoner of America's expectations and needs: there could be no escape. The press, the spin doctors in the White House, and the producers in Hollywood would have it their way.

2

Myth and Tragedy on the New Frontier

Between 1770 and 1776, publishers reprinted the captivity accounts of two Puritan settlers more than nine times. The stories of Mary Rowlandson and John Williams became popular almost a hundred years after Indians captured them. Their stories had been told from the pulpit many times in the early 1700s, but it was only in the years immediately preceding the American Revolution that they gained secular popularity.[1]

These early captivity stories were cast as episodes of divine testing against the alien culture of the American Indian and the "satanic temptation" of the New England wilderness. As religious enthusiasm began to ebb, however, the captivities became secular tales crucial to the formation of American identity. The early Puritan tales gained popularity during the Revolution not because of their religious significance but because they were examples of unique and original American lore that embraced character traits that were useful in the revolutionary struggle. Colonists found the captivity metaphor a politically powerful tool for defining their own oppression under British rule.

Captivities did not lose their popularity after the war was won; they simply took on new forms. Ethan Allen wrote the first published account of a Revolutionary War captivity experience in his *Narrative of Colonel Ethan Allen's Captivity* (1779). Soon afterward, John Filson created an American icon in "The Adventures of Col. Daniel Boone" (1784). Captivity was a defining episode in the story of Daniel Boone. Boone's captivity amplified his strength by showing how he learned with, rather than against, a demonized Indian culture. Boone assimilated the most powerful and useful aspects of American Indian identity to better the Indian. His story became outrageously popular in a fledgling nation whose doctrine of Manifest Destiny led it to execute conquests on a continental scale for a century after Filson wrote the story.

The early captivity narratives adhered to many issues in the new nation's culture. Early captivities highlighted the enforced slavery of the American Indians' Puritan captives. The metaphor of captivity, of America imprisoned by England, fueled enthusiasm for rebellion in British-occupied cities such as Boston and New York. And, of course, what had been a metaphor for imprisonment and enslavement became an unavoidable reality in the context of African slavery. Slave narratives became popular not so much because abolitionist philanthropy kept them in the public eye but because the captivity story itself was central to American identity. Slave narratives became so popular in the nineteenth century that critics were compelled to counter their appeal by dismissing them as "literary nigritudes [*sic*]."[2] But such efforts could not stem the cultural force that captivity narratives like *Uncle Tom's Cabin* continued to have for Americans.

———

E ven before the American public became aware of POWs in Vietnam, the country had developed a set of assumptions about captivity experience. The POW story stands on its own, but it is also part of a persistent American myth. The structure of the Vietnam POW story found in popular narrative literature and film closely matches the plot of earlier American captivity narratives. In order to understand the current story we must first remember the cultural and narrative foundations of the POW myth.

My historical archeology extends Richard Slotkin's critique of early American literature to current POW stories.[3] In his work on the captivity narrative, Slotkin describes three prevailing elements of myth: a "protagonist hero" the audience can identify with; a "universe in which the hero may act"; and a narrative that describes the interaction of hero and universe.4 These structural elements occur in the majority of Vietnam POW stories.

Slotkin expands his conception of the myth to include not only the structure but also the motivations he sees in the production of the myth. For this explanation he draws heavily from Joseph Campbell. Slotkin sees Campbell's "heroic quest" as the "most important archetype underlying American cultural mythology." This quest involved "the departure of the hero from his common-day world to seek the power of the gods in the underworld." The hero's motivation was derived from "the threat of some natural or human calamity which will overtake his people unless the power of the gods can be borrowed or the gods themselves reconciled with the people."5 This dynamic is clearly at work in the majority of Vietnam POW stories. The elements are all present: the pilot as hero-victim, the trial as an "underworldly" experience of captivity, and a structure that relates the quest of the hero, who recovers some important truth that would make at least part of the Vietnam War a victory.6

In the 1960s there was probably no hero more pervasive than the American astronaut. The astronaut was first a pilot, most often a combat pilot, the ultimate American: physically perfect, mentally tough, intellectually gifted, morally pure, and spiritually wild. The image of the astronaut facing the frontier of space re-created the larger-than-life frontier heroes of the American past: historical figures like Puritan Mary Rowlandson and fictional characters like frontiersman Daniel Boone. It was an image consistent with everything the United States needed after Sputnik. The astronauts' efforts came to symbolize America; their success fashioned the American self-image.

The POWs, most of whom were military pilots, were potential astronauts robbed of their destiny by the North Vietnamese. Astronaut Buzz Aldrin's book, *Return to Earth,* implies this displacement in his dedication to POW Sam Johnson: "for Sam . . . whose place I took, who took my place."7 POW pilots were attractive heroes, could-be astronauts, military men bound to but at the same time separated from the political motivations that started and sustained the war.8 Yet they were just doing their job.

Thus, the pilots embodied not only the strength and perfection of the astronaut but also the innocence and complacence of the female victim.[9] Indian captivity lore depicted innocent settlers (who had, in reality, annexed Indian lands and destroyed the inhabitants) going about their daily lives when Indians unjustly attacked and captured them. In the context of such stories the conquering hordes of white settlers became peaceful inhabitants subjected to the savage and irrational violence of wild peoples. Similarly, the POW-pilot would be depicted as the innocent victim of an accident: his shoot-down and captivity. Films like *The Hanoi Hilton, In Love and War,* and *When Hell Was in Session* would avoid the aggressive, ruthless, and somewhat arbitrary bombing attacks prosecuted by the pilots in favor of frantic and traumatic ejection sequences. Inevitably the pilot appears as an unarmed man dangling helplessly from a parachute while being shot at by violent and vindictive Vietnamese peasants ignorant of the rules of war. North Vietnamese insistence that these men were "criminals" seemed ridiculous in this context.

The POW hero could have it both ways: he could prosecute the war as daredevil pilot at the same time that he could transfer any deep responsibility for his activities to the political superstructure he served. The military pilot thus became the ultimate candidate for the quest, an American Adam. He departed, however inadvertently, from his "common-day world" as pilot and was thrust into the trial of a captivity for which he claimed no responsibility.

Although clearly heroic figures before captivity, the pilots in most of the POW autobiographies and films first appear "in a state of relative complacent ease."[10] Virtually all of the pilot narratives begin in the difficult but secure world of the aircraft carrier or air base. Geoffrey Norman's description of Al Stafford is typical:

> Like most fighter pilots, Al Stafford was a blend of individualist and team player. A man could not fly single-seat airplanes in combat without believing he was the best. His ego was as important in a way as his eyesight and his reflexes. Fighter pilots operated at the end of a long and elaborate chain of support. A carrier pilot like Stafford was one of seventy-six men on a ship with a crew of some four thousand. The mission of every member of that crew was, ultimately, to keep the seventy-six pilots flying. . . . A man did not need a hungry ego to feel elite, important, and, in an odd but logical way, invulnerable.[11]

Puritan captivity stories like those of Mary Rowlandson and John Williams began with the pathos of capture. In the case of Mary Rowlandson, she was torn from domestic life, her children, and her husband. Her four-month captivity presented her with a trial of relogous faith and cultural virtue against the godless and alien Indians. For the POWs, life after capture was, according to Sam Johnson, a "cruel joke: to pin a man whose life has been spent in the sky, defying gravity and crashing through invisible barriers to soar above oceans and continents."[12] The "breaking of family ties" and embarkation on the "trial" of Puritan captivity narratives neatly matches the military pilot's transition from the fraternal support of his carrier or air base to the jungle floor and the stripping, both physical and mental, that went along with it:[13]

> A captured pilot quickly found himself without the security that came from training, routine, and doctrine. . . . His armor—flight suit and helmet—was taken from him, along with his clothes. He was stripped to his underwear and tied up by peasants armed with pitchforks and rusty machetes. Pilots accustomed to sleeping in beds with clean sheets, eating hot food off good china, and having their laundry done for them by enlisted men were suddenly reduced to living in conditions that an infantryman would have found harsh and that were for them unimaginable. . . . Finally, the captured aviator was alone.[14]

Not only did the POW venture into and, to some extent, endure his captivity alone, just as the frontier hero had, but he also entered this new frontier without any of the technological trappings of his privileged life as a pilot, trappings seen as an ineffective crutch by many critics of the Vietnam War. Carrier pilot Charles Plumb describes his predicament in those terms: "Stripped of personal possessions, of million-dollar airplanes, of rank and prestige, we suddenly found ourselves at the bottom of a dark pit."[15] The pilot, stripped of his comforts and technological advantages, was prepared for the archetypal struggle with the elements of the wilderness. Jay Jensen in his narrative *Six Years in Hell* describes his captivity as such a test: "It [his POW experience] was a test of faith, courage, and honor. I passed that test. . . . I believe that one of the reasons that God placed us here on earth is to be tested by adversity and problems."[16]

The captive's new "universe" looked like a strange and perverse "underworld." Naval aviator Eugene McDaniel portrays his first moments in North Vietnam as something remote from human experience:

> There was no feeling quite like knowing you are in a strange country, surrounded by a people who know no rule but death to the enemy. On top of that, of course, is the jungle. There is nothing compared to the tropical jungle when it comes to survival. It is thick, thorny, full of unexpected dangers, ruthlessly hot and defiant of man. Flying over it is bad enough— even then it appears sullen, unyielding, merciless—but on the ground a man is soon aware of its immensity, its gigantic suffocating encirclement, its relentless squeeze on life systems that depend on air, good water, and food.[17]

The texts of the POW story endlessly draw on horrific metaphors to figure the environment during captivity, most often simply calling it "Hell."[18] Within this context the Indians of the Puritan experience and the North Vietnamese of the Vietnam experience become inhuman devils.[19] To deal with this figural wilderness the heroes of the archetypal drama must turn inward[20] and rely on an "ethical code" to sustain them in their trials. For the POWs this code was at least superficially the Code of Conduct established by Eisenhower after the Korean War. Some POWs, among them John Dramesi, Ernest Brace, James Stockdale, Eugene McDaniel, and James Mulligan, found the Code was enough to sustain them. But for others "the book—the Code of Conduct—was not enough."[21] Many POWs relied on a higher authority than a national code, most often religion; in the case of Al Stafford it was a new code eventually nicknamed "Bouncing Back."[22]

The hero-pilot eventually wins his struggle with the wilderness, significantly within the wilderness itself. The POWs beat their captors at their own game—they survived material poverty and physical deprivation through implicitly transcendent and nurturing ideologies.[23] The POW story portrays the war as a transcendent, ahistorical struggle. The struggle becomes ahistoric because it focuses attention on the psychological battle and away from the human carnage of the war in South Vietnam. The imminent victory of the POW-hero relies not on his latent physical superiority but instead on the transcendent sovereignty of the individual.²⁴ This victory allows him not only to reassure Americans that they could have won the war if the terms of the conflict had allowed, but reinforces the view that the war was, in fact, a victory: that the real war was fought by the pilots in captivity and not the troops in the field.²⁵ The POW at once resolved the need for an American victory, and at the same time justified the "human calamity" of the war by proving once and for all the evil nature of his North Vietnamese captors.

Although many of the POWs explain their experience in religious terms, most reject religion as the decisive factor in their survival. Most autobiographical narratives concentrate on some essence of the American self that finally saved the POWs from sure death. Ernest Brace is explicit on this point: "I felt like praying, but months before I had rationalized that God hadn't put me here and God wasn't going to get me out."²⁶ Brace is emphatic about his self-reliance: "I was convinced, now more than ever, that no one was going to extricate me from my misery but myself."²⁷

Thus the POW pilot-hero returns to society from the figural underworld "into a higher level of existence and power," which affords him a privileged voice in the uncertain aftermath of the war. His Lazarus-like return from a metaphorical death gives him a privileged and virtually unarguable "posthumous authority."²⁸ The POW was one of the only positive symbols in an otherwise bleak history. The captivity experience thus lent itself to reduction, to "an imitable formula, a literary convention, a romantic version of the myth."²⁹ These stories functioned in the context of a defeated America through their "ritual-therapeutic use."³⁰ The POW was thus taken as metonymic, standing for all prisoners of the war. It was compensatory and satisfying for Americans to deflect the blame for the country's failures during the Vietnam era away from the sacred American self and toward other more distant and less troubling causes. The perceived victory of the POW became necessary to preserve the American self and the American self-conception at a time when all else seemed open to question.

The POWs were time travelers, Rip Van Winkles from an era before Vietnam changed almost everything. Imprisonment in North Vietnam was a human "time capsule."³¹ The POWs carried intact through captivity values and standards that were unaffected by the frictions within American culture in the late sixties and early seventies. They were short-haired victims, blameless heroes who proved themselves ultimate individuals by surviving an unusually difficult captivity. Such images appealed to the "me" generation, which might otherwise reject military figures out of hand after the miscarried war effort. Ironically, the POWs seemed to have preserved their "good" characters better in North Vietnam than they would have if they had remained free on their carriers, at their bases in South Vietnam, or in the United States.

The POWs themselves perceived their experience as productive. Geoffrey Norman depicts a conversation where a female reporter (in many POW stories the consummate figure of imminent betrayal) asks a leading question: "How does it make you feel . . . to know that you wasted all those years?" The POW responds: "Those years weren't wasted."[32] Jay Jensen made the triumph of his captivity experience quite clear: "I conquered adversity, overcame obstacles, and turned stumbling blocks into stepping stones of progress. I returned a better man than when I was shot down."[33]

The POW struggle, in large part, came to represent the whole of the Vietnam war to Americans. The POW experience provided the United States with an ersatz victory, with a face-saving litany that could be read comfortably: the POWs resisted the North Vietnamese Communists at the frontier, thus saving America both physically and psychologically from the threat of Communist infiltration. The POWs triumphed in a war that was at least figuratively seen to "lay waste" and "destroy" America as a cohesive people.

The POWs implicitly redescribe the Vietnam War by representing themselves, however unconsciously, as emblems of the American self. Many of the POW stories are hauntingly similar. This similarity is not based so much on the circumstances of capture and captivity in Vietnam as on the way the captives describe their experience in terms of themselves and their environment. The experiences of the POW-heroes and their tales of pain in Hanoi and rebirth in American society provided a useful ambiguity that allows their violent capture and tortuous captivity to become "an aspect of their cultivation and improvement" in the context of an America that needed compensation for a costly and divisive war.[34]

It would be hard to find an action film, book, or adventure classic that does not include some suggestion of the captivity drama. It is an obligatory element of the American action/adventure plot. "America Held Hostage" was a major theme of American identity long before ABC's Ted Koppel applied the phrase to the Iranian-held hostages in 1980.[35] It should, therefore, come as no surprise that the POWs and their stories penetrated American culture in so many ways.

3

Autobiography and the POW Experience

W
hen Everett Alvarez returned from North Vietnam in February of 1973, the media craved his story. Everywhere, he was confronted with opportunities to appear, testify, endorse, and speak. He was offered a book contract. Autobiography appeared the best way for Alvarez to tell his own story, construct his own self exclusive of the ways he was being used for "endorsing" agendas he "knew nothing about."[1]

When he met with prospective publishers, Alvarez was "disappointed and discouraged" to find that they were not interested in the story he wanted to tell: "I had in mind a sort of Stalag 17 thing, an account of how we survived . . . following our senior officers' directions . . . and so on." But when his agent suggested other elements of Alvarez's experience, "the fact that my wife had run off . . . and my family had been active in antiwar protests," the publishers' interest "came alive then, and I cringed. I didn't even want to talk about those things."[2] Over a decade later, however, he would discuss "those things" in two books and in speaking engagements, magazine features, and television spots. Time may have changed Alvarez's attitude toward telling his story, but the struggle between his own sense of experience and the inscription of that experience in American culture was clear. He became "disappointed and discouraged—not because there would be no book bonanza but because of the additional evidence of a huge gap in understanding between us POWs and the rest of the country." By writing an autobiography, Alvarez had hoped to fill the gap, to reconcile himself with the America he returned to.

Autobiography is a national genre, almost a national pastime. Life writing was virtually the only form of literature written in America before 1820, and there continues to be an "identification of autobiography in America with America."[3] The compulsion for a POW to write autobiography could well stem from a desire to thank the country that brought him home by providing America an example for its youth, "an advertisement for America." The POW-hero wanted to shape his story to what he saw as this "didactic national purpose,"[4] following the example of countless American life writers from the early captivities through "architects of American character" such as Franklin, Whitman, Douglass, Henry Adams, John Adams and yes, even Reagan, Iacocca, Vanilla Ice, and the "Boz" (Brian Bosworth).[5]

Robinson Risner's autobiography about his experience as a POW in Vietnam begins with an explicit statement of his authorial intention. He points to what we might learn from his story:

> Someone asked me why I was writing this book and my honest answer is this: I believe that today's young people are searching for a dragon to slay. . . . I want to show that the smartest and the bravest rely on their faith in God and our way of life. I hope to show how that faith has been tried by fire—and never failed. I would like to say, "Don't ever be ashamed of your faith, nor of your wonderful heritage. Be proud of those things which made America great and which can, with our help, be even greater."[6]

Risner makes the target of his story clear by pointing to "our young people." He speaks from his authorized role as a "threshold bearer" (to use Joseph Campbell's term). His authority springs from an experience that he perceives as hell itself. He and his "faith has been tried by fire." He implicitly places himself and the other POWs in a group of the "smartest and the bravest," those with the right stuff. His hero status authorizes him to bring back the amazing story he is about to tell, a story that attaches his survival to "God and our way of life." This dyad serves as his ideal, the perfection he aspires to in his narrative. He asserts a transcendent self that embodies both God and America. He is both teacher and student: teaching Americans the lessons learned through imprisonment in North Vietnam as they watch how he learned them himself through the "fire" he endured.

POW autobiographers like Risner had to reach for such high aspirations through the figures and tropes of written language. Such efforts exhibit a "straining toward perfection—perfection of a kind that connects the individual with a cosmic pattern that, because it is perfect itself, verifies that individual's own potential perfection."[7] Risner conjures the mythical dragon as a metaphor for things he sees threatening the sanctity of American identity, an identity his exemplary conduct will demonstrate. His life becomes important because of his symbolically posthumous authority. The sharply defined limits of his captivity experience allow him to speak of it almost as if it were another life that he has perspective on because he now views it from beyond.

Since mass communication became a reality, the primary stuff of our experience has become more and more the direct broadcast, real-time imagery, and "eyewitness" reporting of television and radio. But unlike the rest of the Vietnam War, the POW experience had little of such media coverage: the subject, by its very nature, was hidden from such scrutiny. The television images, photographs, and interviews of the POWs that we did get were from the North Vietnamese themselves or "neutral" visitors and were dismissed as propaganda. Even in an age when Americans accepted television as reliable, images of the POWs became material for enemy deception. Therefore, the testimony of the prisoners themselves achieved heightened importance. The only POW text we would believe would be the captives' own voices upon their return. The media hype of Operation Homecoming pointed directly to the imminent revelations of repatriated prisoners. The primary text of the Vietnam POW experience thus became the captives' testimony.

Even though they did not receive as wide an audience as POW films, POW autobiographies from the Vietnam War have been immensely successful. Interest in them appeared to peak immediately after the sensation of Operation Homecoming in 1973, but they have had persistent appeal. Renewed interest in Vietnam literature during the 1980s prompted reprintings of many. From 1989 to 1991, Risner's *Passing of the Night* saw its third printing and James Rowe's *Five Years to*

Freedom its twelfth. Jay Jensen's *Six Years in Hell,* John Dramesi's *Code of Honor,* Dieter Dengler's *Escape from Laos,* and Everet Alvarez's *Chained Eagle* were reprinted in paperback. Gerald Coffee published his auto-biography, *Beyond Survival,* and recorded a sequel, *Beyond Survival: the Next Chapter,* on tape. Donald Fine published *Code of Conduct,* a sequel to Alvarez's prison account. Sam Johnson published *Captive Warriors,* and Ben and Anne Purcel collaborated on their story of the POW experience, *Love and Duty.*

Before looking at the POWs' relationship with the language of journalism, film, television, and advertising, it is important to examine the POWs' relationship with their own written language. By examin-ing how language has made or unmade the POW in the dozens of autobiographical accounts that continue to populate our libraries and bookstores, I describe how that story functions in American culture. The relationship between the POW and the authority he assumes as writer is a fickle one. We have already seen how disappointing this relationship became for Alvarez, and the mythic identifications it im-posed upon Risner.

The autobiographer uses the most volatile material any artist might take on as his subject: his own self. This quality of autobiography is both a blessing and a curse. On the one hand, the writer can draw on and publicize carefully edited experiences. In many ways the autobiog-rapher can remake the self, create a new identity or validate an old one. To do this, however, the writer must expose himself, make a public confession. If the stuff of life were only joy this would still be a difficult task, but when it is pain and suffering, a debilitating experi-ence, revisiting the site of that disaster, even in the mind's eye, can be destructive.

James Mulligan, a prisoner in Hanoi for six years, reveals his feel-ings soon after capture: "I felt like a fallen eagle, captured and caged, now only the object of human curiosity."[8] Everett Alvarez describes himself as a "chained eagle" (the title of his first book). Both men chose the image of an eagle, the symbol of America, to stand for their captivity and, in the poetics of their story, America's. These metaphors of self express the dilemma the POWs faced. Describing the POW experience at once ties the writer to his in this case painful past while exposing that same past to public scrutiny and use. The metaphor of captive eagle signifies both temporary imprisonment in North Vietnam and the more complex and lasting psychological legacy of that experience. The POW author must enter into an agreement, or autobiographical pact, with his reader to reveal intimate details of painful experiences.[9] This is particularly true when dealing with heroes and myth in mass society.[10] Alvarez initially resisted making such an agreement, but he eventually told his story in his two books, in advertising for Philip Morris, in *People* magazine, on "Larry King," and on "Prime Time Live." Alvarez became tied to his experience as a prisoner; the POW experience, whether welcome or not, was inseparable from his public image.

In constructing autobiographies the POWs redefined themselves.[11] They released their experience into the integral and reductive productions of American publishing: their experiences would be, to borrow Phil Beidler's liturgy, "written, designed, typeset, artworked, edited, printed, jacketed, and blurbed."[12] For the POWs the world became remade in terms of a new set of assumptions, a new way of seeing everything. Alvarez and Mulligan remain shackled, not by the North Vietnamese, but by their experience.

James Rowe survived for five years in Vietcong prison camps and successfully escaped in 1968. For twenty years after his escape Rowe used the authority of his prison experience to run for political office, lead in the army, and teach what he had learned. One passage of his autobiography, *Five Years to Freedom*, reflects the struggle to reconcile his prison experience with his life after escape. After escaping from captivity, James Rowe finds himself in a large hospital room:

> My room turned out to be a spacious, well-lit miniature auditorium. I felt as if we could have had a basketball game in it if the ceiling wasn't so low. The idea of staying in a room this large by myself was disturbing. I caught myself estimating how many mosquito nets could be strung inside the room and whistled softly at the final count.[13]

In gauging the size of his new dwellings, he juxtaposes the two metaphors he might use to determine size. His first metaphor is drawn from his precaptivity experience: basketball. But his second metaphor is drawn from his more recent captivity experience: mosquito nets.

His feeling of discomfort, however, springs from the latter experience. Although Rowe struggles to frame his experience in both before- and during-captivity terms, his struggle may be in vain. From the time of his escape, his notoriety, his value as an officer and individual in American society, did not come from his experience and understanding based on basketball, but on the knowing that sprang from mosquito nets.

Rowe's future political and military career came to depend most not on his middle-class American background or West Point education but on his authority as a former POW, a survivor and escapee. He relives his experience again and again in a wide range of cultural spaces for the benefit of voters during his political campaign, for students of special warfare at Fort Bragg, and for readers of his autobiography. In any public life he chooses after captivity, there resides an immanent demand for a confession from his prison experience.

This autobiographical pressure has two very different consequences. By reliving his captivity experience, Rowe becomes a perpetual victim. His captors sought to "unmake" and "make" the world for him in their torture and "re-educational training." This remaking of the world for Rowe was inherently painful.[14] In contrast, however, his experiences as a POW allow him to recast and reunderstand the world in new and gratifying ways. Inherent in each remembered moment of captivity is his return to his present (and presumably better) life as a free individual in America. This perpetual return offers him immediate gratification for reliving his torturous experience and motivates him to do so. This motivation, outside the political and economic valuation of that experience by American culture, chains Rowe to his POW experience.

In a way Rowe ends up being reeducated by his own culture. The pressures on him to tell his tale force him to remake his world. The remaking he resisted from his captors materialized in his life after captivity. Rowe's hope for freedom and his constant desire to escape the circumstances of his captivity are frustrated by the demands of his postcaptivity audiences. His autobiographical muse becomes his captor; his autobiography becomes the site of his pain.

Rowe made his hopes explicit in the final lines of a poem he wrote during captivity: "What happens now . . . cannot last" because "this [the miserable conditions of his captivity] remains behind."[15] Unfortunately, his experiences and memory of captivity cannot be left behind. Quite the contrary. If we have learned anything from the survivor's narrative, we have learned that "what happens now" can never "remain behind" in the context of postcaptivity experience. This is doubly so for the autobiographer and prospective icon, whose value will increasingly be reduced to the validated difference between his experience and everyone else's: captivity.

Rowe believed that he could separate himself from his captors and the five years he spent in captivity by recovering his precaptivity experiences. He also believed he could leave his captivity experience "behind." After he escaped, he learned that several of his friends had died while he was in captivity. He eulogizes them in *Five Years to Freedom:*

> Just as these men stood with us while they lived, they continued to stand with us after their passing. The words, an anthem from the Academy that none of us would forget, never had more meaning than at this moment, "Grip hands with us now though we see not, Grip hands with us, strengthen our hearts; As the long line stiffens and straightens with the thrill that your presence imparts, Grip hands tho' it be from the shadows."[16]

Rowe discusses the positive spiritual essence he has come to believe in. But this passage metaphorically expresses the effect of captivity experience on the way he has come to know the world. Rowe's captors will populate his appearances and stories in public life as much as his friends and West Point classmates will.

When dealing with his past experiences, Rowe grips hands with friend and foe, joy and hardship alike. The account of his return to the United States is peppered with references to his captivity, just as the rest of his life will be. He constantly reaches for his captivity experience in order to understand new experiences—it becomes, in fact, the measure of all things. While describing his welcome by a high-ranking military official, he cannot help describing his pride in terms of captivity:

> Boy, would this frost Mafia [a Vietcong interrogator] if he could see it! I chuckled to myself, remembering the days I sat on a pole floor looking up

at Mafia perched on a chair behind a poncho-draped stand as he conducted an indoctrination. What he must have thought about the ragged,
illness-weakened, fungus-infected POW's in his relative grandeur. In the
land of the blind, a one-eyed man is king.[17]

Rowe's new life and rebirth, however joyful, are bonded to his tragic
captivity experience. His captors have remade his world, although
perhaps not in a way they had intended.

This bond between past and present in no way assures the victim
that he can represent pain and suffering. John McGrath's unique
autobiographical text, which collects both a written account and pencil
sketches of the POW experience, attempts to go beyond words:
"Words alone are not sufficient to convey the experience." McGrath
hopes to achieve an elusive goal, to "succeed in showing what these
and other words meant." But even he eventually concedes that he
cannot convey what he means in any stable way: "I notice my drawings
are too soft."[18]

James Rowe also admits that he cannot successfully do what he
spends the rest of his life attempting to do: convey the POW experience. The focus of his efforts and perhaps the most difficult goal to
achieve will be to convey unfamiliar deprivation and pain to his audience. Rowe describes a question, asked upon his return to America,
that troubled him:

> The only question which had disturbed me was when one individual asked,
> "How were you treated?" I sat back in momentary confusion, searching for
> some sequence of words that would convey, in a matter of seconds, the
> summation of five years as a POW. There was no means of conveying what
> those years were like to an audience who had no concept of the constant
> physical pressures; the filth, the disease, hunger; the crushing mental
> pressure; the frustrations, anxieties, the fears. I couldn't tell him in an
> hour, or a day even, unless he had been there, and there were only a few
> who had been and returned. None of them were in this room.[19]

Rowe grants that his own "sequence of words" as presented in his
autobiographical narrative will never convey perhaps the most essential injustices of his captivity.

The implication of what McGrath concedes and Rowe admits in these passages represents the paradox of representing experience. The subjects are tied to their own experience in ways that preclude "leaving it behind," while at the same time they are unable to convey the stable meaning they crave. Both McGrath and Rowe see their texts as attempts to relate something they consciously lose control of. Yet they realize their own inability to control the possible significations of their account: they are setting that account free to float into an audience that could have "no concept" of what they were trying to say. But, of course, an experience isn't really free at all, it and all meanings that might spring from the text are inevitably chained to the author himself.

There was a positive value in such public confessions, however. Ironically, a POW's persistence in making public autobiographic information that he consistently refused to divulge to his captors enabled his disclosure to function like a religious confession; it seemed to unburden him of his wrongs, liberate him, and promise him salvation.[20]

But the confession might have exactly the opposite effect in the context of mass society. The POW issue received an increasing amount of publicity during the Vietnam War. This gradually rising fame culminated in an explosion of media coverage when the majority of POWs were released in 1973. The scale of this media fame gave each of the POWs instant recognition. This fame seemed at first to provide them with an unprecedented degree of freedom, unknown even before their experience in captivity.[21]

One cost of this fame was reduction to the forms of mass media that demanded image and sound bytes rather than longer representations. And once the story had been told and accepted by the American audience, there came a kind of closure: "Oh, I know what that's all about": "to believe in them as quintessences of human nature [many

POW narratives claim a privileged knowledge of some essence of self] is to believe in their fame as the prefiguring of a fame for all."[22] The public could, in a sense, cut the sound after a while and stop listening. Once the reduced and assimilable baseline narrative was complete, it became increasingly difficult for any individual voice to escape the centripetal forces of POW fame.

In a way, instant recognition as a Vietnam POW meant instant reduction and sudden silence; the image was so loaded with expectations and conclusions that one hardly needed listen at all.[23] The "informational function of the media would thus be to help us forget, to serve as the very agents and mechanisms for our historical amnesia."[24] In this way the POW confession might never be heard. Instead, it became "entrapped in an audience attention that is intimate but impersonal, embracing without nurturing:"[25] simply one-sided. The only remainder of the self in such a context might be the image byte that spoke only through the monologue of the normalized myth.

⸻

For anyone to embark on an autobiographical project requires some degree of belief "in the transcendent sovereignty of the individual."[26] In many of the POW texts we find an inward turn, a withdrawal from the sensuous participation in events and a movement to a detached position as observer: the inevitable effect of carceral architecture where "the cell confronts the convict with himself"[27] and the outright horror of his own condition. The POWs eventually faced an inability to convey their experience in any stable way, as we have seen with Rowe and McGrath. Thus the POW/author must confront the widening gap between his experience and the strategies that might work to close the gap or fill it with "compensatory" material.[28] He must resist "obliterating the line between self and role, body and identity, being and name."[29]

This discussion might explain the dominance of the positive and compensatory narrative structures we find consistently in POW stories. Authors who confront this gap and consciously leave it open are not attractive to an American audience starved for complete selves and images of honest, almost faultless heroes. We will see in succeeding chapters that by not compensating, POW authors like Monika Schwinn, James Daly, George Smith, and, to some extent, John Dramesi exhibit in their text a gaping wound that corresponds with their own aversion to continuing to deal with and foreground their experience.

Those POWs who seem to execute the most confident closure (here I am talking about icons like James Stockdale, Jeremiah Denton, Everett Alvarez, Charles Plumb, James Mulligan, and Eugene McDaniel) reappear on the cultural landscape. Of course, narratives that compensate would appeal more to an American audience that has, however vicariously, experienced the pain and suffering of captivity and now seeks a satisfying resolution to the story. This is one reason that the POW release of 1973 was such an important event: Americans had been drawn into the POW story; they had experienced and been entertained by the various episodes and plot twists and they needed a successful final chapter.

In the end, however, the valorized texts compressed their experience into a set of abstract, "simple rules"[30] or reduced "experience into a constellation of compelling metaphors."[31] Either way the POW stories subverted rather than affirmed their radically experiential mode. The "consolidation of human powers—intellectual, spiritual, and physical"[32] in their own figures sets up the former POWs for an inevitable fall.[33] Their self-conception becomes so ponderous that they slip from their position of experiential authority to reified ideology. "What thus seem initially to be individualistic autobiographical searchings turn out to be revelations of traditions, re-collections of disseminated identities."[34] In this way the POW autobiography participates in a "carceral network" that renders the POWs themselves "docile and useful" within a "system of overlapping subjection and objectification."[35] They become icons, idols, and, in some cases, decal-like clowns wandering from venue to venue searching for the needs their bloated self-image might yet fill.[36] Their images do less to teach us about their lived experience than they do to endorse the political and religious ideologies they serve.

On the very night that Americans saw the first televised pictures from Iraq of captured U.S. airmen, a paid-TV program was in progress on another channel. The program, "Amazing Discoveries," is one of many programs that disguise themselves as open-forum talk shows in order to sell some product. On this night Harry Lorayne was selling his "Memory Power System." The final testimonial for that night's show was from a military man: Colonel Arthur T. Ballard, seven years a POW in Vietnam. Colonel Ballard claimed in a mechanical, uninflected voice that Harry Lorayne and his system helped him through his captivity and was even decisive in enabling Ballard and his fellow captives to survive.

This segment, juxtaposed with the apparently coerced and similarly mechanical and uninflected confessions of American POWs in Iraq, creates a cruelly ironic perspective on American culture. We see that POWs read dubious scripts for the benefit of questionable authorities, whether for their captors in enemy nations or for entrepreneurs of American culture. But this is not the worst to come out of that evening's channel flipping.

The final moments of the TV show feature a teary-eyed Harry Lorayne affirming the ideology of America and the American self. Ballard's captivity experience and difficult struggle become useful and public only as a decal for yet another self-help product. Nothing could better demonstrate the deliberate and complete cultural asphyxiation of the POW story.[37]

4
History and
The Hanoi Hilton

T he mid-1980s seemed the perfect time to launch the definitive Vietnam POW film. Ronald Reagan, the actor-President, had led America into what appeared to be prosperity. Public interest in the Vietnam War reached nostalgic proportions—even though Americans had seemed to avoid reminders of Vietnam in the seventies. Bookshelves overflowed with histories, novels, and various forms of life writing about the war. Film, television, and news media reached back across a decade to recover the war for the next generation.

But no one had yet done the definitive POW film. The POW experience was relegated to short sequences in POW/MIA rescue tales, touchstones for heroes on their way to another adventure. The films made in the seventies concentrated on a single character; autobiographical films like *When Hell Was in Session* seemed to avoid the complications of collective experience. No one had yet used a single prison camp as the focal point as successful POW films about the Second World War had. The time was ripe for *The Hanoi Hilton.*

Lionel Chetwynd, the writer/director of *The Hanoi Hilton,* took great pains to re-create the Vietnam POW experience for his American audience. The jacket for the videotape carries his proud comments about the production:

Nearly a quarter century after Everett Alvarez was shot out of the sky over North Vietnam to become the first US prisoner held in the North, I invited him to visit the set of *The Hanoi Hilton,* a painstaking reconstruction of the infamous Hoa Lo prison where he had languished as a prisoner for some eight and a half years. He was dumbstruck. Said Alvarez, "It was real. They had taken me back."

The implication of this home video sales pitch is that *The Hanoi Hilton* was authentic, the definitive motion picture of the Vietnam POW experience.

The film recruited a host of former-POW advisors and military experts to create the set. It was an impressive effort. Everything seemed to match what the POWs themselves remembered, down to the odd, striped prisoner "pajamas" and claustrophobic concrete cells. The plot locked its focus on the POWs from the beginning. There were no dramatic cuts to home-front footage of separated families, play-action battle scenes, or home-front politics. We enter *The Hanoi Hilton* as the pilots did. In the opening scenes we follow a cocky naval aviator, Lieutenant Commander Patrick Williamson (Michael Moriarty), from his flag-waving interview with a skeptical journalist to his inauspicious parachute ride into the Vietnamese jungle. The first minutes of the film rush us from the comfort of an aircraft carrier wardroom to a cramped, dirty cell in the Hanoi Hilton. From that moment on the film never leaves Hanoi. We live in an appropriate claustrophobia throughout the film. Williamson, initially alone, is eventually joined by dozens of American prisoners. The characters in the film parallel actual personalities closely enough to establish some credibility: a stalwart Every Colonel named Cathcart (Lawrence Pressman) corresponds with a number of actual camp SROs (senior ranking officers); an unfortunate seaman, Rasmussen (Jesse Dobson), blown off the deck of his ship, captures the irony of Douglas Hegdahl's actual predicament; a rather limited number of prison cadre, including Michael Russo as a visiting Cuban, Fidel, who takes a crack at the American "air pirates," completes the cast.

For the most part, however, Chetwynd's "painstaking reconstruction" ended with set construction and baseline character sketches. The scenes of the movie significantly differ from the extant accounts of captivity in Hoa Lo.

━━━━━━━━━━━━━━━━

When I walked into a movie theater in Fayetteville, North Carolina, to see *The Hanoi Hilton* for the first time, I wondered what part of the POW story, which characters, I would see. I had read dozens of POW accounts from Vietnam. Was this story one that I had not read? Was it a fiction constructed around the hypothetical experience of some dead hero like Medal of Honor winner Lance Sijan (*Into the Mouth of the Cat*)? Or was it going to be a documentary, a mixture of personal narrative and experience?

As I watched the film, I was increasingly confused by what I saw. The film presented a homogeneous story, but it was not from any of the stories I had read. Then again it was from all of them. It wasn't a fiction based on some dead hero. It wasn't a documentary either. It was a complete whole: a chronological narrative that included the experiences from many of the autobiographies but represented none of them. The characters were not quite right; the scenes were somehow confused.

When I left the theater, I was bewildered. Whose story was being told here? What was the point? Why had someone altered the characters and modified the scenes from the original accounts I had read? One conclusion might be that the story was developed without the cooperation of the POWs, but more than a dozen former POWs were listed in the credits as consultants. What had happened?

Eventually I was able to understand how the POW autobiographies I had read became the popular film. By comparing specific sequences in the film with similar passages in the autobiographies, I found what had made me so uncomfortable. There was a definite relation between the autobiographies and *The Hanoi Hilton*. These similarities become important because they allow us to consider the strategic alterations written into the film. We can tally these differences to show how the creators of *The Hanoi Hilton* appropriated POW experience to fit certain ideological agendas. An uncanny structural similarity between many of the POW autobiographies, *The Hanoi Hilton,* and early captivity myths allows the assumptions and exclusions of the movie to become visible. *The Hanoi Hilton* emphasizes

POW resistance, which seldom occurred, highlights atrocities, demonizes the North Vietnamese, and, most of all, concentrates on the POW struggle in Hanoi exclusive of more troubling and complex realities of why Americans were staying at the Hanoi Hilton in the first place. The film would again highlight the heroic qualities of the POW struggle. The dream of the movie was to take the plenitude of POW experience and make it history.

━━━━━━━━━━

As we have seen, the greatest problem for POWs in reconstructing their stories was the struggle between advancing some truth, a testimony of their experience, while maintaining a personal voice. Therefore, POWs would often reach for familiar metaphors that might describe the intensity of their experience in terms the American public could understand. They shaped their individual stories to the demands of collective storytelling and narrative figurability. Familiar religious metaphors would appear most often. These structures are evident in chapter titles that contain terms like "hell," "Lazarus," and "resurrection," and book titles like *With God in a P.O.W. Camp, When Hell Was in Session,* and *The Passing of the Night.* The authors adopted popular narrative strategies found in the Bible and patriotic lore to convey the pain, suffering, loneliness, sense of betrayal, hopes, and dreams that would otherwise slip through the rigid chronological structures of the extensive debriefings and written testimony they were asked to submit to the Pentagon when they returned.

Former POWs face a dilemma similar to the one faced by Holocaust survivors. Both POWs and Holocaust survivors struggled to give their stories the force of didactic testimony. James Young explains that Holocaust survivors faced "an especially painful quandary: on the one hand the survivor-scribe would write both himself and his experiences into existence after the fact, giving them both expression and textual actuality, but on the other hand, in order to make his testimony seem true, he would simultaneously efface himself from his text."[1] But neither the Holocaust survivor nor the Vietnam POW could have it both ways: there is neither objective truth nor original experience. Each text is constructed from fragments of information forced into some narrative whole. In this way the texts function less as "documentary evidence" than as "historical exegesis."[2] POW narratives attempt to convey some lasting truths about what the authors' experiences meant. But this kind of documentary certainty was forever beyond their reach.[3]

The POW story operated well at the level of myth, unlike much of the lived experience in Vietnam, because it had remained beyond the reach of television and other forms of immediate press. In fact, it was just this inaccessibility that fueled the press's insatiable hunger for elusive images of the increasingly famous POWs. The North Vietnamese used this to their advantage while the POWs were still in Hanoi. Any bit of information about the POW experience was sure to receive endless display regardless of quality or intent. This dynamic left the POWs wary of television. Most were at least partly aware of the media's effect on the public. Charles Plumb, a prisoner in Hanoi for six years, implies all of this: "What, then, about the people? We envisioned an American leaving work with nail half-pounded, trudging home with his six-pack of beer, propping his feet on the coffee table, and indifferently turning the war on and off with an automatic channel selector. We didn't want to be forgotten; we wanted to mean something."[4] Plumb voices his anxiety about both television and other representations of the POW in American media. He sees television as a means of "forgetting" an experience. He assumes that television as a form strips its subjects of meaning. William Lawrence, a prisoner of the Vietnamese for six years, would echo Plumb's anxiety in an address to West Point cadets on the night the Gulf War began: "One of the most corruptive forces in this country is television." Both Plumb and Lawrence wish to avoid one form of American media in order to escape being contextualized or recolonized in the television landscape of ads, sitcoms (like "Hogan's Heroes"), and paid programming. Unfortunately, Plumb's fears were realized when he and his fellow POWs, through their authority and fame bought at a tremendous physical and mental price, appear in ballpark publicity spots, magazine ads, paid television programming, and *The Hanoi Hilton.*

T*he Hanoi Hilton* probably did little to allay Plumb's original
fears. An unmistakably patriotic musical score backgrounds almost every sequence in the film. In a rapid opening sequence
Lieutenant Commander Williamson finds himself wandering in a
field, looking for his injured crewman. The film gets our blood boil-
ing early with an introduction to the murderous North Vietnamese.
Williamson finds his crewman and they huddle together in some
bushes. Williamson calls for help on his emergency radio—but he is
too late: an armed Vietnamese man and woman appear, seemingly
from nowhere. The Vietnamese woman takes Williamson's radio and
smashes it. Williamson's "backseater" starts to complain. He has a
broken leg. A tracking shot follows the crippled man as he drags
himself away from the North Vietnamese. The crewman pleads for
mercy all the way. Williamson looks on, dumbfounded. The Vietnamese shoot Williamson's injured comrade in the head.

None of the autobiographies describe such a sequence. Brutal treatment, mock executions, and beatings took place, to be sure. But execution of downed airmen was unusual. In at least one incident, in fact,
the opposite was true: an American pilot killed a Vietnamese man
during his capture and survived capture and captivity despite the
incident.[5] Nevertheless, *The Hanoi Hilton* chose to foreground an incident depicting North Vietnamese brutality. It is important to note
what we never see in the movie (and what we continued to avoid
during the recent Gulf War): explicit scenes of the devastation caused
by the machines the now helpless captives piloted. We never see a
dead or maimed Vietnamese. We do get plenty of dead Americans
and graphic scenes of torture.

When the film refers to the bombing it does so with a snicker. While
the POWs sit out one raid, they wonder if they might be hit by their own
bombs. Men who have been shot down most recently assure the older
POWs that it can't happen; in fact, they suggest that the Vietnamese are
probably sleeping in the courtyard for that reason. A group of POWs
sneak to the windows to find out. They cannot contain their laughter.
We might wonder if such a scene is really so hilarious.

James Mulligan, a six-year POW and author of *The Hanoi Commitment,* describes his own resistance against the Vietnamese in his description of an episode most POWs remember: being forced to bow to their North Vietnamese captors. Some POWs thought this was a small issue and decided against resisting, but others, like Mulligan, disagreed. He relates the episode: " 'Boo down!' My God he wants me to bow down to that crowd. . . . 'Bullshit!', I said. 'Screw you! I don't bow down to anyone, prisoner or not!' " The North Vietnamese guards then cruelly wrenched Mulligan's broken, untreated arm until he could stand it no longer, ". . . but I bowed down."[6]

The movie version of a similar episode is very different. A character in the movie, Captain Miles, is escorted into the compound by North Vietnamese guards who ignore the humorous monologue he delivers as they walk down the cellblock. Miles is then pushed into his cell and told, "You bow!" He replies, "You bow!" The guard then clubs Miles to the floor. As unlikely as it may seem, the guard then flees as Miles hurls his latrine bucket at the closing door. He never bows at any time during the rest of the film.

The Hanoi Hilton recovers the bowing scene as a case of successful resistance. It shows that a physically aggressive POW might succeed in making a point with the Vietnamese. If anything is clear from the autobiographical accounts, it is that this type of resistance rarely succeeded, as Mulligan's narrative points out. Yet the makers of the film represent something different, more satisfying than an American losing a one-on-one confrontation with a North Vietnamese guard. The film rarely shows one Vietnamese, armed or not, able to subdue an American POW, yet the autobiographies also contradict this. Several accounts report that Americans seldom resisted an armed guard in Hoa Lo. They point out that the cost of such an act was too high: brutal beatings at least, and probably death.

Although the film admits, through the torture and confessions of numerous POWs, that no POW can resist telling the North Vietnamese what they want to hear, we never see Miles tortured or confessing. He survives captivity without making any visible concessions to the North Vietnamese. It may be comfortable to think of Miles as a possibility, the myth of complete resistance, the embodiment of a dream played out endlessly in the guise of heroic figures from Daniel Boone

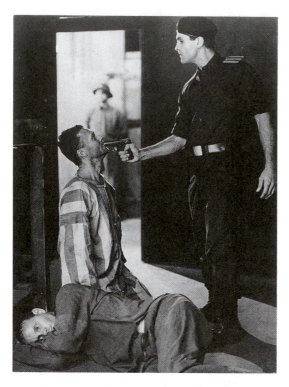

The Cuban interrogator "Fidel" (Michael Russo) threatens Captain Miles (Stephen Davies) with death. Miles defies him, explaining that the ruthless cadre will just be "doing him a favor" by killing him. Commander Williamson (Michael Moriarty) lies helpless on the floor after being tortured in *The Hanoi Hilton. Courtesy of the Museum of Modern Art/Film Stills Archive.* (1987, Cannon Films, Inc.)

to Rambo; but in reality there is only one method of complete resistance in the context of such a captivity: death.

Another intersection between the autobiographies and the movie comes during an episode of captivity many relate: the arrival of the Cuban interrogator called "Fidel." Everett Alvarez names an entire chapter of his autobiography for this interrogator. The confrontation between the American pilot, Lieutenant Oliviero (John Vargas), and Fidel appears both in Alvarez's book and *The Hanoi Hilton.*

In *The Hanoi Hilton* Lieutenant Oliviero attends a "quiz" (interrogation) with Fidel. The Cuban appeals to the American as a brother, but Oliviero quickly rejects this suggestion. The captive gives Fidel a direct answer: "Screw you." This enrages Fidel, who pulls a gun. With the gun pointed at his head, Oliviero spits on Fidel's face. The scene ends quickly with one shot—the POW murdered.

Alvarez tells a different story. He describes in great detail the arguments Fidel makes. Some of them, as I point out in chapter 9, go uncharacteristically unanswered in Alvarez's text. Alvarez explains that he did resist answering questions but did nothing to infuriate the volatile Cuban. He warns a fellow POW, "If they come for you, don't piss this guy off. For Chrissake be nice to him!"[7] Two men do die after being tortured by Fidel, but this happens over a long period of attrition. Alvarez avoids any confrontations and eventually stops seeing Fidel: "Of the eleven guys Fidel had called to quiz, I was the only one he left more or less alone after that initial grilling. Some of us speculated much later that he left me alone on orders from the Vietnamese, who may have considered me 'their own.' "[8]

The film version shortens and remakes the lived experience of the POW in order to make points that Alvarez, in particular, never suggests. First, like the bowing confrontation, the movie suggests that the POWs physically resisted their interrogators. According to the autobiographers, this is clearly not the way things happened. Second, the film foregrounds the confrontation between an American pilot as a showdown between nationalism and race. The Cuban appeals to the Puerto Rican pilot on the basis of their shared ethnicity, but the pilot violently rejects this approach and discounts everything the Cuban says. The pilot commits the equivalent of suicide in order to prove that his patriotism transcends his ethnic ties with Fidel. When the Cuban offers the pilot his freedom, the pilot responds, "I am free." The final frames of this episode show the pilot being dragged from the room, dead.

The Hanoi Hilton is also unfaithful to other aspects of captivity at Hoa Lo Prison. John Dramesi, a six-year prisoner and the author of

Code of Honor, describes thinking about a POW movie. "This, I
thought, will be part of the story that will never be told."⁹ Dramesi
presents many incidents that other narratives and *The Hanoi Hilton*
never reveal: the trial of one POW by other POWs in captivity for
being too "loud"; a general refusal by POWs to help Dramesi and
another POW escape (escape is a form of resistance mandated by the
Code of Conduct);¹⁰ and a group of POWs who refused to show their
dissent while another American was being tortured.¹¹ Other aspects of
captivity similarly left out of *The Hanoi Hilton* account include women
captives, Vietnamese women as prison staff within the compound,
contact between Americans and Vietnamese women, various escape
attempts, and the problematic return of the POWs to America.

Closely linked to this last issue is the problem of accountability.
Dramesi laments: " 'Forgive and forget, live and let live!' Why was it
necessary for us to forgive? Were we so lacking in our leadership?
And why was it necessary to forget? Unless you wanted the other
person to forget what you had done."¹² Basically no one was held
accountable for his actions in Vietnam: not the Peace Committee, not
the officers who collaborated, not the North Vietnamese, and not the
policy that put everyone in the situation in the first place. But this is
the rest of the story, the morning after, which the freeze-frame finish
of *The Hanoi Hilton* seeks to avoid. The movie diverts our attention
from other aspects of the war: bomb damage, the fighting in the rest
of Southeast Asia, the peace talks, unrest in America, and the sordid
politics of United States involvement. In the end, the movie is probably quite right about one thing: Hoa Lo, separated as it was from the
rest of the war, was the only place an American patriot could survive.

In *The Hanoi Hilton* the oppositions are always quite obvious. Equivocations are not useful in the transition from testimony to popular film.
The oppositions must be clear to avoid ambiguity, to avoid giving the
audience pause, and to avoid giving the market a chance for distrac-
tion. *The Hanoi Hilton* narrates actual events "parabolically, even didacti-
cally, around preexisting cultural axioms."¹³ The North Vietnamese
are always flat characters, the nameless enemy lurking in the hall. The
interrogator is the educated, overtly civilized, but ultimately devious
adversary. The POWs compile a long string of nicknames to tag their
captors in the autobiographies: Stag (sharper-than-average gook),

Spot, Soft Soap Fairy, Bug, Big Dumb. But these are carefully left out of the script. Major Ngo Duc (Aki Aleong), the principal North Vietnamese interrogator in the film, is only called the "Cat" in the credits for the movie. The script avoids any language that might sully the otherwise heroic dialogue in the film.

In *The Hanoi Hilton* the only racists seem to be the North Vietnamese and their sympathizers. Major Ngo Duc tells Colonel Cathcart: "They [his superiors] must see that I have helped you put your white man's arrogance aside." Later, Fidel, the Cuban interrogator, would tell Lieutenant Oliviero: "Ain't nothin' you can tell me about honkies." He then asks: "So why's a blood like you stickin' around with white scum?" The visiting peace delegations question Captain Eric Turner (Rick Fitts, an African-American POW), and present the poor treatment of his race in America as a rationale for accepting early release.

Lieutenant Ashby (Doug Savant) meets with a visiting journalist, Paula (Gloria Carlin). *The Hanoi Hilton* features women most prominently for betraying and tormenting the POWs. *Courtesy of the Museum of Modern Art/Film Stills Archive.* (1987, Cannon Films, Inc.)

He flatly refuses, saying: "I'm sorry, boss, but you got the wrong nigger!"

The roles the POW and captor play in *The Hanoi Hilton* are not new. The perspectives have the look of a World War II film made in the forties or fifties. The North Vietnamese in *The Hanoi Hilton* look suspiciously like the North Koreans in *Prisoner of War* and *The Bamboo Prison* or the Japanese in *First Yank into Tokyo* and *The Camp on Blood Island*. The roles were there before the movie even started.

Women play several stereotypical roles in *The Hanoi Hilton*. First, POW wives, so prominent in two other autobiographical POW films, *When Hell Was in Session* and *In Love and War,* are left out. *The Hanoi Hilton* avoids the complexities other movies attempt to engage. The actual roles women do get to play in the film work to amplify the tortured predicament of the POWs. One shot shows a POW reading a letter from his wife. Major Fischer (Jeffrey Jones) stops halfway through the letter and goes into an angry convulsion. He shouts, "Son of a bitch! Why now!" His wife has just divorced him. The Vietnamese who grabs Williamson and clumsily crushes his radio in the opening sequence is a woman. The second peace delegation in the movie features a Jane Fonda clone, Paula (Gloria Carlin), who unwittingly prods the haggard-looking POWs for propaganda sound bytes. Her attempts at sensitivity and concern about the war are made to look frivolous. The final shot of her visit focuses on her expressive embrace with the cruel North Vietnamese torturer, Major Ngo Duc. In a scene depicting the infamous Hanoi March, where prisoners were forced to walk a gantlet of violent North Vietnamese citizens, and in the final scene, showing the POWs assembling for release, the deep focus distracts us with a well-dressed blonde woman with a camera prominently displayed against the background of drably robed, black-haired Vietnamese. The female characters in these sequences are images of betrayal. Their appearance eclipses the activism of POW wives and the deference Vietnamese women apparently showed American men, as discussed in numerous autobiographical accounts, including those of Mulligan, Dramesi, Alvarez, and Plumb.

These episodes show not only the constructedness of the film medium but also the differing interpretations that come from film and autobiography. The differences appear to hinge on the controlling mythologies of the POW experience: the dream of complete resistance, the superiority of American character, captivity as a test in a figural hell. The popular film magnifies these themes, because it must cater to the demands of collective storytelling even more rigorously than autobiography. Film must become accessible to a wider collective imagination; it must normalize the details experienced to reach a larger audience.

The constructedness of the movie belies the memories it pretends to represent. The movie, like most cultural productions, comes in a coherent narrative skein, while memory comes in "freely associated moments, kernels of time around which events gather and accrue significance."[14] By putting their experiences on video, the POW consultants for *The Hanoi Hilton* put their experience within the conventions of narrative film. This form demands contortions—not to meet the needs of the POWs or their experience but to represent the story in ways that satisfy the audience and sell to the mass market. Unlike the narration in autobiography, *The Hanoi Hilton*'s structure, not the speaker, narrates events.

The Hanoi Hilton takes an amalgam of POW accounts, the significant events of captivity, and the most remarkable characteristics of different POWs to produce a narrative whole.[15] The making of the movie could easily be a paradigm for myth production: a normalized story derived from a collection of individuals, many of whom have told their story elsewhere. It is, of course, just this quality of *The Hanoi Hilton* that allows us to read closely the contrast between individual and film account, the transition from autobiographical narrative to movie mythology.

No episode makes this transition more obvious than the Cuban interrogator sequence. Everett Alvarez does not discuss *The Hanoi Hilton* in his book about his postcaptivity public life, but he does lament in his second book, *Code of Conduct,* that the movie "*Platoon* lacks historical and political perspective."[16] The irony of such an observation is stunning when we consider the way Lieutenant Oliviero's *Hanoi Hilton* encounter with "Fidel" was strategically different from Alvarez's own account of the incident in *Chained Eagle.*

Ronald Reagan himself offered a plug for *The Hanoi Hilton:* "Every American should see this powerful and moving film as a tribute to our

POWs and as an exercise in sheer understanding of history." His blurb is prominently displayed on the jacket of the home video release. The impropriety of such a comment from the President of the United States aside, we cannot avoid the naiveté of his statement. He again seemed to be confusing movies with reality. But he was quite right: *The Hanoi Hilton* was meant to be a history lesson for Americans. Whether the movie has anything to do with history is another matter.

———————

*T*he Hanoi Hilton is the site of "cultural poesis—and politics" where there is a "constant reconstitution of selves and others through specific exclusions, conventions, and discursive practices."[17] Predictably, cultural expectations and needs imposed the roles of the characters in *The Hanoi Hilton*. It may have looked like Hanoi to the ex-POWs, but it was really just Korea or Japan all over again in the context of the film. The characters were shaped more from without than within. Foucault calls this process "normalization."[18] The POW story could and has become "legend," but only according to the needs of American culture. The narratives of both the films and the autobiographies reach for a historical reality and political conformity that leave an "untenable historicity in these tales: they are simultaneously history and legend, documentation and art."[19]

In the transformation from experience to narrative the POW autobiographies become "the seeds of new legends, tales that in time will achieve a certain legendary status of their own."[20] These new legends quickly eclipse their autobiographical beginnings, however. By showing themselves as clearly and undeniably heroic, the POWs created an irresistible character, an even more satisfying hero: the POW left behind, the missing in action (MIA). The MIA is a seductive image because it allows us to again recover the POW experience and live the triumph of his imminent return. The POW story has helped America sustain a Cold War logic for the last decade. The POW allows America to ignore the disaster of Vietnam and refigure it as a victory: the MIA allows us to revisit that conflict with a just cause and win in the imaginary realm or "virtual world" of cultural productions. *The Hanoi Hil-*

ton is a pretext for violence that vicariously carries out what some Americans would have had us do: defeat the North Vietnamese, settling once and for all the question of American superiority.

The POW eventually found himself written out of what began as his story. As the figure of Rambo and his clones populated the cultural landscape, the POW lost his mantle of fame. His story, appropriated and extrapolated, jumped beyond his control. POWs showed up less frequently as independent speakers and more often as hired corporate decals and spokesmen in speeches, ads, and TV spots that co-opted their experience.

Whatever good intentions it may have had, *The Hanoi Hilton* ultimately replaces lived experience with something else. The film takes on the meaning and significance of the experience it pretends to represent. In this way such portrayals of the POW in American popular culture are intensely pornographic. However convincing the set of the movie was for Everett Alvarez or Ronald Reagan, the characters who populate *The Hanoi Hilton* were unrepresentative of those portrayed in the POW autobiographies. In many ways the movie succeeds in co-opting the POW autobiographies in much the same way that the North Vietnamese attempted to use the POWs for propaganda: the North Vietnamese attempted to remake the POWs—*The Hanoi Hilton* did it.

━━━━━━━━━

I n her autobiography, *On the Other Side,* Kate Webb, a prisoner of the Vietcong for two weeks, describes well the problem with representing the POW experience in movies: "That's why all prisoner-of-war movies are unreal. They can't film long minutes of boredom, film the straw roof, the texture, the tree outside, the guard fiddling with the sores on his feet—could flashback to me on that, fiddling with my feet. Boring. As film editor I slashed the film with a stamp marked 'Bores me to tears.' "[21] Webb is quite right: television, film, and other staples of American culture can make the actual world appear rather boring. Perhaps we can never adequately reconstruct the POW experience on film. Perhaps we should not even try.

5

Selling and the POW

The language of advertising is the most prolific and aggressive form of rhetoric in our culture today. Advertising covers the surface of our culture: it is the primary text of American communication, the political and economic high ground of media. However well advertising seems submerged in television and magazines, in actuality it dominates print media and punctuates television programming. Nowhere is the collusion of advertising and substantive journalism or television programming so unselfconscious as in the current genre of multipage print media ads that mimic articles and news stories, or paid-television programs that mimic the dialogic motif of the television talk show. Similarly, images of the POW in advertising pretend to inform and teach us about POW experience, but have really used the pathos of POW fame as a decal, almost as involvement media for gaining a wider audience and market. We pause at the POW icon while turning a page or flipping channels because we trust the POW image. We see it as insulated from the confusing and frustrating flow of political and economic agendas that attempt to coerce us. The POW experience seems to have a substance that goes beyond the simulacrum.

It would be naive to ignore how advertising casts the Vietnam POW. Advertising seeks not so much to represent the POW as to identify him with us. The rhetoric of advertising uses the qualities of the POW story that we will identify with most closely to get our attention and convince. In doing so these ads reveal the most adhesive elements of POW lore. The assumptions behind how the ads address us are at the heart of the POW myth.

"You'll never know how sweet freedom can be unless you've lost it for 8½ years."[1] This caption appears next to a photograph of Everett Alvarez, Jr., former Vietnam POW. The black-and-white photograph looks like a candid shot of the former navy flier. Alvarez's tilted stature and side-looking pose give the impression that we have interrupted him. His mouth is open as though he were speaking to someone else and did not have much time to spend talking with us. The implication is that the remark, along with others that frame the picture, are off-the-cuff comments made by a man with people to see and places to go, a man in the midst of an active life.

Alvarez is dressed in a business suit. In the background of the photograph we see the corner of a framed portrait. We see just enough to understand that this portrait has a conventional horizon perspective: a conservative, high-brow art perspective. The image of Alvarez is juxtaposed with more of his comments: "When you're caged up in an alien land you begin to understand the essence of liberty, and what we have here in this country. . . ." The words "alien" and "caged" create a sharp contrast with the conservatively set and dressed Alvarez. This contrast leads us to the punchline of the caption: "The return to freedom was exhilarating. Everything I touched felt good. Everything smelled so good. It was sweet beyond belief. Now, I wake up every day and, no matter what I have to face, I look forward to it with anticipation. I'm here and able to choose, able to do, able to act as a free individual."

Where would such an image occur on the American cultural landscape? It might be interesting to list the political spaces left to images such as this, but it should come as no surprise that this image occurs as one of a series of full-page magazine ads sponsored by an American corporation: Philip Morris. Each of the advertisements in this particular campaign features a similar cameo-style image. Each includes a caption dealing with freedom and individual rights (a footnote to the ad offers a free copy of the Bill of Rights). Others in the series use the iconic qualities of James Earl Jones, former Representative Barbara

"You'll never know how sweet freedom can be unless you've lost it for 8½ years."

EVERETT ALVAREZ, JR.
VIETNAM POW

Everett Alvarez, Jr. was starved, beaten and forced to endure unspeakable tortures.

His years of horror began in 1964 when the U.S. Navy plane he was piloting got shot down over the Gulf of Tonkin. For the next 8½ years he was a prisoner of war—the longest held in North Vietnam.

During those endless months he struggled to preserve his honor and his sense of self. And by his example inspired dozens of other POW's.

"When you're caged up in an alien land," relates Alvarez, "you begin to understand the essence of liberty, and what we have here in this country....

"The return to freedom was exhilarating. Everything I touched felt good. Everything I ate tasted good. Everything smelled so good. It was sweet beyond belief. Now, I wake up every day and, no matter what I have to face, I look forward to it with anticipation. I'm here and able to choose, able to do, able to act as a free individual."

Philip Morris Companies Inc.

KRAFT GENERAL FOODS · MILLER BREWING COMPANY · PHILIP MORRIS U.S.A.

© Philip Morris Companies Inc. 1990

Join Philip Morris Companies Inc. in support of the National Archives' celebration of the 200th anniversary of the Bill of Rights. For a free copy of this historic document, call 1-800-552-2222, or write Bill of Rights · Philip Morris Companies Inc. · 2020 Pennsylvania Ave. N.W. · Suite 533 · Washington D.C. 20006

Jordan, and the former president of Notre Dame, Theodore M. Hesburgh, to convey the same idea: freedom. The array of personalities in the campaign is meant to reach audiences across a broad spectrum of gender, race, occupation, and religion. The ideology behind the advertisement would appear detached from the interests of Philip Morris, even if you look closely at the fine print beneath the corporate logo, which lists "Kraft General Foods-Miller Brewing Company-Philip Morris."

What is left out of this seemingly revealing list of corporate interests is the component of Philip Morris that motivates the freedom theme in this ad: tobacco. In fact, tobacco has accounted for the lion's share of Philip Morris profits during the last two decades. It is interesting that Philip Morris should, at least implicitly, address this ad to the component of its business entirely left out of the subtitle of its logo. It is equally interesting to note the particular qualities of freedom Alvarez chooses. According to the comments in the ad, freedom "felt good," "tasted good," and "smelled so good." Freedom apparently has the sensual qualities of the cigarettes and beer Philip Morris wants to peddle. A more accurate caption to this ad therefore might be "Freedom is cigarettes and beer."

But what is most interesting, and perhaps most troubling, is the range of personalities presented in the ads. In the context of the other figures appropriated by Philip Morris to spread its message, Alvarez's icon value springs from a lived experience rather than from his occupation. On the other hand, Alvarez's status and perhaps even his employment are important and implied. He wears a business suit and appears to be in the midst of some activity, some unspecified upper-middle-class job. The presence and absence of his costume are at once important. He wears not the uniform of his previous occupation (naval officer), but the costume and facial mask of power in this country. In this way he is the emblem of the recovered Vietnam veteran, a functional part of American society and economy. Alvarez appears out of uniform for another reason, too: the military is important, but it most comfortably exists in a synchronic past, a remembered but never present Vietnam. He is an emblem for Americans who not only have put the war behind them but also have learned and profited from their wartime experience. His image is an implicit refutation of the negative effects of Vietnam and accompanying post-traumatic stress disorder. His appearance is an antidote for American anxiety in the aftermath of Vietnam.

The immanent qualities of the Alvarez image are amplified through his costume and mask (both present and absent). These qualities constitute Alvarez's icon value. This value allows him to appear at the national level in media publications framed by deceptive claims. Philip Morris has appropriated Alvarez and the POW story from Vietnam to spread its message of "freedom." Of course, this concern for freedom is not so much a philanthropic gesture as an appeal for public support to thwart the increasing restrictions on cigarette smoking in America. In the context of the advertisement freedom is a coercive abstraction. At least implicitly, bans on the use of cigarettes equate with imprisonment by the North Vietnamese.

Among the popular POW figures Alvarez is unique. He has held senior positions in both the Peace Corps and Veterans Administration; his name is familiar to many in government and veterans' groups; and he is a minority member from a poor migrant background. These factors make Alvarez attractive. The key components of the Alvarez icon are explicated in a short (and therefore typical) character spot in *People* magazine.[2] The *People* article opens a window on Alvarez as a promotion for the book *Chained Eagle,* which he co-wrote with Anthony Pitch.

People distills Alvarez's autobiographical product into the most juicy yet tasteful issue bytes. What the Philip Morris ad touts as "unspeakable tortures" become in the context of the *People* article explicitly described scenes of physical and psychological torture. The article begins with a focus on the various injuries Alvarez received as a POW. These bodily reminders are then related to the psychological ills that the book will apparently help readers to purge. *People* highlights the most brutal incident of torture from the book as the link between the bodily pain Alvarez still experiences and the psychological pain he has yet to deal with. This initial image shows an example of what we might find in the rest of the article and the book: the public display of Alvarez's very private psychological anguish and the revisitation of his wartime horror.

The implied purpose of the *People* spot is to help Alvarez deal with his experience as victim. By reading Alvarez's story, by buying his book, we are sympathizing with his misfortune. We embrace Alvarez and his family by listening to intimate details of his personal struggle. Alvarez's story is as sentimental as it is tragic. Revelations of his experience appeal to the religious qualities of confession while hinting at the secular possibilities of psychological trauma and recovery: another 911 success story for us, another self-help success story for the American individual. Alvarez's "confession" appears to unburden him of his painful past while promising him salvation in our sympathetic gaze. Audience interest in Alvarez's life seems almost philanthropic.

But presentations of pain in such popular tabloids seldom function as catharsis for distressed individuals. Instead, such stories offer up their subjects for the pleasure of our analysis.³ As readers of Alvarez's story of physical punishment and witnesses of his play-action psychological struggle, we in effect assume the position of torturer, vicariously experiencing the site of human anguish without having to experience the physical pain. The reader becomes the torturer, exhorting Alvarez to tell all, to display his pain and confess his hidden feelings. If the American market is a reflection of American people (because we elect what we want to see through purchase), then the Alvarez spot reflects our desire to assume the role of torturer and confessor. In this way the *People* article functions much like the "forced confession" extracted by the North Vietnamese. The article re-creates the confession and points to the book where Alvarez has "told all." The coauthored book and article are in many ways like the "dictated letter" written by Alvarez in captivity, except the book and article are written through the conservative discourse of Reagan America rather than the convoluted Marxist doctrine of the North Vietnamese.

The *People* article also highlights Alvarez's minority status, a factor obviously important in the Philip Morris ad. The ad may, in the end, be just another in the series of cigarette advertisements that overtly target the poor and minority groups who may have suffered most from use of the implied product. In the *People* article Alvarez's minority background is predictably emphasized: he is characterized by his earliest memories of his "Mexican-American father" and "working in a vegetable field the summer after he finished the sixth grade." Although the ad foregrounds his family and uses Alvarez's father extensively, there is no indication in the article that his parents are divorced. So much for the great American family *People* uses as a contrast in order to indict Tangee Alvarez (Alvarez's first wife, who divorced him while he was in captivity). In order to heighten the tragedy implied by Alvarez's own involuntary wartime divorce, the *People* article says nothing about the home-front problems between Lalo and Chloe (Alvarez's parents).

The Philip Morris advertisement says even less. It makes no mention of Alvarez's minority status or family problems. Instead, he is tied to an abstraction: freedom. The difficulties and complications of race, class, and the cigarette as a harmful product are smoothed over by this abstraction, just as the painful and debilitating experience of the POW is buried in order to give the Alvarez cameo a privileged place in the discourse on freedom.

But Alvarez's minority status is important. He plays a definite role in the array of personalities portrayed in other versions of the Philip Morris ad. He was attractive to Philip Morris because he had a definite appeal to minority audiences. Alvarez himself remarks often on his fame as a minority figure in his book about life after captivity, *Code of Conduct*. But he was ambivalent about issues of race from the time of his return: "I felt I was one of them [in this case a group of Mexican-American workers shouting "Alvarez! Alvarez!"] in many ways, but not in the political and social-action areas."[4] However Alvarez felt about helping others, Philip Morris was able to buy his minority status and fame for their purposes.

Alvarez's experience as a POW affords him special status, gives him a privileged position that we will "never know." One of the leading television news magazines, "Prime Time Live," featured Alvarez at the end of a show just prior to Thanksgiving 1989.[5] Alvarez was pictured in casual clothes strolling along the wall at the Vietnam Veterans Memorial in Washington. Alvarez spoke a brief essay on the meaning of "Thanksgiving." In the context of this television spot Alvarez functions as a bearer of national values. In the context of popular culture he has achieved the position required to define a uniquely American holiday.

Alvarez's post-POW life has a metonymic quality that allows him to stand for all Vietnam veterans. He is a kind of living scar, the embodiment of a divisive conflict that still haunts America. Alvarez still may be crippled by the conflict, but his image on television and in popular magazines and ads confirms that he was strong enough to survive the war and his tortures. It implies a transcendent and essential American self that defines America in much the same way Thanksgiving does. The spin doctors producing *Prime Time Live* could think of no more appropriate testimonial for the Thanksgiving holiday. Thus, in the television spot Alvarez's own horrible experience, which we might vicariously experience through his image, becomes an immediate and assumable pretext for giving thanks.

T he ironies of selling with the POW image are even more conspicuous in a quarter-page ad that appeared in the *New York Times*.[6] This advertisement also used the icon quality of the Vietnam POW. It was published during the height of the battle between Frank Lorenzo and the Eastern Pilots Association. The advertisement, sponsored by the Eastern Pilots of the Airline Pilots' Association, features a picture of five former Vietnam POWs framed in union rhetoric exhorting "fellow Americans" to "join with the 3,400 proud Eastern pilot men and women, many of whom flew to protect America." The picture and description are meant to stand for all Eastern employees who have taken up arms against yet another "nightmare": "They Are Now Fighting Against The American Nightmare—Frank Lorenzo!" Dressed in their corporate, paramilitary uniforms, they re-create their moral/political victory over the North Vietnamese oppressor. The POWs here serve as an emblem for the struggle against another oppressor, Frank Lorenzo.

What is perhaps most interesting about this particular ad is the story it implies. The headline proclaims that "These Former POW's Fought For The AMERICAN DREAM." The words "AMERICAN DREAM" are in the largest and boldest type on the page. The POWs are apparently still fighting for that same objective, only now they face a new enemy: Frank Lorenzo. The ad parallels the POW experience with the fight against a corporate Godzilla.

These Former POW's Fought For The
AMERICAN DREAM

They Are Now Fighting Against The American Nightmare—Frank Lorenzo!

Striking Eastern pilots (from left to right) Gerry Gerndt of Milwaukee, Wisconsin, Air Force veteran and prisoner of war in Vietnam from August 1967 to March 1973; Hubert Buchanan of Amherst, New Hampshire, Air Force veteran and POW from September 1966 to March 1973; Charles Brown of South Hadley, Massachusetts, Air Force veteran and POW from December 1972 to March 1973; John Anderson of Montgomery, Alabama, Air Force veteran and POW from December 1972 to February 1973; and Ron Mastin of Marietta, Georgia, Air Force veteran and POW from January 1967 to March 1973.

Courage, dedication to duty, and a belief in a man's obligation to moral principles have always been the hallmark of what America represents.

Nowhere are these standards better exemplified than by these former prisoners of war, who now are striking Eastern pilots. They are joined by 3,400 of their fellow Eastern pilots, 1,500 of whom served in the armed forces and are Korea and Vietnam veterans.

Frank Lorenzo recently said that the striking Eastern pilots have been "brainwashed." These men, who, unlike Lorenzo, have seen war and brainwashing first hand, know exactly what they are doing. They are fighting another war—a war against greed and power...a war to protect the safety, pride and dignity of the aviation profession.

Frank Lorenzo has reduced our American Dream to an American Nightmare. His management is stripping away everything all of us have worked to build. As Congressman Doug Bosco (D-CA) said on the floor of the House of Representatives, "Frank Lorenzo is the neutron bomb of the airline industry. The assets remain as booty, the people lose their jobs, their livelihoods, their pensions, their health benefits, yes, even their airline tickets." He protects assets and destroys people. Frank Lorenzo is not an airline builder. Instead he is a destroyer of families, a pillager of the American Dream.

Fellow Americans, today we need your help! Please join with the 3,400 proud Eastern pilot men and women, many of whom flew to protect America, who are now honoring the legal IAM picket line.

PLEASE HELP PROTECT OUR AMERICAN DREAM AND DON'T FLY EASTERN UNTIL THE STRIKE HAS ENDED.

THIS MESSAGE FROM THE EASTERN PILOTS, AIR LINE PILOTS ASSOCIATION

Of course, it is Lorenzo who threw the first stone in this battle of metaphors. The ad points out that Lorenzo said "the Eastern Pilots have been 'brainwashed.' " The ad doesn't need more than this one word: "These men, who, unlike Lorenzo, have seen war and brainwashing first hand, know exactly what they are doing. They are fighting another war—a war against greed and power . . . a war to protect the safety, pride and dignity of the aviation profession." The ad shows two causes the pilots must fight to protect in the current struggle: the American Dream and the aviation profession. The implication of the ad is that we should consider the union, the aviation profession, and the American Dream interchangeable parts of a romanticized whole—a difficult antic at best.

The next paragraph of the ad extends the POW struggle metaphor that Lorenzo supposedly opened up. The rhetoric of this paragraph is meant to have referential value. It draws on a historical mythology (the Vietnam POW story) accessible to the target audience. In both the POW and union struggles the "American Dream [has been] reduced to an American Nightmare"; the oppressor is "stripping away everything" in a quest for "booty." Lorenzo (and by implication the North Vietnamese) "destroys people" without physical effect; he is a "neutron bomb," a "destroyer of families, a pillager of the American Dream."

Unfortunately, the ad conflates much of what exists in war-POW lore. The headline itself attaches to the Vietnam war a cause that, if taken alone, could hardly stand. The headline says that the POWs were fighting for the American Dream, but it is unclear whether their struggle as POWs or their bombing attacks or both are counted in that struggle. In either case it is dubious at best to say that these men were fighting for the American Dream in Vietnam. If they were fighting for an American dream it would have to be an American dream abstracted, invented, and then imposed on South Vietnam. Such rhetoric recovers the war in terms of an abstraction (the American Dream) that was hardly U.S. motivation in Vietnam. The American Dream is arguably not the most stable abstraction in 1990s America. The concept of the American Dream is under serious renegotiation in American culture, even if one accepts that it did once exist as a collective vision or stable construct. In most POW autobiographies, there is no suggestion that the American Dream was the motivation for the POWs' struggle, when they were prisoners or otherwise.

The ad exploits the breach in Lorenzo's rhetoric by focusing on the term "brainwashing." But "brainwashing" was never associated with the Vietnam POWs in anything but idle speculation during the war. The image of POW brainwashing exists largely as a construct from the lore surrounding the prisoners in Korea, not Vietnam. In fact, few of the mass media, clinical, or experiential texts that concern the American Vietnam POW characterize the experience in terms of brainwashing. There were similarities between the two experiences, but brainwashing was an image Vietnam POWs attempted to work against rather than with. The Eastern Pilots Association ad claims that "these men . . . have seen war and brainwashing first hand." But this claim transfers the brainwashing of the Korean POW experience to the Vietnam POW experience, an aspect of the experience that most Vietnam POW accounts refute.

Another part of the brainwashing analogy becomes significant when the ad takes the POWs as one group. The five POWs pictured spent differing periods in captivity. One spent seven years, but two spent less than four months in North Vietnam. The latter two men were captured in the Christmas 1972 bombing, which was credited with forcing an agreement on POW release. The problem with grouping these men together in any rhetorical/political economy is that the experiences of the "old guys" were significantly different from those of the "new shootdowns." This distinction is played out endlessly in the representations of the war, from written autobiographies to *The Hanoi Hilton*. The greatest issue separating early and late shootdowns appears to be treatment by the North Vietnamese. Torture, mistreatment, and segregation were characteristic of captivity until the POWs in Hanoi were placed in collective lodgings. The period after 1971, commonly referred to as "camp unity,"⁷ saw the most lenient treatment of POWs. This was particularly true of the first months of 1973, when the POWs in Hanoi were being "fattened up" for repatriation. So it is hard to accept the claim that all of the POWs pictured were the victims of brainwashing, even if one takes the license to label the harsh treatment received by the early POWs as such.

Another aspect of this struggle analogy is at least mildly ironic. The labor union characterizes Lorenzo, a legitimized corporate tycoon, in terms of "booty," "stripping," and "pillaging." These are exactly the terms used by the North Vietnamese in their ham-handed critique of capitalism and American involvement in Southeast Asia. The union rhetoric and the "brainwashing" by the Vietnamese and Koreans share a political locus in that they both criticize capitalist ideals and excesses. The irony comes when we realize that the union rhetoric endorses the "brainwashing" conducted by the enemy in two wars. At least part of what the North Vietnamese told these POWs appears to have been correct: the POWs found themselves victimized by the unethical practices of corporate capitalism (hence the current struggle, loss of employment).

Another irony in the image of the POWs pictured against the background of an enveloping American flag occurs when one puts the ideology of the union against the dynamics of corporate economics in America. The union wants to appropriate the same symbols that legitimize the corporate structure they are fighting. What's more, the average annual salary of the unionized workers in this struggle is $65,000. If this is a class struggle, it is a struggle within the upper strata of the American economy. If these people are prisoners of Frank Lorenzo, they are perhaps better kept than other prisoners.

———————

T he Eastern Pilots advertisement is at best a mixed message. The co-opted union stretches to recover a Vietnam wartime opposition (which never really existed) in a dubious analogy with current worker-management struggles. What is perhaps more important is the use of the POW as icon, abstracted from any actual context, at once trivializing the POW experience as comparable with unemployment while reenacting the very criticisms of capitalism used by the group they wish to make a demon-other, the North Vietnamese. The ad claims that the union is involved in the moral equivalent of war and that the union is being held hostage in an experience comparable to the torturous imprisonment experienced by the Vietnam POWs.

Such messages, however implied, are nothing more than useful and pathetic lies. If Americans accept such claims uncritically, they will produce a truth that defines itself in terms of polarizing analogies and groundless images. Yet such messages appear to have access to mass media in ways that elude all but a privileged group of people in this country, a country which would appear to shun censorship. Apparently, the political economy of mass media has little to do with freedom or democracy. As we survey the ever increasing body of representation surrounding the Vietnam POW, it is increasingly clear that certain stories germinate and grow while others are marginalized and die. It is this struggle that is most interesting: the negotiation of the POW story in American culture. This reading of the Philip Morris and Pilots Association ads is a paradigm for reading POW texts. Such readings accomplish what the "truth box" does for political campaign advertisements: analyzes the message in these representations in order to offer alternatives to the valorized, authenticated, normalized, and complacent readings the ad makers hope for.

"Idea advertising"[8] is nothing new, of course, but the line of ads under discussion has less to do with idea advertising than with outright deception. Philip Morris is not trying to sell an idea without a product; rather, the ad tries to sell an idea that has traction in an immediate political debate. Moreover, the product is specifically written out of the advertisement. By using freedom as an abstraction, Philip Morris diverts attention from its rather controversial agenda of selling cigarettes in spite of public health warnings. It is no coincidence that this particular ad, although it at least implicitly promotes tobacco, avoids the government statute that mandates the warning box required on explicit cigarette advertisements. By avoiding the debate entirely by an abstraction, Philip Morris not only promotes its products but does so under the guise of philanthropic concern for human freedom and national sovereignty. It misleads the reader who cannot decode the politics of the ad, it promotes a questionable product, it allows the company to pretend to be concerned with an abstraction that has nothing to do with the explicit motives of the corporation, it uses a popular minority figure to sell a product perhaps overused by the race and class represented by the personality selected, it appropriates a painful experience from American history and implies a connection between it and a controversial product, and it gives a very painful and perhaps unnecessary experience a positive, privileged value that might encourage rather than discourage a re-creation of the site of the very pain portrayed in the ad. The very existence of this ad and its privileged place in the mass media points away from and not toward the concept the ad pretends to promote: freedom.

The Eastern Pilots ad stretches to recover a discredited and painful struggle as a paradigm for current union-management dysfunction. It also uses certain facts in a creative way to obscure distinctions within a very diverse group of prisoners. Its rhetoric functions in an economy of information presented in support of a white, male, bourgeois organization that seeks to expand and consolidate its power base in the context of an increasingly capitalistic corporate America. Wrapping the POWs in the flag attempts to identify the union with American values in opposition to a legitimized and successful capitalist. The pathetic irony and unintended message of the ad is that these POWs are parroting the critique of capitalism they were forced to listen to and resist as prisoners.

The "giant killer" of ad-alley,[9] Philip Morris, selected the Alvarez image because it had an emotional appeal and a referential value. Similarly, the POW struggle depicted in the pilot advertisement reconstructs the oppositions of the Vietnam POW struggle to fit a contemporary context. The ad points to a history that is known and accessible; its referential value springs from the popularity of the Vietnam POW experience. It is the further representation and function of the POW experience that I want to explore in the rest of this book. The POW story implicit in the image bytes presented in the ads is one so well known in American culture that it has become a kind of lore. Ads, news stories, self-help tapes, popular movies, and even political power today appropriate the latent image of the Vietnam POW in order to send messages and promote ideas that often have little to do with the original lived experience. The hostage dilemma faced endlessly in the Middle East is a prime example of how the prisoner, particularly the illegitimate captive of competing factional and national interests, has come to occupy a central place in the American national conscience.

Everett Alvarez saw his fame as problematic: "My 'celebrity' status had not ended . . . at the airport . . . I was . . . looked on as a hero.

There wasn't anything I could do about it. In some ways I had little more control over what began happening to me in freedom than I had had in prison."[10] The fame accorded the POW has become a kind of "costume," a term that Leo Braudy has used in his critique of "fame and its history."[11] Braudy sees the "desire for fame" as a "culturally adaptive trait by which the individual retailors traditional standards of distinctive personal nature into a costume by which he can succeed before his chosen audience."[12] But for the POWs this "costume" was not something derived from or constructed by the individual. Rather, it was figuratively handed to the authorized POWs when they walked off the plane upon return to America after captivity.[13] Thus, the POW who appears in the ads I have read might be seen as a kind of clown, an individual given a remarkable "costume" of fame and provided with a particular routine to entertain a particular audience.

In a way, the POWs have become just another set of talking heads, speaking only when authorized by economic and political interest. They seldom speak for themselves but instead are appropriated into images that speak for them in a voice-over, dubbed discourse. This discourse is the POW story, normalized through various narrative structures and political economies that are seldom foregrounded. The POW story in the context of the advertisements discussed here has become a mythical whole constructed from the needs of special interest and existing power. But, as we shall see, this dynamic is not limited to advertising: it has become part of the history of the Vietnam War.

6
Errors and Expectations

In "Beyond Survival: The Next Chapter," Gerald Coffee describes his life as a navy aviator and his seven years as a POW in North Vietnam. In order to make his audience (a recorded presence in this "live" audio program) understand his experiences, he uses comparisons to cultural artifacts that parallel his experience. While describing his early career as a pilot, Coffee explains: "You all saw *Top Gun?* That was me." Later he uses other films to describe his expectations upon capture: "I was lookin' for that classic old Hollywood version of a POW camp. Right? Like we've all seen in the movies: *The Great Escape,* you know, Steve McQueen doin' it, or *Stalag 17* or 'Hogan's Heroes,' the TV program. Right? The guards are kinda rolypoly, the guys race mice, bet cigarettes and play the guitar; little volleyball. Not too bad. You can last out the war that way. That wasn't how it was in World War II of course, but that's what I was looking for. That was my concept."

Like many other POWs, Gerald Coffee points directly to movies, books, and other popular images that influenced his conception of captivity. The autobiographies explain how POWs got their ideas about captivity and how those ideas and expectations served them when they became prisoners. The POW narratives worked both with and against dominant images of captivity in American culture.

For example, in the first few minutes of his speech, Gerald Coffee validates the popular *Top Gun* image of the military pilot while fore-grounding vacuous popular conceptions of captivity. Although these images may seem contradictory, his use of them testifies to the currency they have for a wide variety of American audiences. Coffee relies on such imagery to communicate his otherwise remote experiences. By using key referents from film and television, he is able to identify with his audience to better sell his "lessons learned." Popular conceptions of captivity in film and television, credible or not, are critical to our common language and understanding. They exist as icons of the imagination, which we must work with or against in order to communicate.

We cannot let the contradictions of Coffee's presentation remain unchallenged, however. *Top Gun* may entertain audiences, but the imagination it fosters has a dubious relation with lived experience. Coffee validates for his audience the same popular images that so disillusioned him early in his captivity. By calling attention to and using such stuff, he endorses its value, if not as lessons for captivity, then as effective tools for discussing the dilemmas of captivity. Such approaches leave POWs in a limbo between myth and the dark prison cells they inhabited.

⸻

Robinson Risner, a senior-ranking POW and leader of resistance for his seven-year stay in Hanoi, encountered the gap between his expectations and reality during his early days as a POW. He recalls his first hopes: "We'll have games, and there will probably be a big compound." Risner goes on to relate how he foolishly missed the opportunity to get information about the Korean POW experience from a friend who had lived it. "I had never asked him if he had been tortured or had gotten enough to eat. I remembered him saying that the Koreans had given the POWs some padded or quilted clothes in the winter but that it had not been sufficient. That was all I could remember."[1] In the end he concedes, "All my information had come through the survival schools and from what I had read in fiction."

This "information" proved wholly inadequate. "But some things I remember quite well. None of them jibed with my concept of a prisoner-of-war camp."[2] He found increasingly that his precaptivity conceptions of a prison camp were based more on the needs of the American public than on any actual experience. Thus Risner, when he wrote his own story, had to fill the gap, compensating for his errors by constructing some new ideas and recovering some old ones about himself and his predicament.[3]

James Stockdale affirms the positive effect his military training had on his conduct during captivity. He mentions experiences at survival schools and the Naval Academy that prepared him for his experience. But even given such precise and directed training, Stockdale admits that his conception of captivity was somewhat naive. At one point he lost his patience: "I was getting damned tired of sitting there in Heartbreak [a particular cell block in Hoa Lo] watching all these other new shootdowns spend about ten days there and then have the heavenly experience of being taken out and put in a jeep and taken to a real prison camp of the sort I dreamed about." Stockdale eventually found out the truth: "A man who had been to that outlying camp . . . was sent back. Only there was no campfire; he hadn't had a cellmate."[4] Thus Stockdale confronted the errors of his expectations.

The vast majority of POWs describe various parts of Hoa Lo prison with names from American prison lore, but they scrupulously avoid comparing their prison experience in Vietnam with prison in the United States. Few of the narratives explicitly compare the POW experience with the experiences in or images of the American penal system. It is strange that no one dared reach for familiar stories of American prisoners to relate their experience (the captives in Hoa Lo prison do refer to one building as "Alcatraz," but never elaborate on the implied comparison).[5] The punishments, solitary confinement, and prolonged imprisonment that promoted such a watershed of privileged knowledge from the officer-pilots of Vietnam failed to do the same for "criminals" in the American penal system in the context of American lore. The stuff of instant fame in one context became legitimately suppressed in another.

Kate Webb, however, a journalist who spent two weeks as a prisoner of the Viet Cong, explicitly compares herself with the prison inmate:

"Johnny Cash, where are you now? Do the San Quentin inmates sweep the floors of their cells? They have news. Surely they do. The warden would say Pakistan blew up today. Well, maybe he wouldn't. He'd say something like Pete was getting out on parole."[6] Webb begins this passage by describing her captivity as worse than that of a prisoner in America: "They have news." But she soon reverses her conclusion, and thus implies that the prison experience in Vietnam might be quite similar to the prison experience in America. This is an analogy that others who portray their experience as religious, patriotic, or somehow linked to the essential American self would consciously avoid. Such a comparison would erode the hero image of the POW and at the same time affirm the label the North Vietnamese endlessly attempted to attach to the American pilots: criminal.

James Rowe implies his kinship with Holocaust victims in the final chapter of his book. At one reception upon his return, he explains an episode that particularly moved him.

> Lou, Tom and I proceeded from the aircraft to a small Operations building amid a barrage of flashbulbs and questions from indistinct faces behind outthrust microphones. I do remember one man who broke from the crowd and came up beside me, grasping my shoulder for a moment, "I escaped from the Nazis," he said. "God bless you." Then he was gone.[7]

By retelling this incident near the conclusion of his narrative, Rowe discovers a ready-made metaphor for his captivity and experience. In doing so he is able to characterize his Vietcong captors as "Nazis" and to find a vehicle for conveying at least some of the pain and suffering he consciously represses.[8]

Rowe's reference joins a long list of "reapplications" of the Holocaust detailed by James Young in his study of Holocaust representations:

> The Holocaust and its suffering Jewish victims have thus figured the suffering Russians in Yevgeny Yevtushenko's poetry; gulag prisoners for Andrei Sinyavsky; poets for Paul Celan; Angela Davis for James Baldwin; psychic pain for Sylvia Plath; and Palestinian refugees in the poetry of contemporary Israeli writers.[9]

The Holocaust functioned for the POWs because it corresponded with their experience in a number of satisfying ways. First, it polarzied the participants as either good or evil. It made the POWs victims instead of soldiers. Second, retrieving the events of the Holocaust cast the POW experience in terms of ultimate human misery and injustice. The hunger, torture, and murder of POWs could be expressed in terms of a larger, previously examined event. Then, too, the Holocaust provided textual evidence of a comparable experience unavailable from other representations, which romanticized or softened the cruel realities of captivity.

One POW seemed to have found a fiction that aptly fit his captivity and did not produce a gap that had to be filled with compensatory images. George Smith refers to Joseph Heller's *Catch-22* a number of times in his narrative. "All of us were put in the position of being a soldier in an Army not at war, captured by an organization that did not exist in the eyes of my government, which was fighting that organization. It was straight out of *Catch-22*."[10] Even though the message of *Catch-22* should, on the surface at least, have been of little comfort to Smith, it apparently provided a model for him to identify with and embrace—at least somebody else had seen what he saw. He realized he was living a black comedy where people died for reasons he could not accept. His narrative relied less on mythic POWs in World War II camps than on allegorical critiques of his ridiculous circumstances. The bittersweet, black humor of *Some Kind of Hero* would attempt a similar critique, but Richard Pryor's slapstick performance could not revive the serious tone of Smith's plight. Smith did not ennoble his experience with images of *Top Gun* or John Wayne. He saw himself more as tragic clown than romantic warrior.

Two German POWs never reach to the Holocaust, prison, or other fictions to describe their captivity. Monika Schwinn and Bernhard Diehl altogether shun the use of such metaphors. Their cultural background aroused far different conceptions and explanations for their years in North Vietnam. Monika Schwinn and Bernhard Diehl, West German nurses, spent five years in captivity. Mistaken for CIA agents or some incarnation of South Vietnamese military assistance, their captivity remains difficult to describe, explain, or justify. Schwinn begins

her narrative with probably the most sobering and prophetic POW
story from a previous war:

> Prisoner. I had grown up in the shadow of that word. It stirred old and
> frightening memories. I was born in 1942, in the middle of the war, and I
> was barely three when it ended. But I was never able to forget my father,
> who had been taken prisoner by the Russians and did not return. . . . I
> remember only two things about the war. One is the bomb shelter. . . . The
> other is the image of my mother sitting by the kitchen window night after
> night, mending clothes and watching for my father to appear in the door
> of the railway station. She wanted to have a clear view of the station, so
> often she did not cover the window at night. Seeing that she was not
> observing the blackout, the police kept coming to our house to complain;
> but my mother ignored them. She was waiting for my father. His body was
> never found. Thus she went on waiting until her death in 1956. I never
> knew my father. All I knew about him, all anyone ever said about him, was
> that he was a prisoner. When I was a child, the very walls seemed to echo
> with that word. . . . When my brother started school we acquired an atlas,
> and I searched the maps for Russia, where my father was. On the map
> everything looked very small and not at all far away. "Why can't we go
> there and get Father? Why doesn't he run away?" My mother shook her
> head, saying, "My God, child, you don't know anything about being a
> prisoner." Now I was a prisoner too.[11]

Schwinn's passage is remarkable for a number of reasons. First, her
country's history and her own experience go a long way to explain
how she understood so much about captivity in a way others could
not. She brought no Hollywood figures or military training with her
into captivity: she had only the tragedy of her own father. Second,
Schwinn's experience is a true episode that parallels America's ongo-
ing, unsubstantiated, and feared legacy of the Vietnam war: the MIA.
As the daughter of a confirmed POW who never came home Schwinn
lived America's most persistent nightmare of the Vietnam War. She
derives her expectations of captivity from a sense of history radically
different from that of American POWs. She grew up in a nation
divided and forced to face its complicity in the Holocaust, and a nation left with few myths about its own hegemony. She survived her
experience without the heroic figures and absolute qualities other
POWs claimed as essential for survival. In contrast to the battery of

redeeming denouements that appear in many American POW stories, Schwinn claims to have found no transcendental self, salient ideology, or guardian angel during her captivity. Instead she found only pain and suffering:

> Now, four years later, did I really know much more? I understood a few things better. I understood how many enemies these people had to combat, beginning with nature, the jungle and the rain, the floods and the drought. The *my's* [Americans] were not their first enemies, but simply the most recent. A thousand years ago it had been the Chinese, then the Japanese, and for the last one hundred years, the French. I understood how a people who had known nothing but enemies could learn to be enemies themselves.[12]

Schwinn's insightful epilogue contrasts sharply with other narratives. As a veteran of a country routinely bombed by the United States, she perhaps had a better appreciation of the suffering of the Vietnam War than some of her fellow POWs who, before shootdown, had seen Vietnam exclusively through the canopy of their aircraft or the imperial cartography of aerial photographs and electronic imaging. Schwinn and Diehl had also witnessed and treated the casualties of the war in their abbreviated work as nurses on a hospital ship off South Vietnam—another experience remote from American pilots attacking Vietnam from unthreatened aircraft carriers in the Gulf of Tonkin or safe bases in Thailand. Their culture, experience, and sense of history had fostered no zeal for creating superstructures. For them there was little gap to fill, and thus they offer little compensatory religion, ideology, or inflated self-image.

Bernhard Diehl had a realistic and cynical appraisal of his homecoming:

> I imagined what it would be like when we got home—the reporters asking questions, the special attention, the receptions. For a few days or a few weeks, we would be treated as celebrities. People would tell us how brave we had been and what shining examples we were to our fellow men. They would cite us as victims of Communist oppression and cruelty and boast of the superiority of their own system: for we of the free world, of course, had never unjustly deprived anyone of his liberty.[13]

Diehl foresees the structures that will endlessly fill popular notions of the POW experience in Vietnam. His sarcasm is direct and telling. He, like Schwinn, concludes his narrative with a counterpoise to what he sees as the spurious justifications and compensations the American POWs will claim for their years of captivity. He sees with great clarity the "theater" that is about to begin. Diehl, like Schwinn, fails to find either "God in a P.O.W. camp" (as the title of Ralph Gaither's book does) or an essential national identity during his captivity. He seeks no redemption from the captivity that he will deal with for the rest of his life. Diehl would like to have preempted the press and the politicians who would find some usable past in years of imprisonment. He implies that "the free world" has, in fact, been equally cruel, although the pretension of the POW release will play differently. The congratulations will valorize the experience so "the free world" might continue the war against "Communist oppression and cruelty." Bombing, invasion, taking prisoners, torture; it has all happened before. Making the POWs celebrities will make sure it happens again, keep the status quo, continue the struggle that keeps us at work, at war.

Lest we think that celebrity dreams were not among POW expectations, Dieter Dengler speculates with a fellow captive about what would happen if they successfully escaped: "Maybe we'll be invited to President Johnson's ranch for a barbecue. Think of it! . . . Hell all the astronauts do is fly around up there. . . . If they got a parade, just think of what we'll get!"[14] But Dengler never got an audience with the President. The POW issue was not important to the Johnson administration in 1966 when Dengler escaped. It would be seven more years and after Watergate before an American President would host a highly publicized dinner for the collected former POWs at the White House. The POWs would eventually become exactly what Diehl had cynically predicted and Dengler hopefully dreamed: "celebrities."

John Dramesi, another long-time Vietnam POW, acknowledges the fame he expected. He recalls reaching through layers of feces to unclog a drain to please his unhappy cellmate: "Marlon Brando isn't going to like this scene."[15] Albeit jokingly, Dramesi hints at the fame he expects upon return. Ironically, Marlon Brando played not the heroic POW but the insane Special Forces Colonel Kurz in *Apocalypse Now*. The best actors would not be playing POWs in post-Vietnam

America. The autobiographical events of the POW story would seldom catch center stage in the POW drama. The honest and historical portrayals the POWs expected to see of their experience would seldom materialize. Instead, the POWs would wear the mantle of fame much like other figures in America. Portrayals of the POWs would be less about an archeology of POW experience and more about satisfying America's needs after a lost war. Dramesi's comment, however revealing, would not be prophetic.

James Rowe voices anxiety about his coming fame in *Five Years to Freedom:* "In all the stories I had ever read about things like this, there was a moment of truth as the main character reestablished contact between his foot and terra firma, usually accompanied by some profound comment. Should I start rehearsing now, I wondered?"[16] Rowe sees himself as the protagonist of the vague fiction he describes, but nevertheless seems uncomfortable in that role. His uneasiness, coming as it does during his triumphant return to America, indicates a new gap in his perceptions: the gap between what he knew he had experienced and the image waiting for him in the presses of American popular culture. Rowe struggles to control the fame that is about to engulf him. But in the end he has nothing to fear. He and the other former POWs would not be the focus of attention. Instead, their images and incarnations would be what mattered most to literary agents, film directors, advertising firms, and campaign managers in America.

In their narratives, former POWs often discuss a gap between the "received wisdom" of captivity, and what they actually experienced.[17] Expectation is a critical element of how we cope with our day-to-day lives. Expectations at once guide our access to the past, prompt our reactions to the present, and create the horizon of our future. Images from film and television, significant influences in American culture, often left the POWs with impossible, unrealistic expectations. The POWs most often remark on how the POW myth differed from experience. In doing so they make visible the consequences of believing in the prevailing myths and confess their own naiveté. The imperative for reconciling the conditions of their captivity with ponderous baggage from American culture left them partially unprepared for long years of captivity. As a result the overwhelming rhetorical aim of the

Vietnam POW narrative became didactic, an attempt to shape future expectations: "lessons learned."

Ironically, most POWs, however consciously, help make myths themselves by injecting their stories into American culture of the seventies, eighties, and nineties. As we shall see in coming chapters, although the image of the Vietnam POW achieved unprecedented popularity, representations of captivity would not necessarily prove any more helpful to future POWs than *The Great Escape* was for Gerald Coffee.

The POWs' homecoming would come to signify a victory. The POWs themselves would be "fabricated as commodities"[18] and used as involvement media to peddle the ideologies, exciting tales of escape and rescue, self-help regimes, and marketing agendas of the America they thought they had defended while they suffered. The POWs' celebrity would slip from experience to the Cold War ideologies and vacuous generalizations Bernhard Diehl had feared. American culture would quickly erase the boundary between experience and film, real-life hero and actor. The force of fame elided and sometimes even inverted the roles. This inversion of actor and hero becomes explicit when we remember that it was John Wayne who was asked to address former Vietnam POWs at a White House reception in 1973, rather than surviving POWs who were asked to speak to a collection of Hollywood actors and media celebrities.

Larry Guarino confronted what he saw as the irony of Wayne's appearance at that dinner. Guarino and Wayne were seated at the same table. Guarino tells of the conversation midway through his account of the eight years he spent in Hanoi:

> "Duke," I said, "I tried to think about how *you* might have handled the interrogators." He listened intently. "So when they asked questions I told 'em to go to hell, when they asked me to do something, I told 'em to stick it up their asses. . . . And do you know what, Duke? They beat the shit out of me!" The Duke shook with silent laughter, but there were tears in his eyes.[19]

Guarino had laid bare the errors of his own expectations.

7

"Young Men, Husbands, Sons, Brothers, Fathers"

In the early 1970s when the National League of Families was attempting to publicize the POW issue, a film about wives of POWs and MIAs seemed like a good idea. After all, such a film could portray the voices of those most closely associated with the explosive POW issue (besides the men themselves, who were naturally unavailable). The wives and families were, perhaps by default, the focus of substantial scrutiny by the media already. But Mark Robson's movie about the POW/MIA wife, *Limbo,* ran into problems early on.

When he asked for help from the Department of Defense, he was turned down. Robson modified the script, but the Pentagon still would not cooperate. Scenes of POW wives opposing the war and having affairs angered the Pentagon. The Department of Defense felt that such a film could have propaganda value for the North Vietnamese.[1] Such fears, however noble they may have sounded, glossed other misgivings the military had concerning the POW family issue. *Limbo* would have helped authorize female voices that threatened the intensely patriarchal authority the Defense Department was otherwise having such trouble defending. POW wives, partially free from the authority the military usually exercised over them through their now absent husbands, posed a dilemma for the Pentagon.

The roles were reversing. Imprisonment feminized the POWs by making them silent objects of sentiment, subjects of rescue, and pawns of public attention.[2] The active, masculine role vacated by the POWs was assumed, to a degree, by their families. POW wives inherited traditionally male roles with political and media muscle that politicians

Three POW wives console each other and ponder their plight in *Limbo*. Only one husband will return alive. *Courtesy of the Museum of Modern Art/Film Stills Archive.* (1972, Universal)

had to reckon with. While their husbands languished in the physical and psychological claustrophobia of North Vietnamese prisons, the POW families struggled with newfound freedoms to activate stagnant political and media powers back in the United States.

At the time, a Nixon administration memo talked about "keeping the families on the reservation" as though the spouses and children of the POWs were somehow a danger to national security.[3] The reservation metaphor worked quite nicely. The administration and the military could count on using implicit boundaries within the military family against anyone who might speak out. The rationale for enforcing those boundaries tied the rubric "keep silent" to national duty and concern for POW welfare.

As we have seen, however, "keep silent" had more to do with Nixon's paranoid ambitions and the initial negative political valence ascribed to the POW issue than with POW welfare. Women and the families of the prisoners were supposed to remain confined in their private, nonpublic, nonwork roles, thus stabilizing the social, economic, and political definition of domesticity in a society where such roles were coming into question. But the forced imprisonment and helplessness of POWs in Hanoi mirrored and consequently aggravated the frustration of POW families in the United States who were instructed to "keep silent."

Like the casualty figures shown daily on network television, POW wives were painful reminders of the war's cost. Dorothy McDaniel, wife of six-year POW Eugene McDaniel, explained what she represented to other soldiers preparing for Vietnam: "I was a grim reminder to them—and to their wives—that some of them might not make it back next time."[4] To others the families of the POWs were exactly the kind of "grim reminder" America needed. Images of POW families may have been uncomfortable to some, but their images were becoming a sensation worthy of the entertainment market. Robson was eventually able to direct and distribute *Limbo* to both theater and television audiences.

Apparently the film never fell into the hands of the North Vietnamese as the Pentagon had feared it would. The North Vietnamese, of course, could hardly have cared—by the time *Limbo* was released the POWs weren't being forced to make statements. The Pentagon had little to worry about from *Limbo* anyway: the POWs were receiving plenty of direct evidence that some of their families were opposed to the war and that some wives had given up on their husbands.[5] Such news came in letters, newspapers, and magazines that the North Vietnamese were happy to pass on to the demoralized American prisoners. Could a fiction like *Limbo* have been more damaging than such news from home?

Popular accounts and histories of the Vietnam POW experience often neglect or downplay the role of women. The line quoted in the title for this chapter comes from a so-called definitive history of the Vietnam POW. John Hubbell's "history" emphasizes the masculinity of the captivity experience in his introduction: "They [the POWs] were living, breathing, walking, talking, smiling young men, husbands, sons, brothers, fathers, friends."[6] Many POW autobiographies present women in just this way: as an absence. But the story is not so simple. Women were a part of the Vietnam POW experience in all respects. Monika Schwinn survived the Hanoi Hilton along with the men. Other women were also captured during the course of the war, although their stories are seldom told. Women played an instrumental role in securing the POW release of 1973. And then there are the "other" women: those faceless, voiceless Vietnamese who either suffered with or provided for the American POWs. But perhaps the most prominent women of the POW story were those who failed to carry out their duty as wives and mothers: the women who betrayed the POWs.

Male narratives and popular culture (terms that are all too often synonymous) use gender and sexual preference to negotiate the POW story in several ways. In many male narratives women are relegated to secondary roles. The essence of these secondary roles lies in either steadfast support for or sensational betrayal of the absent men. The male narratives also appropriate female stereotypes to evaluate the Vietnamese. The more popular narratives damn the North Vietnamese by portraying them as less "developed" and feminine, while describing how the emaciated bodies of American POWs become the object of Vietnamese women's desire. In the overwhelming majority of POW texts women and the Vietnamese, who were all implicitly feminine, were defined in terms of the imposing American male.

L oyal and hard-working POW wives became icons in the POW story. Sybil Stockdale, represented in the book and television movie *In Love and War,* and Dorothy McDaniel, author of her own account of the POW issue, *After the Hero's Welcome,* were both leaders in the National League of Families. Their political activism played an important role in forcing initially reluctant media and political powers to negotiate the POW issue before the American public. Their narratives are amazing accounts of how women's roles could expand beyond the claustrophobia of tradition and domesticity. Their narratives identify gender boundaries as they describe the struggle for POW repatriation. What is perhaps even more remarkable is how these hard-won, expanded roles snap back into traditional domestic structures once the POWs return. POW autobiographies highlight the "homecoming" of the male to emphasize the comforting and proper return of domestic order. By returning to their economic and political spaces within the nuclear family, prominent POW wives deferred to renewed and returned POW men.

Almost twenty years after the POWs came home and fifteen years after her husband published his autobiography, Dorothy McDaniel wrote about her experiences and published them in a separate volume, *After the Hero's Welcome.* Almost twenty years after Robson's *Limbo,* she attempted to tell the POW story from the perspective of the POW wife. Her unique account and its late appearance point out just how difficult it has been to escape gendered roles in American culture. The Pentagon's fears of breaking gender barriers had been internalized by Dorothy McDaniel.

She had come to see her years of potent media and political activism as "amateur efforts to bring Red [her husband, Eugene McDaniel] home."[7] For McDaniel the expanded role she achieved in her husband's absence collapsed when the POWs returned. While sorting through the "stacks" of POW/MIA files in her home, ample evidence of the tremendous effort she made on her husband's behalf, she recalls: "The children helped me select the papers we thought would mean the most to Red. . . . I bundled up the rest and built a big bonfire in the backyard, ignoring fire regulations, to celebrate 'the end of Mom's public life.' "[8] Dorothy McDaniel attempted to destroy the efforts of her activism: she defined her efforts only in terms of what they might mean for her husband.

But what she had learned and tried to forget in her political struggle over the POW issue during the war could have been of great help to her husband. In the 1980s Eugene McDaniel pursued the MIA issue, only to find the same bureaucratic and political resistance that his wife had found a decade before. Dorothy McDaniel could not fail to remark on the irony: "He didn't want to give up his belief that the system would work. . . . So he had continued doggedly, in the face of fierce opposition, to get the story of the abandoned men out before the public, on the front pages of the newspapers, and into the halls of power."[9] But this was exactly what Dorothy McDaniel had done successfully a decade earlier. Eugene McDaniel would eventually conclude: "The flak I've taken since I got into this battle here for the POWs is much worse than the torture and isolation I endured in the Hanoi Hilton."[10] But Dorothy McDaniel couldn't say that. Even though her own "battle . . . for the POWs" in the late sixties and early seventies mirrored the struggle her husband faced, she effaces her original efforts to tell the story of her husband's postcaptivity political career in her book. She repeatedly returns to the "scars" of torture on her husband's body to symbolize the pain of her family and to gauge the righteousness of her struggle.[11] She consciously directs our gaze away from herself and toward her "towering six-foot-three husband who stands ten feet tall in my eyes."[12] She feels it is important to abandon her activist role so as not to threaten her husband, who has been feminized by his captivity in Hanoi. She seems to slip back onto the "reservation" where the Nixon administration had wanted her.

Jim and Sybil Stockdale's *In Love and War* is probably the most closely collaborated of the POW texts. The Stockdales juxtapose their experiences in order to tell the story of the war from two perspectives. Sybil Stockdale's first chapter, "The Navy Wife," establishes the context of her story. She begins by talking about "spinning tales of romantic fantasy" in her childhood. This passage is clearly ironic, but not because Stockdale sees romance as "fantasy." The section becomes ironic because of how the fantasy fails. It does not fail because it is hopelessly romantic to begin with, but because the Stockdale family was betrayed along the way by an illegitimate imprisonment in Vietnam where according to Admiral Stockdale "a generation of young Americans would get left holding the bag."[13]

Although Sybil Stockdale transcends the female stereotype, her narrative always returns to what she sees as her essentially subordinate and "ladylike" position. After a forceful and apparently productive confrontation with Alexander Haig in which she assumes a very aggressive posture and demands support for the POWs, Mrs. Stockdale is quick to recoil: "We all shook hands and were our ladylike selves again."[14]

In Love and War concludes with Admiral Stockdale's physical absence and figural impotence resolved in the hospital where the POWs are convalescing. Sybil Stockdale is eager to point out "how completely wrong they had been about the sexual impotence." Jim Stockdale echoes Sybil Stockdale's jubilation by replying in a telephone call from a high-ranking naval officer with "yes, sir, everything is just fine here at the hospital and Sybil is right here in bed with me."[15] Sybil Stockdale's victory is achieved by proving the "briefers" wrong a final time by asserting her husband's potency. Admiral Stockdale reasserts his dominance by speaking for a silent Sybil in a situation serving as emblem for his returned sexual potency and natural male dominance.

In other male narratives the wives have even less space. James Mulligan, a six-year POW of the Vietnam War, admits the phallocentric assumptions of his narrative, *The Hanoi Commitment:* "Like most 20th century male Americans I felt quite self-sufficient."[16] Yet Mulligan is eager to point out gender bias in the surrounding culture: "The Vietnamese women were free like the freedom that the beast of burden enjoys." In contrast, Americans (particularly American men) know how to handle women: "Back in the U.S. we put our women on a pedestal so that they can help bring out the best that's in each of us males. What a contrast there."[17] Mulligan's attitude toward his wife amplifies his earlier account and conception of women: "My body ached to be with her, to hold her in my arms and never let go."[18] Although Mulligan does make other remarks about his wife, her value and role are secondary, barely supportive of his resistance in Vietnam. His desire for his wife emphasizes her "bodily" role, while silencing her political role and voice. Only at the end of his account does James Mulligan reveal Louise Mulligan's leading role in forming an East Coast POW wives' organization. None of her efforts is recorded in the narrative. Such an exclusion highlights Mulligan's self-reliance, the solitude of his struggle.

In many of the autobiographies, women are merely objects, if they are mentioned at all. John Dramesi, another six-year captive, titles one chapter of *Code of Honor* "The Golden Key and Nancy." "Nancy" gets only five lines in the ten-page chapter. Her identity and significance are revealed in a short passage at the beginning of the chapter: "When the radio was turned off someone began to play Western music. It was Nancy Sinatra singing. Training, discipline, and physical strength were on the verge of failing. It was the woman, Nancy Sinatra, at that critical moment who kept me loyal to my purpose."[19] Nancy becomes an idol for Dramesi. The "woman" serves as emblem for American culture. Dramesi objectifies her as a spiritual force (a traditional female role) in the turning point of his struggle. As such, she exemplifies the woman's role as helper, nurturing a soldier in his struggle with the forces of evil.

L oyal and patriotic women had distinct but limited roles in POW autobiographies, film, and magazine biographies. They would share equal time but not equal importance with their husbands in television movies like *In Love and War* and *When Hell Was in Session*. But they attracted less media attention than the more sensational female betrayers: Jane Fonda and other women who visited Hanoi, Tangee Alvarez and wives who abandoned their absent POW husbands, and wives and mothers who opposed the war. When Everett

Alvarez went looking for publishers for his autobiography, the people he met keyed their interest to the story of his absent wife and his antiwar activist sister. They seemed less interested in the details of Alvarez's record eight-year stay in Hanoi.

Probably the most prominent figure of national betrayal in POW narratives and American culture is Jane Fonda. Alvarez's sister comments on Everett Alvarez's perspective on Fonda:

> He was less subtle in his disdain for Jane Fonda and everything she had come to symbolize. Delia [Alvarez's peace-activist sister] knew it would have made no difference to him if she had told him that Jane Fonda herself had been used by the Vietnamese as a letter carrier to bring home letters from POWs, including one from Everett.[20]

Other women who visited Hanoi were more remarkable for James Mulligan:

> On 27 September 1972 the three latest fink releases left for home. I was glad that they took with them the American bitch that had caused our museum troubles. On more than one occasion in the past, a big-mouth American female visiting Hanoi had caused us to be mistreated.[21]

For Mulligan, of all the peace activists who had visited Hanoi, the women were the most difficult for him to accept. Apparently these women had fallen from their "pedestal."

In film, the woman as betrayer interested producers as it had Alvarez's publishers. Even though the Pentagon explained to the creators of *Limbo* that less than one percent of POW wives were unfaithful, few movies would do without highlighting a woman's betrayal. Few autobiographies could keep from mentioning the adulterous wife. The adulterous female betrayer would become a stock character in POW films like *The Hanoi Hilton, Rolling Thunder, Some Kind of Hero, Welcome Home,* and *Limbo.* "Son of a bitch! Why now!" Major Fischer proclaimed to his fellow prisoners when his wife's Dear John letter arrived in *The Hanoi Hilton.* Major Charles Rane's unfaithful wife would be shot by greedy bandits early on in *Rolling Thunder.* Later, Rane would shoot a prostitute; his ex-POW accomplice, Johnny Vohden, would ruthlessly pistol-whip another prostitute. Apparently the women deserved it. In *Some*

Kind of Hero, before ex-POW Eddie Keller and his wife can enjoy their first night of postcaptivity domestic bliss, his wife reveals that she has married another man and spent all the family savings. These women were bitches and whores for not being able to keep their legs crossed while their husbands were systematically starved and tortured in Vietnam. Perhaps fiction had already made the American woman an essentially adulterous character. Audiences had always been fascinated by indiscretions played out endlessly through distorted incarnations of America's founding adulteress, Hester Prynne of Nathaniel Hawthorne's *The Scarlet Letter.*

But when it came to the man, there was no such self-righteousness. In the film *Intimate Strangers,* ex-POW Sally Berman would spend a year trying to muster the courage to apologize for her rape and resultant child, while her husband, shacked up with a nurse in his expensive private practice on the home front, would not have to agonize over any such explanations. It was just natural for a man, but a crime for a woman.

The betrayal theme appears in the *People* article on Alvarez and in "Betrayed," the fifteenth chapter of Alvarez's *Chained Eagle.* "The book and magazine article include portraits of the Alvarez women back home: his mother, his sister, and his first wife. The Alvarez story has such appeal to the American consciousness partly because of the complex relationships he, as the male POW, has with "his" women at home. He is betrayed in some way by nearly all the women in his life: Delia, his sister, becomes a "prominent anti-war activist," and Tangee, his wife, gets an illegitimate "Mexican divorce" and marries another man. His mother, although supportive during captivity, is remembered for coldly telling Alvarez's uncle, "Don't pay him . . . Just teach him to work."

Anthony Pitch, Alvarez's coauthor, highlights the significance women had in the experience with this passage: "But two in particular . . . stood near the altar close by their friend, just as they had done in the bitterest moments in the Hanoi Hilton when Everett had suffered from a woman's betrayal."[22] In comparison to the solitude, starvation diet, and physical beatings, Tangee Alvarez's lack of faith tops the list of crimes committed against Alvarez during his captivity.[23] There is apparently no darker crime than a "woman's betrayal."[24] But even their betrayal backhandedly endorsed the POW fight by proving the free choice that Alvarez fought for. Both Tangee and Delia might have used their choices incorrectly, but the point becomes that they had a choice and were simply not strong enough to make the right one.

The final woman in the Alvarez story is his current wife, Tammy. After his ordeal in Hanoi, she ushers Alvarez into a secure and lasting marriage where "Everett [can] tell his story for our grandkids." Tammy arrives as a rescuing hero just in time to preserve the woman's domestic role and save Everett from postcaptivity gender chaos. She recovers the female from incorrect choices and re-creates the proper domestic role for women. Tammy arrives as the just reward for a betrayed hero, thus recovering a happy ending for an otherwise tragic experience.

The Alvarez women are in many ways problematic. Alvarez's own father, who is quoted in the *People* piece, is forgiven for treatment implied by this passage from "Betrayed":

> Sometimes, when Lalo was home and Chloe sat quietly knitting, she saw her husband cry for his absent son. But she could not give him the consolation that she herself needed so desperately. However much she regretted the disintegration of her own marriage, she gave her husband credit where it was due. He had been a good father to their children, even though he had at times been impatient as many others. And he had always been an exceptionally dependable worker. . . . But when they were together there was strife and she cowered if he raised his voice. . . . Her doctor advised her to release the tension by crying and screaming or even throwing a few pots and pans, but she could not become what she had never been. So she suffered. And then, in a cruel twist of timing, she felt the hot flashes and melancholia of her change of life.[25]

Chloe suffered at least verbal abuse by her husband. Yet the narrative places the value of work above patience with children and spouse, implicitly vindicating Lalo's neglect. In a cruel irony Chloe all but reenacts the captivity of her son at the hands of her husband and "doctor." The unintended implication is that the plight of women in America is not unlike that of the Vietnam POW.

In another ironic twist Alvarez becomes the victim of his own gender and racial stereotyping, which echo throughout *Chained*

Eagle. The stereotypes Alvarez constructs foreshadow the demise of his marriage to his first wife, Tangee. Alvarez admits at one point that "they [his family] approved of her because she was cast so securely in the traditional Mexican mold. Shapely and feminine, she could be expected to raise a loving brood with solid virtues and values and be the warm-hearted center of the family."[26] Tangee eludes this stereotype and covertly remarries while still collecting Alvarez's military service benefits. However improper Tangee's conduct, it becomes obvious that she has entered a world where there are very different expectations: one for men and one for women. She fails to fit the stereotype of "Mexican wives [who] lived at home and waited years for their [migrant farmer] husbands to return from jobs up north."[27] These readings of particular episodes in *Chained Eagle* tell a story of betrayal and imprisonment that undercuts the patriarchal structures on which Alvarez and Pitch prefer to rely for the sensation of their story.

A

lthough women on the "home front" are the central feminine figures in the Alvarez story, his narrative does acknowledge other aspects of the gender issue. Unfortunately, these aspects deal in the stereotypes most useful in promoting the POW myth. Alvarez is not alone in this effort. Many of the POW narratives construct and use the figure of the indigenous woman and homosexuality to promote sensation and triumph in their own experience.

Vietnamese women appear in Alvarez's narrative much more frequently than they do in other POW stories. He describes one woman who took showers in sight of his cell: "This one had tight thighs and whispering hips and walked like a woman, every step reaffirming her mystique. We figured she must have French blood so we called her Frenchie." After a more detailed description of the episode, Alvarez goes on to say that "not a man forgot that day when Frenchie bared her elongated body beneath the azure summer sky."[28] Few other narratives are so candid as to remark on the pleasure of such an incident, however. Predictably, such events are written out of many stories to preserve the uniformly stoic picture of imprisonment.[29]

In the first few paragraphs of his "Americans" chapter, Alvarez describes a particularly offensive guard who "always had a finger up his red, bulbous nose." This guard is labeled a "homosexual." When Alvarez took a shower, "he [the suspect guard] sat down, staring at me unabashedly. One day he came into my cell with my food, put it down and stared for a while with a finger up his nostril. 'Whoosh! Whoosh!, you!' he said suddenly, waving his arms like a floundering swimmer. I couldn't understand what he was getting at so I ignored him and ate my rations."[30] Alvarez concludes that "like most guards, Rudolf was a simpleton." Apparently, Alvarez and his coauthor place this at the beginning of the chapter entitled "Americans" to highlight the difference between Americans and Vietnamese. The difference emerges in terms of the implied "homosexuality" of the guard (an obviously damning characteristic in the context of this narrative). The guard also appears in *Chained Eagle* as a "simpleton" because he cannot effectively sign to a resistant Alvarez. Even though Alvarez gives the guard credit for "lacking the meanness of other guards," he damns him out of hand as a "simpleton" and homosexual on the basis of his failure to act within Alvarez's own adopted cultural and sexual assumptions. One interpretation of the guard's apparently inexplicable gestures regarding the food might be that he wanted Alvarez to bathe. This is hardly a damning episode and does little to credit Alvarez's conclusion that the guard is a "simpleton" or a "homosexual."

Charles Plumb defines the Vietnamese in similar terms. In his *i'm no hero* Plumb devotes several chapters to assessing the North Vietnamese culture from his glimpses through the cell walls. Plumb describes the Vietnamese in terms of their inverted and corrupt gender roles:

> The women not only were the principal workers but assumed the aggressive role in the battle between the sexes, teasing and chasing the males who often appeared completely indifferent. Perhaps the wartime ratio of men to women was so favorable to available males that they could play hard to get. In any case, the men seemed to have little use for female flirtation. The men did, however, display an especial affection toward their male comrades. On rare occasions, guards even propositioned POWs, but they never pressed the issue.[31]

Apparently if women take an "aggressive role" some aberration of social structure must have occurred. As for the men, Plumb also makes what he believes to be the damning allegation that the Vietnamese men were homosexual.

Doubting the masculinity of his captors is a strategy Plumb uses to assert himself as superior to the culture which imprisons him. A later passage amplifies his observations on the sexual preferences of the North Vietnamese: "Even so, these men had no qualms about sexual exposure to each other. It was common to see two V guards or officers holding hands, walking arm-in-arm, reaching hands under one another's clothing, or lying in the undergrowth with their bodies intertwined. Of course they exhibited this conduct without the awareness that we could see them."[32] Plumb's problem becomes obvious in this passage. However exciting it might be to reverse the observation vector between guard and prisoner, his observations assume that the social practices and sexual stereotypes that exist in his America are universal and apply directly to the people of North Vietnam. Even if we again make the assumption that homosexual practice is somehow damning, there is no basis for assuming that physical contact between men is an indication of something other than friendship. Of course, this discussion assumes that Plumb neither mistook nor invented what he saw. Either way he attempts to attack his captors' masculinity, a perhaps self-satisfying but nevertheless crude psychological ploy.

Many POW autobiographies amplified their authority by depicting the North Vietnamese as sexually perverse. The passages on Vietnamese culture in *i'm no hero* and *Chained Eagle* are meant to amplify the POW's status as a hero by presenting yet another foreign and testing aspect of captivity the POW was forced to endure.

But when it came to Americans, bodily exposure, however unintentional, served to validate American superiority rather than to indicate homosexual tendencies. Larry Guarino, Jeremiah Denton, and other POWs describe the interest the Vietnamese had in naked Americans. Larry Guarino explains how "captors were able to see the pilot's exposed genitals, and they were astounded." Apparently "qualms about sexual exposure" were only appropriate when you had less to offer than the "astounding" bodies of Americans.

Denton describes how North Vietnamese women were awe-struck

by the superior physique of Americans. At one point Denton describes one woman who was particularly kind:

> There was one North Vietnamese, however, who gave me a lift from the drab loneliness of my existence. Nursie was a breath of fresh air in a putrid atmosphere. In her early twenties, she was tall for a Vietnamese woman, and quite slender. Best of all, she was gracious, smart, and capable.[33]

This woman helped dress a bandage for Denton during an early episode of his captivity:

> I discovered all of this on my second day in prison when she came to my cell with a female guard and Dipshit [the attendant male guard] to inspect the bandage he had put on my leg. At first I refused to take down my shorts in front of the women. They left the cell and seemed to be flattered that I would presume their innocence, but in a few minutes they were back. As soon as Nursie saw the bandage, she looked at Dipshit in disgust and rolled her eyes. It was much too small and was clumsily applied. She gently removed it and put on a bigger and much better one. Dipshit, abashed by her reprimand, pretended not to watch.[34]

Denton views the North Vietnamese woman in the traditional role of care provider but implies a solidarity with her through their mutual revulsion for the treatment afforded POWs. But any philanthropic motivations Denton might have applied to the woman are quickly dashed:

> Nursie and the female guard were hanging around, watching as I walked into the bath area. Vietnamese women seemed to enjoy looking at the American prisoners. Because of poor diet, most of the North Vietnamese were underdeveloped, and the women obviously admired our muscular bodies and hairy chests. The two women stared at me quite unselfconsciously as I walked toward the shower building.[35]

Denton assumes that the racial differences he observes between Americans and North Vietnamese are simply a matter of underdevelopment. The implication is that the North Vietnamese are somehow less developed because their bodies do not match the obvious perfection of the American. This logic would have us believe that with adequate food, these people would end up with physiques just like Americans', complete with "hairy chests." More to the point, the women are apparently motivated to treat the Americans with more kindness not out of human compassion but because they admire the sexually superior American men.

Such is the obvious implication of the second Rambo film, in which the Vietnamese woman, Co (Julia Nickson), is attracted by Rambo's partially clothed and overmuscled physique. In the film *Rambo: First Blood Part II* the Vietnamese woman falls for the half-naked, distracted John Rambo at first sight. But this was OK. How could she not choose the bigger, overmuscled American over underdeveloped, faceless Vietnamese "seconds"? The only other good-looking white men were the Russians, and they were just plain evil. Co would do anything to help Rambo get a few emaciated Americans across the border. The Vietnamese woman could seduce the American male. She was just trying to better herself: it was only right. American women in POW narratives had no such justification for pursuing their own interests, however. John Rambo could never fall for an American woman in a film about Vietnam: the American woman was inherently unreliable, the image of imminent betrayal.

Larry Guarino's autobiography makes Vietnamese fascination with American sexuality explicit. Guarino, a prisoner of the North Vietnamese for over seven years, describes a story he heard about a recently captured, "particularly well endowed" American who became the subject of "gaping visitors" in a rural Vietnamese village. Finally "they brought a lovely young woman . . . and . . . wanted her to have his child." The pilot refused, but then feared that "his genitalia might be amputated and mounted on a stick in front of the tribal long hut, for viewing by generations to come!"[36] However fanciful such a story might have been to the POWs themselves, it does make the radically phallocentric assumptions of Guarino's narrative clear.

One part of James Mulligan's narrative is particularly revealing. Mulligan spent a portion of his captivity with another POW, Jeremiah Denton, who produced one of the earliest POW autobiographies and the earliest popular movie based on Vietnam POW experience. Denton's *When Hell Was in Session* became a paradigm for later accounts of captivity, and he went on to become a United States senator and powerful POW voice in American politics.

Mulligan's candid account mentions one aspect of captivity that Denton leaves out: Denton's relationship with a Vietnamese woman. Mulligan observes that Denton began this relationship after five harrowing years of captivity. "The reason for his irrationality was a dumpy short Vietnamese water girl we named the Tank. Jerry became convinced that the Tank was his way out of Hanoi." Denton persistently pursued a relationship with "Tank" by attempting communication (and therefore risking torture): "Pretty soon all Denton was doing was coughing [a form of covert communication for the POWs] every time he even suspected Tank was near." Denton also confided in Mulligan an escape plan that prefigures the subplot of movies like *Rambo: First Blood Part II:* "Then he would imagine a wild escape. His plans were complex and he was so convinced that he even had a contingency plan in the event he and Tank were fleeing south and the rest of us were suddenly released. He wanted me to lead a flight of A4's to look for him."[37] Denton's scheme occurs nowhere in his own narrative, and the water girl in Denton's account departs much the way she does in Mulligan's telling of the story, "sailing off into oblivion."[38] Apparently this was the rightful fate of all Vietnamese and other women who failed to support the plans of their men in captivity.

Denton relates the experience that corresponds with the "water girl" episode described by Mulligan: "The young women who worked in the camps as cooks or watergirls seemed to be fascinated by the American prisoners, and each appeared to have her favorite. But prisoner-women relationships were usually confined to an exchange of meaningful glances, more sympathetic than sexual in nature."[39] This last remark is undercut by the issue Denton uses to introduce this section, however. "On some rare occasions, they tried to entice prisoners by offering them a woman."[40] Denton is eager to foreground how his captors exploit the sexual value of "their" women, but he preempts an insinuation that there were sexual relationships between prisoners and women by dismissing the covert gestures as "sympathetic." In any case, he implies that the Americans would be uninterested in such "underdeveloped" women.

John Dramesi's account is no less arrogant, but a bit more revealing. Dramesi's account is less self-conscious about his own desire to see North Vietnamese women, or at least one of them. His narrative, unlike Denton's, proves that American POWs were human:

> I shuffled to the door to peek from my favorite hole. There, walking away from me, was a shapely Vietnamese girl with a long pony tail that went all the way down to her lovely rear end. With the tip of her pony tail swinging as if to say, "Goodbye, John," she turned the corner. That girl has most of the sex in North Vietnam.[41]

Dramesi highlights his contact with another prison worker, Pia:

> I motioned for her to come close to the bars and she did. As she came close, I lifted the necklace that I wore so that she could see it. Then I held the string wide with both hands outside the bars and coaxed her to come closer. She came closer, bowed her head slightly, and I put it around her neck. Then, without releasing the string, I moved very close to her face and through the bars our lips touched.[42]

Denton's point in recalling the "water girl" incident is undercut by the candor of the previous passage. Denton's account differs significantly from Mulligan's. As Denton remembers it, the girl's name is "Greta." "Greta . . . made frequent visits to the peephole [apparently admiring Denton], spending as many moments as she could before the sound of an approaching guard would cause her to close the peephole."[43] Denton reverses traditional roles to emphasize his plight as prisoner and reassert his racial and sexual superiority by describing the insatiable desire North Vietnamese women had to observe his tortured body,

Denton portrays himself in the incident as ultimately faithful[44]: "By sign language she asked my age. I signaled forty-three. She signaled that I didn't look over thirty-five. I showed her a picture of Jane and the children, which had arrived in Jane's letter. By pointing to my heart and then to Jane, I indicated my love for my wife."[45] Despite Denton's confession, the girl continues to pursue glimpses of him, at one point climbing "halfway up the tower outside my window."[46] Denton reveals none of his escape plans nor does he discuss any of his own efforts to communicate with the girl. This one-sided account functions both to preserve the sanctity of his faithful commitment to his wife and to highlight the depravity and bankrupt sexuality of the Vietnamese women, who took inordinate risks to view the emaciated bodies of the Americans in their cells. Denton, Alvarez, Dramesi, Plumb, and Mulligan make Vietnamese woman appear suspiciously like Co. Co's obvious fascination with and attraction to Rambo's muscular, partially naked American male body leads her to risk all to betray her country and assist an American in his covert plan for POW escape.

Denton's apparently awe-inspiring body, Guarino's incredible tale, Dramesi's shower episode, and Stockdale's reunion with his wife relate

POW wife Sandy Lawton (Kate Jackson) waits for help from military authority in *Limbo*. Actual POW wives and the film itself were stonewalled by Defense Department officials during most of the Vietnam War. *Courtesy of the Museum of Modern Art/Film Stills Archive.* (1972, Universal)

the phallus to American hegemony. The stories of the superior American sexual organ are meant to provide us with concrete evidence of God-given American superiority. These stories compensate sad captivity experience with a phallic victory over the "medieval," "underdeveloped," and "effeminate" Vietnamese.

———————

By juxtaposing different and sometimes conflicting accounts of captivity, we have seen the various roles women played in the male POW narratives. The women in these texts are either objects and reflections of male desire or surrogates for masculine action. Even though the support given the POWs during their very real and physically difficult imprisonment was perhaps the key to their survival, the roles women played were almost always qualified by the roles of the absent ruling men. Such roles highlight how women are represented in the accounts of the Vietnam POW story and make visible the political spaces available to women within that structure.

In an America where the female voice was moving toward autonomy, the activist voices of women in the POW story remained directly subordinate to men. In this way popular POW stories helped "remasculinize" our thinking and left precious little space for female voice and action. In the narratives we have examined so far, women play a finite set of limiting roles. They speak only when authorized within the context of the male narrative. These are the roles we see most often on the popular culture landscape in movies like *When Hell Was in Session, In Love and War,* and *The Hanoi Hilton* and in popular articles and TV appearances. But there is another tale to tell—where women do speak from firsthand experience as prisoners. We will examine these voices in the next chapter.

8
Another Tale to Tell

When French journalist Michele Ray found her way to a South Vietnamese army camp in 1967, the South Vietnamese and their American advisors were astonished. Twenty days earlier she had disappeared from a back-country road. When South Vietnamese soldiers searched for her, all they found was her automobile buried in a rice field. She had obviously been captured.

Before capture Ray had been anxious to learn how she might be treated. She asked the Vietnamese Government Information Service, the South Vietnamese agency that questioned all enemy POWs, "What would happen if I were captured?" One interrogator speculated on what the enemy would do: " 'You would first be tried and then condemned. . . . No torture will be good enough. Your ears and your nose will be cut off. But to begin with. . . .' The interpreter refused to translate this last remark. I imagine that it was my femininity that was to be violated."[1] Despite the interrogator's dire and somewhat stereotypical predictions, Ray was held for a short time and then released by the Viet Cong.

After walking out of the jungle, Ray was flown to a field hospital for a medical examination. She was surprised by what the American doctor asked her: "Were you forced?" Ray was confused: "I didn't understand, and I looked at him in astonishment." The doctor made his question more explicit: "Did they abuse you?" Ray was incredulous: "I burst out laughing, but I really wanted to cry. Yes, I am really on 'the other side' now. White Teeth, Lynx Eye, the Beatles, the professor [her captors] . . . have all become Vietcong again, 'Victor Charlie,' a black mass, impersonal—the enemy."[2] When she realized that the Americans assumed she had been raped during captivity, Ray was astounded. She makes it clear in her narrative that this assumption has more to do with making an enemy than concern for her health. She wants to "cry" because the doctor has missed the point. She sees that even this "doctor," someone supposed to be concerned with healing, shares in the objectifications that fuel the continuing war. The doctor's assumption participates in the demonology that helps objectify and reduce "Victor Charlie" to "a black mass, impersonal—the enemy." The assumption and its satisfaction would make the Vietcong less human and consequently easier to kill.

Most Americans have never heard Ray's story. When her book was published, Hollywood was busy collaborating with the United States Army on *The Green Berets*. Images of female captivity did not appeal to the mass audience unless they focused on the near-pornographic. Female prisons, which might have provided a film history on which to draw—should any studio have wanted to—have always had their audience. But only so long as the lusty captive women wore clingy outfits and garish cosmetics. The home video markets of the 1980s exploited the women's prison theme with a new cycle of "action/adventure" films, but clearly such vulgar, blatantly exploitive fictions were not based on actual accounts. The popular image of female captivity exploited the woman's body and her sexual desire and rarely if ever depicted any wisdom she might have gained from her experience.

Captive women seldom learned anything worth talking about. Whereas captivity had given male POWs of the Vietnam War a privileged voice and a special knowledge of God, family, and self, female captivity seemed to hold none of that same interest. Captivity for a woman had a functional importance with pornographic implications, but no epistemologic value.

Everett Alvarez briefly discusses some of the prisoners he saw in Hoa Lo Prison in Hanoi:

> Through the peephole I saw the daily arrival of long lines of men and women, chained together by their ankles. Some of the women were scraggly, others, clearly young prostitutes, flirted brazenly with the guards, seductively making eyes and swishing their long black hair.[3]

Later Alvarez remarks on hearing their screams; an apparently typical incident ignored in other accounts:

> From nearby came the lash of whips and the cries and screams of female
> prisoners. . . . the torturers were moved neither by the gender nor by the
> pain of their victims. Were these the hordes of young, shackled women,
> brought into the courtyard daily, whom Chihuahua [a North Vietnamese
> interrogator] had testily identified as prostitutes? If so, it said something
> about the severity of the regime if this was its method of correction.[4]

But Alvarez goes no further to speculate on the implications of
women held in the same prison as his male-pilot companions. He does
not explicitly discuss rape and sexual molestation, but it is implicit in
his text. However intriguing (or titillating) these images are for Alvarez, he is more content to contemplate women in roles other than as
fellow prisoners in Hoa Lo, possibly suffering the same treatment he
receives from his captors. But, of course, these are Vietnamese
women who cannot speak across the "cultural divide" Alvarez sees
between himself and the Vietnamese.[5]

Other narratives look hard for explanations and attempt to project
possible explanations for the women captives. Larry Guarino remembers how he, too, had heard the "screams of women prisoners and
assumed they were political prisoners being tortured." But Guarino's
assumptions turn out to be false. He later learned what had been
happening from a fellow prisoner: "Ben said the screaming came
from pregnant female prisoners in labor."[6] Although Alvarez and
Guarino probably were hearing different events, their assumptions
seemed to be remarkably similar and perhaps equally false.

Richard Dudman's *forty days with the enemy* describes the capture,
captivity, and release of four American journalists in Cambodia. At
one point Dudman describes being separated from Beth, another
recently captured journalist: "As we were waiting for whatever was to
come next, I heard in the distance what seemed a high-pitched shriek
of a woman in pain. I was sure Beth was being tortured."[7] Dudman's
anxiety, based on his conditioned male fear of female captivity, prove
wholly false. Beth later rejoins Dudman and explains that she had
been taken to a small hut: "She was in a schoolroom. A young Vietnamese stood guard near the door. He walked over to her and pulled
her silver rings from her fingers and made a timid effort to seduce
her. 'This is not necessary,' she said, 'you are my brother and I am

After being abused by their Vietnamese captors, women prisoners take matters into their own hands in *Five Gates to Hell*. Tales of female captivity, which
began as staples of Indian captivity lore, have been suppressed in Vietnam
POW media. *Courtesy of the Museum of Modern Art/Film Stills Archive.* (1959,
Twentieth Century-Fox)

your sister.' Her words were in English. He put the rings back on her
fingers and made no more trouble."[8] Dudman never makes a further
effort to explain the screams.

Surrounding the debate about women in combat has always been
the hypothetical question of exposing women to possible captivity.
The assumption seems to be that women have never been exposed to
captivity and that if they were they would be raped. The popular
captivity story involving women seldom does without the subplot of
rape or some other form of physical molestation. For example, in
films like *First Yank into Tokyo* (1945), *The Secret of Blood Island* (1964),
Five Gates to Hell (1959), *Seven Women From Hell* (1962), *Brushfire*
(1961), *Opposing Force* (1986), *Intimate Strangers* (1986), *Women of Valor*

(1986), and *Savage Justice* (1987), sexuality is an essential part of female captivity. Films like *Savage Justice* foreground the rape of the
protagonist as a pretext for revenge, on the part of either the woman
herself or some male hero. As Sarah Howard (Julia Montgomery)
explains in *Savage Justice:* "I did what I had to do to survive." The line
has become cliché. The female protagonist in such films must always
apologize for the unspeakable but prominently displayed rape scene.
Rape of female captives has become a mythic taboo we transgress for
entertainment and invoke for policy.

Intimate Strangers, one of the few movies that depicts a female POW
of the Vietnam War, treats Nurse Sally Bearson's (Teri Garr) rape as a
suspenseful secret. The television movie emphasizes the Bearsons'
troubled marriage and dark secret (her rape in a POW camp) at the
expense of dealing with anything else from her ten-year captivity. The
flashbacks to her captivity experience consist entirely of images surrounding her rape in a bamboo cage. The plot of the film and its limp
suspense revolve around Sally's admission that she was raped and that
her refugee companion is, in fact, her son, fathered by one of her
captors. The final scene of the film shows Sally begging her husband,
Jeff (Stacy Keach), to make love to her. Sally spends the entire film
reliving her experiences so that she might confess and be forgiven by
Jeff. Typically and ironically, Jeff's love relationship with another
woman (Cathy Lee Crosby) requires no such apology or explanation.
Whereas Sally must suffer and apologize to redeem her tarnished
image in the wake of her captivity and rape, affluent Jeff affirms his
manhood by loving another woman and reveals his sensitivity by for-
giving Sally. Such representations subordinate feminine captivity to
the experience and approval of the stay-at-home male. In popular
lore, captivity for a woman is not an experience that empowers or
enlightens. Unlike men, who are typically shown learning and benefit-
ing from such experience, women must struggle to reveal, apologize,
and compensate for their own captivity.

There are, however, women who have been prisoners of war, who
have been mistreated but not raped or otherwise sexually harassed
during their imprisonment. There are also literally millions of women
who have suffered a captivity arguably worse than anything experienced in North Vietnam: those who experienced the Holocaust. Many

women did, in fact, suffer captivity during the Vietnam War, and many suffered a greater injustice than any of those who have since written autobiographical narratives about their POW experience: they died. In short, women do have experiences much like and worse than those valorized in popular lore surrounding male captivity. But their stories are seldom heard.

Monika Schwinn's narrative in *We Came to Help* exemplifies the contradictions inherent in the POW gender issue. Schwinn spent six years as a prisoner of the North Vietnamese. Only one other POW text refers, albeit offhandedly, to Schwinn. Her story and those of other female prisoners are otherwise ignored.

Some might contend that female prisoners like Ray and Schwinn were not really POWs at all. Whatever frame we might wish to impose on the experience, however, it was made brutally clear to female captives that they were "prisoners of war."[9] Perhaps there is no better testimony of this than the remark made by Benjamin Purcell, a seven-year prisoner and the senior army captive held by the North Vietnamese. Purcell writes in the introduction to *We Came to Help*, "The many accounts of the treatment we received from our Communist captors are so varied that one might draw the conclusion that prisoners were not treated alike, but the aim was the same in every case."[10] At least in the beginning the plight of the journalists and the German nurses was more difficult: the initial stage of their captivity consisted of their interrogation as suspected spies, members of the CIA. However marginalized the female narratives might become, their accounts are important to the captivity experience of the Vietnam War.

━━━━━━━━━━

K ate Webb, like Michele Ray, was a journalist captured in Cambodia. Her account, *On the Other Side,* is an interesting study in the dynamics of female captivity. Webb's text pretends to be exactly what it is not: apolitical. Much like Charlie Plumb's *i'm no hero,* Webb's text wants to concentrate on the people and "instant comparisons . . . between the soldiers of the two sides." Her introductory claim is, in retrospect, quite naive: "It's a simple book, not involved in politics."[11] Webb would like to pretend that her position as an American female journalist in wartime Southeast Asia is somehow objective and uncompromised. She spends most of her narrative trying to level the role her gender plays in the story. By effacing her gendered role, politics, and distinctions between combatants and journalists, Webb struggles to find a space for her narrative in the context of a war that thrived on such distinctions. The attempt to erase such boundaries eventually keeps Webb from sorting out the assumptions that fuel the conflict she seeks to describe.

Webb's very first lines juxtapose "sitting in a ditch" with her UPI bungalow in Phnom Penh. Her predicament results from her "damn fool" behavior. Through an act of incredible arrogance, negligence, or perhaps a little of both, she suffers the fate of many journalists in Vietnam. She appears to believe she is some sort of privileged spirit who should be able to move from bourgeois "bungalow" to squalid "ditch" and back every day without compromising her perspective. She seems to assume that she should be insulated from the hardships of the war for two reasons. First, she believes her press pass serves as some elaborate cloaking device that makes her observation untainted by her presence. Second, she believes her exclusive position as a Western woman marks her as a noncombatant.

Webb's own narrative undercuts her apparently privileged position as nonparticipating observer at the point where she is captured: "I'd seen ambushes as violent as this in Vietnam, but there were radios, helicopters, tin pots to protect your head, some kind of organization. I'd seen worse mortar attacks, but in fixed positions, where you could hope to find or dig for some kind of cover."[12]

Ultimately she finds that she must reexamine the distinctions she has previously found so satisfying, so comforting: "Civilians—military, military—civilians. The military are civilians; soldiers are civilians in uniform." But when a soldier is wounded and there comes a choice between running and aiding the wounded, Webb seems to have less trouble with the distinction: "Soldiers have a sergeant, a general, a paycheck, and have to stay there. . . . They marched out here together, and they'll march back together—those who are left. But reporters, we went alone."[13] And so her conscience remains intact: "I thought of that wounded paratrooper and felt like a heel." But she realizes what apparently is the operative truth here: "Dead reporters look like dead soldiers. Soldiers, reporters, civilians—they all die the same." She sees that in captivity they all will become the same.

The plight of the fleeing reporter collapses with the realities of the fleeing pilot as Webb and her fellow reporter flee a government column ambushed on Highway 4.

> I hugged my knees. To my embarrassment, I'd wet my jeans in the thirteen hours of running. Dodging through [North] Vietnamese lines so close that we lay frozen on the ground with ants crawling over us . . . sometimes separated from one another . . . sometimes huddled together . . . while their voices (which told us they were Vietnamese) sounded clearly, seemingly just over our heads. I was not going to drop my pants and be caught with them down. Moonface had split his tight Phnom Penh trousers right around the crotch. He was hanging out front and back. He'd taken off his shirt and slung it around his waist for modesty. Strange place for modesty— and embarrassment.[14]

She wants to express her anxiety while effacing her gender. What is curious about this passage is that it shows quite plainly the breakdown of the civilian-military distinction during evasion. Webb points out the ridiculousness of her colleague's and her own modesty. This incongruity applies equally to their plight as reporters and her own apolitical aspirations for her book. The reporters, who are at least implicitly noncombatants, must flee from the enemy much the same as the soldiers. Her own book might be a "strange place for [political] modesty."

What is remarkable about Webb's narrative is the explicit absence of gender. Her fears are unsettlingly nondescript. She explains her fears in almost generic terms:

> Prisoners—it began to sink in. Not shot on sight. Prisoners. I sounded out myself for fear, almost looking for it as a touchpoint with reality. Thirst, yes; weariness, yes; even a tickle of amusement at walking carrying tree branches under the planes. The closest thing to fear was a dull apprehension coiled like an endless rope in my stomach.[15]

Her fears of captivity are apparently not gender related—if they are, she consciously avoids them in her text. Despite the apparent gloss of the gender issue in her initial chapters, she does remark on her frequent separations from "the others." The men of her party are housed, tied, and observed differently. Other than pointing to the distinctions, Webb makes no comments that might explain her captors' reasons for, or express her reactions to, these realities.[16] But later in the narrative her reportorial, apolitical account begins to crack:

> I had to stomp on the uneasiness in my mind by spelling it out. Either I was believed to be an American and they had a different fate mapped out for me than the others, or they didn't want the others to talk to me for similar reasons; possibly because I was a woman and they were abiding by the basic decencies, or because they were just trying to scare me.[17]

Despite this admission, Webb most often levels the qualities of her own fear with that of her fellow (male) journalists: "We all had the same fear of our feet giving out, similar stories in the backs of our minds about prisoners who can't keep up."[18] From her account there is little indication that her sex was an issue for her captors. She was not mistreated as popular lore would have us believe. There were, of course, private moments, exchanges, but these were not threatening.

Webb describes her uncomfortable position while taking her first bath: "Grinning, he waved for me to wash my sweater too. His eyes were glued to my psychedelically patterned Pucci bikini briefs. No dice. I shook my head firmly, but grinned back at him. . . . I walked wetly back up the path wishing I had been able to shave my legs."[19] Even though such incidents seldom occur in the narrative, Webb hints at her desire to return to the "bungalow" and her habits as a woman in a "civilized" society. During an interrogation session she recalls, "the girl says something, and the Finger [her interrogator] laughs. I want to go take a bath and be smooth-skinned and in control again."[20] She wants to recover her exclusive status as a female reporter in her "Doll's House" back in Saigon. She tires of her image as "idiotic mixture of Maid Marian, a badly miscast Liberation fighter, and the object of a none-too-devious camp joke."[21]

Webb eventually realizes that the distinctions she makes between soldier and journalist, civilian and soldier, combatant and noncombatant have all collapsed. Her own pretensions of finding truth as a reporter and making a difference in the war eventually dissolve in the day-to-day misery of her terrifyingly boring existence as a prisoner. So, too, her own images of herself as a woman in the wilderness, an aberration, a novelty, clash with the realization that she wants to have it both ways: she wants to be "Liberation Lady" but with soft, bathed skin and in a bungalow: "My attention was diverted from an unleashed flood of doubts and hopes that afternoon by the uncomfortable knowledge that I needed a Tampax." Her detachment collapses into her hidden expectations. "I was embarrassed and bemused. Never would make a jungle heroine. Goddamn reality keeps intervening. Wonder what the women in Dachau did, or the women in Japanese POW camps?"[22]

At the precise moment when she discovers that she cannot separate herself from her gender or live the stereotype, she half-jokingly reveals one of the tragedies of the POW myth. She cannot find a structure, a figuration of a woman's captivity, the scaffolding to deal psychologically with the experience. The lack of previous experience robs her of any effective role she might play in the captivity drama. In comparing herself to World War II POWs and to the victims of the Holocaust, Webb struggles for an unavailable paradigm for her own POW reality.

Inevitably, perhaps sadly, she consequently subordinates her experience to the "real prisoners" in Hanoi.

> Whatever I wrote [during interrogation] could be twisted and taken out of context, appear on a Radio Hanoi broadcast as "UPI correspondent Kate Webb says . . ." I thought of what the American prisoners in Hanoi would think when their guards had them listen to the broadcasts. I could almost feel them flinching, as they struggled with their minds, not believing that yet another of their own people had "gone soft."[23]

In this extraordinary passage Webb at once destroys her own confidence in her profession and cements her own captivity experience to the extensive lore surrounding the POWs in the North. She fears that her words will be extracted "out of context" in much the same way she has quoted sources for her own stories. But now she realizes that her own words will be taken and "twisted" just as she has taken the words of countless others and "twisted" them for her own stories. As she watches her own journalistic strategies turned back on herself, she surrenders the value of her own experience to the prisoners in Hanoi. By imagining this audience for her own responses, she places herself in a subordinate position, creating a situation where she is judged, where her comments can be approved or rejected only by males. By deferring to the apparent importance of the POWs in Hanoi, falling into their rhetoric ("gone soft"), and remaining mute in order to spare them, she becomes the soldier she claims she is not.

When Webb assumes for herself the role of prisoner of war in solidarity with the "prisoners in Hanoi," she undercuts her own contention: "I don't consider myself a prisoner of war; I am not a soldier."[24] This is complicated by her implied aversion to falling into the feminine role of betrayer sensationalized in earlier accounts (Alvarez and others). Her fear of going "soft" as a woman journalist discussing the prisoners in Hanoi shows an aversion to the Jane Fonda stereotype, the role of the betrayer. In accepting the metaphor of going "soft" for not resisting communism, while also telling of her own feminine desire to be "soft skinned" again, Webb inadvertently amplifies feminine stereotypes.

The symmetry she tries so hard to establish between the military on the opposing sides of the conflict can be applied to her captivity as well. By falling into and supporting the established role of Vietnam POW, however self-consciously, she effaces her own narrative, relegating it to the position it will eventually fall to: occluded by the male POW texts.

If there is a real tragedy, a terrible irony in the Vietnam POW experience, it is perhaps the one that is least often heard. Monika Schwinn and Bernhard Diehl's *We Came to Help* tells the story of five West German nurses from the Aid Service of Malta who arrived in An Hoa, Vietnam, on a hospital ship to provide medical assistance. Their status and role were roughly that of the Red Cross, although less well known. Their mission, which was supported by South Vietnam and the United

States, was meant to be neutral. They provided assistance for those left uncared for by the competing military machines. Members of the Aid Service of Malta succeeded in treating thousands of civilians during their stay in Vietnam, and from their own account, the service treated those from both sides of the conflict.

But distinctions during war are always hard to make, as Webb makes clear in her text. During an outing along the Khe Le River, these distinctions fell apart for Monika Schwinn. She and her companions were captured by the North Vietnamese. Five members of the Air Service had gone on a sightseeing trip: Bernhard Diehl, Marie-Luise Kerber, Hindrika Kortmann, Monika Schwinn, and Georg Bartsch. Schwinn and Diehl were the only survivors; they returned to Germany some four years later. Even though they were nurses, they were never able to prove their status to the North Vietnamese. They were imprisoned in various camps and two, Schwinn and Diehl, eventually shared the Hanoi Hilton with hundreds of American prisoners.

We Came to Help is highlighted here primarily to add Monika Schwinn's voice to the fraternity of the Hanoi Hilton. It is her presence and commentary on captivity that contrast to other accounts of the captivity experience and work to dissolve the male monologue of the Vietnam POW experience.

Perhaps the most important aspect of Schwinn's narrative is what she does not say. Schwinn and her companions were never mistreated . . . based on their gender. These women were never raped or molested. They were, however, treated with much the same cruelty as other POWs.

If we take the group of German nurses and compare their mortality rate (three out of five) with that of American soldiers in captivity, the chances of survival were actually much worse for the German nurses. In fact, their official status was also worse: their names appeared on none of the lists submitted by the U.S. delegation to the Paris peace talks.[25] They were systematically starved (although perhaps not deliberately) in much the same way as other prisoners:

The word "hunger" conveys nothing of the horror of slowly starving to death. . . . I lost weight and, worst of all, my hair fell out until I was almost bald. When it began to grow back it was no longer dark, but a sort of brown fluff. At our hospital in Da Nang, I had treated children suffering from severe malnutrition. Instead of blue-black, their hair was brown.[26]

The conditions at the first camp where Schwinn and one of her female companions were held could hardly have been worse. The South Vietnamese prisoners she shared her first camp with were walking dead: "The prisoners looked straight through us. . . . They had been in camp for three or four years, and by now they had lost interest in everything."[27] In contrast with what the mythology would have us think, female prisoners drew no special attention. At one point Schwinn carried her dying companion to the latrine: "Neither guards nor the other prisoners paid any attention to me and my burden. Only a few observed without interest the spectacle of one woman trying to carry another across the prison yard without falling down."[28]

On the day of her death from an undiagnosed fever, Schwinn's companion appealed to the qualities of her own gender as a pretext for hope:

> Mrs. Binh in Paris. The woman who represents the NLF at the Paris peace talks. As a woman, she is sensitive; she must understand what life is like in these camps. She knows all about conditions here. Why doesn't she help us? The men won't help us, but Mrs. Binh is a woman.

The woman's pathetic and "delirious" comments point out that far from marking them as prisoners accorded some special status, their gender made them, if anything, more anonymous, an embarrassment with no representative, no voice. Their captivity had no value:

> The Vietnamese attitude toward women profoundly affected my life for the next four years. A woman, and a prisoner to boot, possessed no rights whatever. Female prisoners were assigned the worst clothing and lodging, and their needs were always ignored. When the Americans bombed the region around Hanoi, all the male prisoners were removed from their cells and taken to dugouts. The guards never bothered to take me along, for, after all, I was only a woman; it would make no difference if I was killed.

As opposed to narratives by other women, Schwinn reflects on her gender and how it affects her captivity:

In the prison camps, a woman had only two advantages. Women were considered nonentities; therefore, female prisoners were assigned the most thick-witted interrogators, who could easily be gulled into believing anything. . . . The second advantage lay in the fact that the Vietnamese would never lay hands on a woman prisoner. . . . But in four years, no one physically molested me. To have touched a female prisoner, a creature without rights or honor, would have been an unpardonable crime.[29]

This testimony directly contradicts the images described by prisoners who claim to have heard women being tortured and, at least implicitly, violated in some way by their captors.

There was, however, one incident where one of the German women was physically approached. Bernhard Diehl explains that when Rika Kortmann left camp "to gather wood, Bob followed her, sat down beside her, and put his arm around her. Rika ran back to us."[30] "Bob," however, was not a Vietnamese cadre, but an infamous American, Robert Garwood. Some have alleged that Garwood served as a "guard" in the jungle POW camps and fought with North Vietnamese units in South Vietnam. Whatever his status, Garwood, in contrast to the Vietnamese, distinguished himself with this incident. Diehl later questioned Garwood about his conduct: "To hear Houng [Vietnamese cadre] tell it, Viet Cong soldiers are above that sort of thing." He [Garwood] laughed again. 'Oh, it's the Americans. They're corrupting everybody in this country!' "[31]

The Vietnamese were certainly not benevolent captors, however. Later in her account, Schwinn expands on her initial statement: "At no time did the Vietnamese show any consideration for my feelings. They never made sexual advances to me, but neither did they respect my privacy. If they saw that I was partially undressed, they used to stand there and watch me or even come closer."[32]

However damning this conduct might be, it is hardly peculiar to the North Vietnamese. James Daly, one of the few prisoners whose narrative mentions Schwinn's captivity, wrote about Schwinn and her female companions. Daly's comments are hardly flattering:

All four [one German had already died] of the Germans were very sick. Even though the women were in really bad shape—and looked it—their just being around turned all the guys on. Everyone tried to catch looks at them through the fence that separated the two areas, especially when they went to the latrine. It was our job to wash their clothes, since they weren't up to doing it themselves. Whenever one of the guys would get his hands on a pair of panties, anyone would have thought it was the most exciting, valuable piece of cloth in the world. He'd hold it up, wave it in the air— even pass it around to be smelled.[33]

Although Daly's tone indicates his own reservations about what "the guys" did, his observations indicate again that North Vietnamese guards were seldom as sexist and intrusive as the American prisoners themselves.

What Dudman, Webb, and Schwinn show is that the assumptions implicit in representations of female captivity are the stuff of myth. The fears of sexual mistreatment and female vulnerability do not address the recorded experience of women captured during the Vietnam conflict. Rather, these narratives make it quite obvious that the fears of female captivity are a reflection of American male desire and need rather than prisoner testimony. The titillation of female captivity continues to carry the evil valence it came to have for religious fanatics at Salem. The female captive myth also expresses the male fear that his possession, the woman, will be violated and his dominant position surrendered to a male "other."

If we are going to speak in terms of racist or nationalist assumptions, it should be clear that the offenders in the molestation and exploitation of women were the Americans and not the Vietnamese. Like the American Indians, the Vietnamese were remarkably well disciplined when it came to Western women. The female captives who speak here make it clear that neither side was particularly sensitive to gender boundaries. If anything, the narratives show that the North Vietnamese policy specifically avoided gender differences while American prisoners highlighted them at the expense of the women they came in contact with.

The three narratives by women are interesting, but typically dismissed in the story of the POW experience. They have ceased to function in the Vietnam-era captivity myth, and they therefore disappear from the cultural landscape. Webb mutes her voice in order not to "betray" her male counterparts in Hanoi, Ray's story was dismissed as the "gushing of a society columnist," and Schwinn tells a story that is seldom heard and never integrated into POW lore. These narratives are marginalized because women are not supposed to be captives. If they do become captives their experience, because of their gender, becomes not the almost-divine experience capitalized on by male captives, but a troubling manifestation of loss. They tell a very different tale of captivity, one not heard in popular accounts. They get left out because of both their gender and how they describe their experience. It is therefore important to remember *how* they get left out, all but intentionally ignored, in the popular imagination. They bring to the surface issues that destroy male assumptions about the captivity experience. Webb erases the distinction between soldier and civilian, captor and captive. Schwinn proves the soldier/civilian distinction invalid and goes on to illuminate racial, national, and ideological boundaries that remain opaque to other POWs. How these boundaries of difference become useful is yet another tale to tell.

9
The Uses of Difference

One of the few war films in production when the Japanese surrendered in August of 1945 was a "B" movie few remember. *First Yank into Tokyo* gained some notoriety as the first popular film about the atomic bomb, but the bomb plot was tacked on after the film was in production. The movie is primarily concerned with getting an American agent, Major Steve Ross (Tom Neal), into a Japanese POW camp to rescue an important scientist, Louis Jardine (Marc Cramer), who has built a supergun. When the existence of the atomic bomb was acknowledged in the summer of 1945, the supergun became "the bomb."

The film is important to this chapter because it makes radical and obvious racist assumptions in a representation of POW experience. *First Yank into Tokyo* begins with Steve Ross as a promising bomber pilot. He is unique because he spent part of his childhood in Tokyo and speaks Japanese fluently. This makes him a prime candidate for a secret mission to rescue the important scientist, Jardine. In order to penetrate the POW camp, the Caucasian Ross must undergo plastic surgery and learn "every kink in their [the Japanese] corkscrew mentalities." Ross emerges from his transforming surgery complete with slanted eyes and a set of prominent buck teeth. The colonel who briefs Ross warns him how difficult it will be to pass as Japanese even with the face change: "As we know from experience they [the Japanese] have a completely reversed approach to things."

The plot works through a whole series of improbable circumstances: Ross's fiancée, Abby Drake (Barbara Hale of Perry Mason fame), who Ross believed died in the Philippines, turns up in Jardine's camp along with Ross's ex-college roommate, who happens to be the Japanese camp commandant. Ross succeeds in springing Jardine and

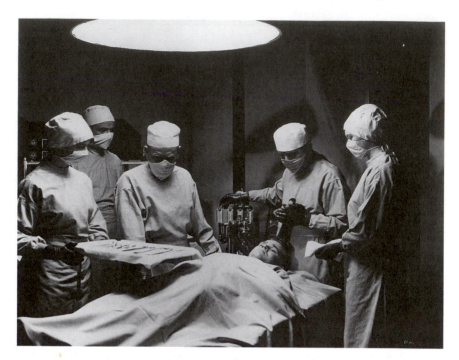

Major Ross (Tom Neal) prepares for a POW rescue mission by undergoing "irreversible" plastic surgery to make his cover plausible in *First Yank into Tokyo*. Although his mission will be a success, he will decide to die rather than return to the United States with his "Jap" features. His decision to die is an admission of the racist assumptions that underlie the film's plot. *Courtesy of the Museum of Modern Art/Film Stills Archive.* (1945, RKO)

Drake, only to end up cornered on a beach while a rescuing submarine awaits. At the end of the film Ross sends Jardine and Drake out to the submarine, explaining that he and Abby Drake "couldn't find any happiness together." Ross, pointing to his "Japanese" face, says, "I'm saddled with this." Ross concludes that "no matter how close people have been to you, they seldom look past your face." The voice-over in the film claims that Ross sacrifices his life for his country. But Ross remains on the beach for another reason: his life will be a constant struggle against those who will associate his modified face with the essential "corkscrew mentalities" of the Japanese. The odd and apparently unintended irony of the film is that the same racism that makes possible Ross's improbable transformation and secret mission forces him to commit the equivalent of suicide by remaining on the beach holding off Japanese soldiers while Jardine and Drake escape to freedom. Ross's acknowledgment of racism in America kills him.

First Yank into Tokyo, however improbable the plot, carries the racist assumptions essential to American thinking during the Second World War. Nine years later, in a film discussed in chapter 1, Web Sloane (Ronald Reagan) in *Prisoner of War* would go on a mission strangely similar to Steve Ross's. *Prisoner of War*'s racial stereotypes of the North Koreans mirror the racial assumptions of *First Yank into Tokyo.* Both films did poorly at the box office, but the second would have a powerful advocate playing the principal actor. Ronald Reagan's claims about the documentary accuracy of *Prisoner of War* may have been well founded, at least in regard to questions of race. In this context it might be interesting to look at how assumptions about racial and other forms of difference changed in representations of the POW experience of the Vietnam War.

━━━━━━━━━━

Gender, race, class, and cultural boundaries amplify the misunderstandings of captivity. Such differences are at the heart of prisoner experience. The arbitrary and seemingly artificial difference between prisoner and captor is probably the most unjust, unfathomable, and immediate structure the prisoner must face. Kate Webb describes it this way: "How different they are, the captor and the captive. The water had cleared some of the dullness from my head, but not the thirst. The captor is master; the captive is slave. It isn't just the guns, though if the guns were not there, we would have been just eight people—two Vietnamese, four Cambodians, a Japanese, and me."[1] As Webb points out, there was a line between them, but the line was complicated and exaggerated by the differences between the people. These differences became useful to prisoner and captive alike. Most often difference was useful in a pejorative way: it provided a way to objectify, make radically "other" the prisoner or captor. It could strip captive or captor of humanity, replace rational thinking with hate, and replace understanding with labels so that "other" might more quickly be assimilated into a psychology that could justify brutality, starvation, confinement, resistance, theft, or deceit.

Racial and cultural differences worked in a variety of ways in the POW narratives. The uses of difference are visible within the discourse of the prisoner, and are actively at work in the ideology and psychology of captive and captor.

At best, the various boundaries in the Vietnam War were problematic. At worst, racial, cultural, and national distinctions were most often made on the surface. A major issue for American forces in the theater was how to separate enemy from friend on the basis of race, cultural wardrobe, or national uniform. How do you tell North Vietnamese from South Vietnamese? The problems of this question could be emblematic for the problems of the war. How is difference useful? How do you identify difference? What do you call it, and what essential qualities do you attribute to certain kinds of difference? How does difference become useful in structuring experience?

Charlie Plumb's account of North Vietnamese culture stands out as the most remarkable. Plumb spends five chapters of his prison autobiography, *i'm no hero*, discussing Vietnamese culture. The names of the chapters detail Plumb's amateur ethnography in the areas of Vietnamese "Pastimes," "Behavior," "Culture," "Construction," and "Propaganda." Plumb makes his observations by conducting a "peep-hole reconnaissance" from his cell and draws his conclusions from many years of idle deliberation.[2]

Plumb's narrative begins with a sequence that undercuts his title, *i'm no hero*. He begins where his story ends, at the new Kansas City Royals' stadium, which he dedicates:

I had been waiting in the dugout, accompanied by the owners of the Royals ball club, Muriel and Ewing Kauffman, who epitomized warmth and compassion—qualities which the North Vietnamese radio had endlessly hammered to be nonexistent in the American social elite. That those of the moneyed class were ogres or mechanical robots bent on persecuting the poor, as promised by North Vietnamese propaganda, could not have been further from the truth. The Kauffmans were congenial, down-to-earth human beings.[3]

Plumb gives an example of American life that will certainly prove that his captors in North Vietnam had gotten it all wrong. Apparently, by showing that people who had money in American were not "ogres or mechanical robots," Plumb believes he is making North Vietnamese assertions about the United States appear utterly ridiculous. The point of North Vietnamese propaganda may not have been the lack of congeniality of the "elite," however, but that there were such economic classes, and an "American social elite," in the first place. By pointing to the radical economic differences at the ballpark, Plumb affirms the distinctions of class at the heart of Marxist doctrine. It is difficult to accept his argument for another reason. However congenial the Kauffmans might have been, their demeanor is not convincing evidence that the class differences he affirms are appropriate. Slaveholders may have been "warm and compassionate," but this did not validate the institution of slavery. Plumb seems to be missing the point.

He later expands on his view of the class issues implicit in his treatment at the stadium.

> I was on the move again, approaching an area kept under close surveillance—the Kauffman suite. What a grandiose sight! . . . The spacious suite, done in blue, was softly lighted by crystal chandeliers. Drinks, hors d'oeuvres, diamonds, expensive gowns—the affluence was overwhelming. It was not at all the mustard-stain ball games I had so often pictured in dreams from the Hanoi Hilton. Ironically, this kind of baseball had been occurring for years, but ten thousand miles away I had no reason even to consider that it was happening. . . . I felt out of place. Instead of wealth, I had known only abject poverty, not seeing so much as a humble button, much less faceted diamonds. But it was gratifying to know that because I had tied my raveled drawstrings and had paced in battered sandals, I had in some small way helped protect this system wherein worthy individuals could attain material success. The influential people who were gathered in this suite were depicted by North Vietnamese propaganda as dangerous capitalist warmongers who exploited the poor. . . . During the seventh inning stretch, I was to be interviewed. . . . A blue cloth with a Royals emblem was hung opposite the camera as a backdrop.[4]

This passage highlights the contradictions in the ideology that powers Plumb's narrative. Plumb wants to impress us with his good impressions of the elite whom the North Vietnamese attempted to criticize. He was proud to have served the system that had produced such good people, people rewarded by material wealth found in few other countries. By juxtaposing American riches with North Vietnamese poverty, he wants to affirm the hegemony of American culture.

But Plumb's own narrative works against itself. First, he admits that there is an "elite" that sits in glassed-in booths while his own relatives wait elsewhere—"the bleachers where my dad, three uncles, and my date Kathy Melcher waited." He admits the class gap when he says, "I felt out of place." Plumb sees that his struggle in Vietnam played a role in the protection of this Kansas City wealth—but this is a Cold War logic that assumes that the North Vietnamese had it in their minds to somehow threaten Royals' stadium. Another irony emerges when Plumb, apparently not a member of the "social elite," observes that the Kauffmans and their guests were not "capitalists ... who exploited the poor," immediately before he is interviewed in front of the advertising logo of the Kansas City Royals. Obviously the magnanimous Kauffmans are capitalizing on the fame, political value, and notoriety of a returned POW to provide a sideshow for their profit-making ball club.

Plumb calls the plight of his captors "paradoxical" and "tragic" because under their socialist ideology they "labored and sacrificed in order to win the ultimate victory over intruding evil."[5] But such a frame of mind hardly seems "paradoxical" or "tragic" when we consider that he himself had quite recently been dropping bombs on these people. It is odd for Plumb to criticize the Vietnamese for defending their culture against attacking planes when we consider the terrible captivity he has endured, ostensibly to defend the rights of "elite" people to sit in cushy booths and watch baseball games while sipping champagne.

Plumb also would have us accept the behavior of the prison guards at Hoa Lo as somehow metonymic, standing for the entire Vietnamese population. Such a jump in logic is questionable at best. It would be like taking a group of prison guards from some maximum-security prison in America and accepting their behavior as representative of all

American society, or surveying the owner's box at some baseball park and taking the scene there as somehow representative of all of American society.

The logic of Plumb's descriptions of the North Vietnamese are equally flawed. Plumb points out that "the North Vietnamese frequently seemed childish and immature." Plumb makes this comment after he observes two guards pretending to drive an inoperative jeep. He points out how their " 'ego' extended to 'private' possessions. . . . Whenever a Vietnamese claimed a pen, pocketknife, or a wristwatch as his own (not the state's), he perpetually showed it to anyone he thought was watching. If he had a watch he'd raise his arm ostentatiously every two minutes to check the time."[6] He apparently forgets what his flights over the North confirmed: the Vietnamese people lived by a different standard than Americans. They had no cars, no watches, no pens, not even pocketknives. These were all luxuries, curiosities. The men pretended to drive the jeep, just as other young soldiers might pretend to fly aircraft or pilot ships. They marveled at their very rare possessions just as a relatively poor man in America might marvel at the opulence of a baseball team owner's personal booth at a ballpark and write about it with admiration in a personal narrative.

Plumb goes on to discuss his estimate of "fashion":

> Maintaining current wardrobes was never a problem for the Vietnamese. Fashions remained the same. Men wore khaki shirts and pants with legs cut off above the knees if they had to slog in the rice paddies. Women wore the same kind of shirts and black baggy pants. On Sunday afternoons, the women exchanged their work shirts for high-collared white blouses, but the pants were the same. Seldom did I see makeup or jewelry. . . . they had no awareness of fashion.[7]

It is not clear what Plumb feels the Vietnamese should be wearing, but the implication is that it should match his expectations as an American. It is not hard to understand why people dressed in similar clothes, especially considering, as he points out, that "guards resorted to stealing our food because they, too, were hungry."[8] Plumb fails to put this observation next to his critique of the material goods he sees around him. He fails to realize that the drab clothing, the trinkets, and the "black lacquer" used to repair teeth might be all that they have.

Plumb has a hard time understanding the Vietnamese culture, including their music:

> What did the Vietnamese do for a pastime? Mostly nothing. They "fiddled around" a lot. A few could play, and many would try to play, a bamboo flute or a guitar or mandolin. Regardless of their talent, most of the sounds they produced were, to me, noise.[9]

He fails to understand that the difference between American music and Vietnamese music might be considerable—a fact that should be obvious.

It may seem that I have chosen some passages from *i'm no hero* that indicate immediate impressions and not careful observations, but Plumb seems confident that these are valid observations:

> As in the case of any ethnic group, the Vietnamese make an interesting but complex study. Interpretations and generalizations are admittedly mine, based on thousands of hours of observation. Initially, I often misunderstood Vietnamese behavior or intent. As the years dragged by, however, I became more adept both in my observation and in my understanding, because I was compelled to discover some subtle clue to help me escape or endure my fate.[10]

He summarizes his observations in this passage: "To me this was a nation of people with misdirected energies. They teased animals, they threw rocks. They beat birds' nests with sticks. They chatted, they smoked, they dozed." Exactly what "directed energies" might be is unclear in this particular passage, but we might assume Plumb is again talking about ballparks and opulent press boxes. He observes that "the Vietnamese seemed more content than Americans, often smiling and laughing at work and play."[11] Although puzzled, he chalks this up to "childishness" and "irresponsibility." He fails to see that cultural differences might compromise his entire frame of reference, that he might be judging this strange culture by standards taken from his own culture. But Plumb is still an expert, most recently appearing on the

"MacNeil/Lehrer Newshour" to offer his expertise and criticism along-side the beaten faces of American POWs in Iraq.[12]

Sometimes anger remains unself-consciously expressed in the narratives. Clearly, the physical and psychological pain of captivity and torture do not make friends of captor and captive. James Mulligan (*The Hanoi Commitment*) is very frustrated with the cultures in which he finds himself: "I couldn't make out any of their jibberish."[13] He goes on to make an observation that reflects an assumption, similar to Plumb's, that the Vietnamese should be as familiar with motor vehicles as Americans: "These little monkeys aren't even smart enough to know how to use the clutch properly."[14] Although hardly in a position to be objective, Mulligan nevertheless uses the same pejorative and stereotyped language and images to characterize the Vietnamese years after his captivity has ended. His anger and racist hatred become an obstacle to his understanding of the "enemy": "Once again his [an interrogator's] devious Asian mind was too much for me to fathom."[15]

Like many POWs, Mulligan remains confused about the intentions of the Vietnamese and the war in general. Such misunderstandings complicate the difficult conditions of captivity. Rather than understanding the difficulty of their situations, many of the POWs pack their misunderstandings into the culture that frustrates them and seems continually to resist their understanding. Kate Webb, however, observes animosity in the face of her captives and offers an explanation for it that goes beyond racial epithet:

> His [an interrogator's] eyes told me he would gladly have jumped on my head till it was pulp. . . . I had seen those eyes too many times in the faces of American, Vietnamese, and Cambodian soldiers. The anguish of having to fight on and reduce oneself to an animal with no time to mourn or save friends; all that ground into a passion to strike back at the cause of it all.[16]

Webb quite rightly points to the frustration and anger directed to the "other." Such displays function for both captor and captive and most often involve investment of emotions into the most accessible qualities of difference. For Plumb and Mulligan those differences are racial and cultural.

These cultural differences are overlayed with an intensely opposi-
tional ideological framework that confuses an already problematic
situation. Tortured, starved, and in some cases maimed for life, the
prisoners understandably returned to American culture with tremendous relief, joy, and pride. Unfortunately, inherent in their painful
recollections are the prejudices and misunderstandings found in
Plumb's *i'm no hero* and Mulligan's *The Hanoi Commitment*. However
understanding we might be of such judgments, it is important to
remember that Plumb and Mulligan were not randomly selected members of American society: these were college-educated officers of the
armed forces, by definition leaders of the nation, and, at least partly as
a result of their experience as POWs, they would become icons of
American culture. Their experience as POWs made them the "threshold bearers" of American values.[17]

One testament to the cultural awareness of the pilots, some of
whom eventually became POWs, is provided by Robinson Risner in
The Passing of the Night. Risner discusses his flying in Panama:

> We did little to endear ourselves to the local populace. Most of us flew at
> least five and a half days a week. A favorite pastime was to blow the roofs
> off the little native huts. The P-39 was ideal for this. You could stick the
> nose in the air and it would "mush," the tail sticking close to the ground. At
> full throttle it would not start climbing for a while. You could mush along
> blowing the roofs off one at a time. And if the huts were not available,
> sailboats were fair game. Hardly a sailboat ever escaped.[18]

Although he acknowledges that his antics did "little to endear" him to
the local population, this passage appears in a chapter he names
"Shaping of the Future." It is unclear why he included this passage in
his narrative. Whatever his reasons, the passage does reveal how insen-
sitive he and his comrades might be. Such experiences, juxtaposed
with the insensitivity of Risner's captors in Hanoi, may have led him to
understand his own prejudices. His own assumptions about the Vietnamese are made explicit: "I thought my captors would probably be
cruel because they were Asians."[19]

Naming is perhaps the most prevalent and blatant mark of racial
and cultural bias in the narratives. Naming the various characters in

the POW story from both sides is an act of objectification. The names attach qualities to their referents based on some physical or social characteristic. Although the names are sometimes endearing, they most often reflect the intense prejudice you might expect. The act of naming functions in two ways in this situation. First, naming a person who already has a name dismisses the original name as somehow unusable or irrelevant. Although this dismissal is often done out of practical necessity (not understanding the language of the "other"), the act nevertheless implies that the original name has no value. Second, the new name provides a means of objectifying the person named. This objectification, in removing the individual from his cultural context, at once puts the subject on the name-maker's own terms and distances the subject from the name-maker. The names also provide some essential referent that makes identification quick and easy. The name also might carry hatred, fear, or some other form of emotion that would satisfy a need of the name-maker or his community. The act of renaming a person of another culture is essentially an act of linguistic imperialism that gives the name-maker the illusion of control over (even possession of) the named, while making that person radically "other." The act at least implicitly rejects the cultural and ethnic context from which the original name springs. As one POW points out, there was a "Western pattern of arrogant indifference toward learning other languages."[20] The act of superimposing the name over another disregards both the culture and the identity of the subject.

This process occurs in one form or another in virtually all the POW narratives. Admiral Stockdale takes part in the somewhat self-conscious renaming of his captors:

> To us [American POWs in Hanoi], these Vietnamese military jailers remained not only rankless but nameless, and thus naturally they acquired American nicknames. I was later to find out that my tall stretcher-bearer was "Dipshit." The short stretcher-bearer was a junior officer; I soon learned that he spoke English, claimed to be a mathematics professor, and was called "Owl" by the Americans.[21]

Stockdale points out that "to us" the North Vietnamese were both "rankless and nameless": they had no legitimate military status or

valid identity. These assumptions apparently justified "American nicknames" like "Dipshit," "Pigeye," "Bug," "Fairy," "Spot," "Big Dumb,"
"Stag," and "Cat." Such "nicknames" hardly enhanced the conditions
of the prisoners or fostered understanding. The names functioned
instead as psychological crutches in captivity to reassert the superiority of the captives over the captors by creating an insider code among
captives and naming the "other" in ways that reduced them to unflat-
tering physical characteristics or mannerisms. Such reductions were
necessary if the POW was going to be physically and mentally prepared to resist, dismiss, and possibly harm his captors. Former POW
Ben Purcell saw his experience as "an investment in understanding. I
have never found it in my heart to hate Armband, Hooknose,
Goldtooth, Crisco, or Spit."[22] But, even in reconciliation, Purcell cannot escape the pejorative language he imposes on his experience. We
must wonder just how much understanding one can have for someone you would call "Spit."

Only one narrative I surveyed becomes overtly critical of using this
renaming practice. Although George Smith uses his own vocabulary
of pejorative names extensively, he eventually becomes uncomfortable
with the renaming process:

> By this time I wasn't feeling too comfortable with the names we had
> pinned on the Vietnamese. They were still the same people they had been
> a week ago—we'd known some of them for nearly two years—but after
> they announced our release I began to realize that most of the names
> simply didn't apply. After you've called a guy an asshole for two years it's
> hard to sit down and smile at him, and be honest, look him directly in the
> eye. I felt a little guilty about it. At the time I named them I'd thought the
> names were appropriate, but now they didn't seem so right. I had been just
> a little bit nasty.[23]

Smith, whose entire POW experience was a composite of harsh treatment, escape, punishment, and release, brings a unique and remarkably objective approach to his narrative:

> I regretted not knowing more about each of them [his captors]. They'd
> never told us much about themselves, but then we'd never asked. We just
> lay in our beds feeling superior. "You silly bastards, here you are giving me

stupid rice and sardines and I'm making something like eight hundred dollars a month—I'll be eating steaks when I get out of here, and you guys will still be living in shit. Even if you do win the fucking war, what have you got—nothing."[24]

He makes the reciprocal nature of the captor-captive relationship visible, saying that "they'd never told us much." Both sides of the conflict worked to keep the struggle intact. One way of doing this was to objectify, make the enemy "other" in the lowest possible terms. The structure most conducive to POW discourse was also well suited to captor: distance yourself from the humanity of the "other" in order to give torture, hatred, and blame no friction in the conscience; make it morally antiseptic. Mechanisms like naming make the otherwise biased, pejorative, and illogical conclusions of POW and captor at least seem believable in their contexts.

Smith does not end his remarks on naming without a deeper critique of the racism and cultural bias implicit in much of the American presence in Vietnam:

> This [naming] was a holdover from being an American—that you're superior to Asiatics—the thing they teach you at Fort Bragg and in high school and in grade school. Gradually I had changed. I had learned humility, I believe. It's something to learn; I hadn't had it before. . . . I changed from my arrogance and nastiness to liking people, from my superiority to feeling that the Vietnamese were pretty good people. Some of the honest culture of an oppressed people must have worn off on me.[25]

This remarkably candid passage is unique among the POW narratives. Then again, Smith was radically unique among the POWs. He was imprisoned on both sides: first he spent two years in Vietcong prison camps and then he spent months incommunicado in American custody on Okinawa. His release and his status as a Special Forces enlisted man fueled suspicions and prompted unusual treatment by both sides. The Vietcong voluntarily released him. The circumstances of his release made the United States Army suspicious of Vietcong motivations. He sat out a detailed investigation of his POW conduct by the army. No charges were ever brought against him, but he lost his position in Special Forces and was eventually discharged from the army. His narrative is, predictably, marginalized in the history of the Vietnam POW.

Ernest Brace, although showing solidarity with the members of the Hanoi Hilton fraternity in other aspects of captivity, is consistent with Smith's account regarding the character of the majority of North Vietnamese:

> After nearly eight years of captivity, there was no bitterness in me against my captors. They had punished me severely when I had tried to escape in the jungle, but it was punishment I had expected. For every guard who had abused me, there were several who had loaned me needles, taught me Vietnamese words, and given me extra helpings of food. I had felt after leaving Korea that I wouldn't mind living in the Orient someday, and though this had not been what I had in mind, I hadn't changed my views about the Orient.[26]

Brace's equivocal stance contrasts with other, more skewed statements on the difference between captor and captive.

We should not be surprised that captives do not like or understand their captors. But the degree to which this hatred manifests itself in the narrative structures and interpretations of POW authors is vitally important. The POWs, by virtue of the qualities of fame that I have discussed, have a privileged voice: the authority to write autobiography, speak on the meaning of Thanksgiving, endorse the authenticity of motion pictures, or establish their experience as an essential test of character for public office. Therefore, how they come to tell their stories and the logic of their interpretations become essential to the credibility and wisdom of what that privileged voice might have to tell us.

Some POWs, quite unself-consciously, compare their experiences as prisoners of war with earlier experiences of military indoctrination. James Daly suggests that many of the same structures and assumptions are at work in both basic training and the prison experience. The objectifications, the making of "other," and the fostering of cohesion and intense community are all aspects of both prison and military hierarchies.[27]

James Daly's critique of his early military training points to some of these troubling assumptions and structures. Daly's critique of military cadence songs points to the explicit gender bias practiced every day at physical training (PT): "I thought the words were really stupid. Actually insulting. Like, 'Jody's got your girl and gone—Jody's got your mama, too.' Or your sister. Or somebody. While everybody else shouted out the marching cadence, I kept my mouth shut tight."[28] He goes on to critique the methods used to train him. He deftly juxtaposes his United States Army experience with his treatment as a prisoner, highlighting what he sees as a fundamental problem in both disciplinary frames:

> The further along into the eight weeks of basic I went, the more I came to realize the way the trainees were treated was completely wrong—that it could never accomplish the goal of building disciplined soldiers who respected the military and the leaders. How can a man coming into the army have any respect for the first noncommissioned officers he meets when he's constantly cursed and insulted, when he marches in cadence to words that call his mother and his sister a whore, when he's put down time and time again?[29]

The structure of basic training, Ranger school, Special Forces qualification courses, Recondo, Airborne, Air Assault, Jumpmaster, Combat Diver, and freshman year at a service academy have disciplinary structures in common with the experience of being a POW: spatial restriction, verbal abuse (the making of "other"), enforced stripping of all material and physical trappings and identifications with other communities, restriction of basic necessities, conversion of basic rights to privileges, and reduction of human existence to legitimated terms of status and action. It should come as no surprise that the military and other national institutions would place a high value on captivity as an experience, since the experience mimics institutionalized indoctrination and military basic training. In the end, the military structures common to both America and Vietnam were pretty much the same for Daly: "But the military mentality—whether it's Vietnamese or American—doesn't allow for individual's concerns, or a sense of compassion."[30]

Perhaps Daly's most astute observations concerned the difference between Vietnamese and Americans. He uncovers what he sees as the basic assumptions behind American policy in Vietnam:

It didn't take me long to find out that, to the army's way of thinking, Vietnamese lives, even hundreds of them, were not as important as the life of one American. As far as the military was concerned, forget the ideas that we're all God's children.[31]

His observations are confirmed by Vietnamese prisoners he meets at a jungle camp:

Jose spoke to a number of the prisoners, and the story they told, in great anger, was that just when it looked as if the Americans could fly in food and supplies, a number of US planes were shot down. Immediately, the remaining helicopters in the area concentrated completely on rescuing the American pilots, forgetting about the Vietnamese completely. And then, when the Americans left, the NVA troops moved in. Thinking back again to the many times I'd faced the military philosophy that one American life was worth more than a thousand others, no matter who they were, the story was not hard to believe.[32]

Daly finds the cultural logic of Americans portrayed in this passage lacking. He makes visible some of the most damaging assumptions of U.S. involvement in the Vietnam War. By pointing to this kind of thinking, he frees his narrative and his own interpretations from the weight of hatred. He fails to load the boundary of difference with the hatred and frustrations he has as a POW.

Racist attitudes were not exclusive to one side or the other. Most texts, however, tend to highlight treatment of Americans "at the hands of" the Vietnamese. Daly points out how his captors viewed his race. "He [a Vietnamese prisoner] told me how the Vietnamese believed that Negroes were so strong they could overcome illness without even needing any medicine. Great!"[33] Interestingly enough, it is Kushner, the officer Daly suspects of racism, who explains to him that the Vietnamese treat foreigners as one homogeneous group. When the German nurses are brought into camp, Daly wonders why they are being held as prisoners, but he then explains: "Kushner had a theory about that. 'The VC refuse to draw a line when it comes to foreigners coming over here.' "[34] In much the same way, Americans did not distinguish between Asian cultures and were frustrated by their inability to do so.

In the end Daly crosses the enemy/friend boundary. Whether he was forced across by his treatment "at the hands of" the American military when he returned or out of conscience is unclear. But his conclusions are instructive when compared to those of other POWs: "The honest truth was, the Vietnamese just weren't the monsters we'd been told they were."[35] However naive we may find Daly's narrative, his conclusions stand in contrast to those of the other POW narratives. In fact, if anyone has distilled the problems of difference down to local, human terms that make sense, Daly seems to do it in an observation he makes after his critique of his basic training experience in the army. "I was raised to believe that the best way to have a man learn respect for you is by showing respect to him. And that never happened during basic training."[36]

Fred Cherry, the senior black air force officer held in the Hanoi Hilton, echoes Daly's sentiments. By his own account Cherry told his captors, "I'm still an officer in the United States services. I will respect that, and I would hope that you will respect that of me."[37] Whatever this "respect" might consist of, Daly moves toward understanding how difference and ways of dealing with difference were at the core of the POW experience. Like his basic training experience, his POW experience demystified the system of beliefs that had formed around difference on both sides. He saw that racial difference was at the heart of American and Vietnamese misunderstandings during the war, if not at the national level, at least at the local, personal level. He shares his position with George Smith, whose POW narrative was acquired by the North Vietnamese and handed out as reading material to some POWs, including Daly.[38]

Ideology was a significant point of difference; it transcended race and culture on both sides. Nowhere does this become more evident than in the mass imprisonment of South Vietnamese by the North. A similar division existed between the halves of Monika Schwinn and Bernhard Diehl's country. At one point in their captivity they were visited by representatives of the East German embassy. Schwinn had hoped to receive help from her fellow Germans, but when they seemed concerned only with her obedience to the Vietnamese, she could not help but point out their shared origins: "At one point I tried to remind the men that we were all Germans. They answered in chorus, 'We have nothing at all in common. Not even our language is the same!' They seemed to me more cruel than the Vietnamese." Schwinn responds to what appears to her as a betrayal with confusion:

> From that moment on, I could no longer bear to look at them. I stared at the flag [North Vietnamese] hanging on the wall above the commandant's bed. It was a red flag embroidered in gold, but it was not new like the flags that fly from flagpoles or hang down outside windows. The cloth and the embroidery were old and faded, and the lower end of the flag was in tatters.[39]

She focuses on the flag in her narrative to convey a message. The disreputable flag is a metaphor that cuts two ways, showing at once the feeble ideology that backs the distinctions between Schwinn and the people she faces, and the disrepair, perhaps irrevocable futility, of national unity.

It is perhaps naive and ironic for Schwinn to express belief in national or cultural unity at this point in her narrative. After spending years in captivity among the starving and neglected South Vietnamese prisoners, she still believed her nation, similarly divided, would be different. Her nation, like Vietnam, had been arbitrarily splintered by Cold War interests anchored in questionable ideological formations on both sides. Her encounter with the East Germans highlights the havoc such divisions had visited on the various Cold War fronts.

Ideology also collapses for Kate Webb, who ultimately rejects such distinctions in her narrative. Seeing the war from "the other side," she realizes that ideas are driving much of the horror around her and she wants no part of it. "All being equal, I would rather be killed as a nuisance than for an idea."[40]

After years of captivity, Schwinn distilled the global ideologies she saw destroying what was left of her life down to a simple, local reality. She eventually gave up on both the East Germans and the Vietnamese. She expressed her frustration by ultimately blaming her captors. Moving from the flag to the commandant who slept underneath, she vented her anger on the Vietnamese: "What did he matter to me, what did I care about any of the Vietnamese? I did not want to understand these people, for they had not bothered to understand me. . . ."

Schwinn, whose whole purpose in visiting Vietnam was to provide nonpartisan help, constantly confronts the contradictions of her captivity and the arbitrary divisions that divide her from others. "A spy who was happy when she did not need to betray her victim; a prison commandant who liked to sleep beneath a tattered flag; a turnkey who was sad when his prisoners did not eat. I was lost in a world where nothing made sense."[41] Implicit in these contradictions is the belief in human community she maintained throughout her captivity. Constantly confronted with an array of prejudices (gender, racial, cultural, national, ideological, and religious), she eventually stopped making sense of her belief systems. She ultimately falls upon the crux of the problem, the reason for the war, the reason for her captivity: "I did not want to understand these people, for they had not bothered to understand me. . . ."[42] Schwinn's own ellipses serve as a pause to emphasize the realization of her own folly and her discovery of the Mobius strip that drove both the continuing war and her captivity.

Everett Alvarez concludes his second book, *Code of Conduct,* by musing about how life after captivity has tempered his feeling toward the North Vietnamese. He goes as far as suggesting that he might some day, if the opportunity presents itself, return to the site of his tragic imprisonment. He is convinced that "the final day of healing of the wounds of Vietnam for me, and for this nation, is at hand." But just a page before this final line, Alvarez makes a revealing comment. In addressing the fate of MIAs, he points out, "Having experienced the sometimes strange quirks of the Vietnamese mind, I wouldn't rule out any possibility."[43] It is hard not to hear a chilling echo of Steve Ross's comment about the "corkscrew mentalities" of the Japanese in *First Yank into Tokyo* in Alvarez's comment about the "strange quirks of the Vietnamese." It makes one wonder just how much, if any, "healing" has occurred in our perceptions of the differences that divide us.

10

Stop Making Sense

The American POWs of the Vietnam War suffered longer in captivity than any other POWs in American history. They spent most of those years confined alone in cells the size of an average bathroom. They were systematically tortured for years. Yet when we read their stories, we find that they ended up being better for their experience. The POW autobiographies speak of better selves, closeness to God, the strength of the family, the strength of America, and victory in a war most Americans thought had been lost. This chapter is about how the Vietnam POWs shaped their personal and political identity in the context of post-Vietnam America. It is about how the POWs created order and meaning for their debilitating experience in Hanoi. It is about the cultural logic of representation and myth.

When John Hellmann critiques *The Deer Hunter* in *American Myth and the Legacy of Vietnam,* he concludes that the "captivity experience is the pivotal episode." He finds this particular captivity episode "deeply disturbing on the most resonant level of cultural myth." He goes on to say that the "final third of the film develops the consequences of the captivity experience."[1] Despite the uneasy success of the film, its images were not satisfying because, according to Hellmann, they portrayed "the traumatic fall of the Kennedy-version of the frontier hero." The film implied that the American mission in Vietnam was a failure that not only destroyed South Vietnam but also eroded the American self. The consequences of captivity in *The Deer Hunter* are profoundly negative.

Representations of captivity in America before and after *The Deer Hunter,* however, portrayed the triumph rather than the erosion of the American self in Vietnam. The negative critique of the Vietnam hero in films like *The Deer Hunter* and *Apocalypse Now* created a reactionary

Michael (Robert DeNiro) and Steven (John Savage) await their fate in the crucial and disturbing POW sequence from *The Deer Hunter.* Courtesy of *the Museum of Modern Art/Film Stills Archive.* (*1978, Universal City Studios, Inc.*)

backlash in the 1980s. The "Kennedy-version of the frontier hero," embodied by the characters played by Chuck Norris and Sylvester Stallone, who both use the POW issue as a pretext for aggression, recaptured center stage in the American imagination. The POW story became popular because it worked against representations of American failure in Vietnam. POW autobiographies and articles, and the press in general, worked to recover the American hero and preserve the American self.

Americans were somewhat astonished, but relieved, to learn from countless POW testimonials what Jay Jensen's autobiography, *Six Years in Hell,* makes explicit: "I returned a better man than when I was shot down."[2] Jensen's remark and others like it would echo into American lore. When *Rolling Thunder's* Major Rane (William Devane) gets his first chance to speak in public after 2,555 days as a POW in North Vietnam, he has very little to say. The 1977 movie's opening scenes show Rane's hometown arrival and triumphant speech: "This experience has made a better man, better officer, and a better American out of me." Five years later ex-POW Corporal Eddie Keller (Richard Pryor), besieged by hungry reporters in the movie *Some Kind of Hero* (1982), reluctantly made his own statement to the press, with somewhat less conviction than Rane: "The experience, I think, helped me be a better person, a better husband, a better father."

Major Rane (William Devane) claimed to be "a better man" after his POW experience in the film *Rolling Thunder.* Courtesy of *the Museum of Modern Art/ Film Stills Archive. (1977, American International Pictures)*

The majority of Vietnam POW stories and images depict captivity as the true test of the American self—a test passed with flying colors: "It was a test of faith, courage, and honor. I passed that test."[3] The "ideal vision of the American" was not the traditional Green Beret-guerilla fighter Hellmann identifies, but the POW and his rescuers (the "new" Special Forces epitomized by Charlie Beckwith's "Delta Force"). Thus, unlike John Hellmann, who sees the legacy of Vietnam causing a "disruption of our [the American myth] story," I see the legacy of Vietnam, if read through the POW narrative, as a radically positive myth that, to use Hellmann's own definition, becomes "an explanation of history which can also serve as a compelling idea for our future."[4]

Rather than seeing their past as a terrible tragedy brought about arbitrarily in the context of a miscarried war effort, most POWs choose to see their experience in the context of coherent structures that make sense of the otherwise incomprehensible events of their captivity. As with survivor narratives of the Holocaust, as James Young points out, "even if no event actually occurred to redeem a particular tragedy, the promise of redemption implicit in the governing mythos nearly always did appear to the victims." Young also notes that the "destruction-redemption dialectic thus seemed to cut two ways: it shaped experience and perception on an illusory basis but possibly also preserved life (or the will to live) on an equally 'illusory' basis."[5] Thus the same belief systems that scaffold POW narratives also may have functioned to save the subject's life during or after the experience.

The structure of the experience also depended on the role pilots played as participant-observers in the POW experience. Pilots, accustomed to observing the ground from above, were literally yanked from their platforms and thrust into a totally alien environment. "Men trained to fly sophisticated machines at incredible speeds and breathtaking heights were caged like animals. No more horizons to scan, no more clouds to soar above, no more barriers to break through." Soldiers accustomed to a tightly knit and highly directive community were required to face moral, political, and psychological problems alone: "But worse than that, no people to be close to."[6] The POWs were not only faced with these problems during and immediately after capture, they were also faced with a life filled with "suffocating monotony" punctuated by episodes of incredible physical and mental pressure. Their plight often caused them to detach themselves from the pain, monotony, and horror of their lived experience and become observers. This is the perspective many of the POWs take when recalling the general outline of experience, the monotony that was a major, unrepresented share of their experience.

Inevitably the POWs had to face their condition and situation. Such is the dilemma of the POW autobiographer, who, faced with the task of reconciling his plight as captive with his duty as soldier, must reach beyond his physical surroundings and lived experience for an explanation of his predicament both as POW and autobiographer. Thus "we may observe the widening of that chasm between seeing and being as well as the compensatory strategies designed to overcome it" within the POW narrative. The formidable string of successful closures and positive effects that surround the problematic experience of the American POWs in Vietnam might well be explained as compensations for these perceptual chasms.

The POWs had to account for gaps between their experience and their expectations. Eugene McDaniel begins his narrative with a catalog of possible "qualities of resistance" that might at once explain and nurture him in the ensuing struggle with his North Vietnamese captors. "From where? Was it my old athletic discipline? Was it the hating to lose, drilled into me early in life? Was it the military code I had followed for the past twelve years—the pride in sticking to it, no matter what? Was it my fragile faith in God?"[7] Although McDaniel finally settles on the latter, this bit of self-reflection reveals an imperative present in many of the POW narratives: the search for a "technology of the self"[8] that will sustain his ego in a hostile environment.

Perhaps the most positive aspect of the postexperience narratives is that the author(s) have, in fact, survived the experience at all. James Young points out that "the memoirist documents nothing more persuasively than his own existence after the Holocaust. The survivor's literature thus becomes testimony not so much to the deaths at Auschwitz but to his life after Auschwitz. A survivor's writing after the Holocaust is proof that he has defeated the 'final solution.' "[9] In this way each of the POW narratives asserts the "self over experience." But such inventions of self invite either Hegelian "consecration" or Derridean negation.[10] In the case of the marginalized narratives of James Daly, Monika Schwinn, Kate Webb, and George Smith,[11] the overwhelming negative valence of the experience induces a consequent negation of their selves. This is brutally obvious in the passage of Webb's narrative in which she subordinates her own experience to the POW experience in Hanoi. In doing this Webb at once foregrounds and foreshadows her own negation.

In the case of the majority of the POW texts, written by white male officer-pilots, however, there is an unsettlingly smug consecration of experience. The POW in these stories most often emerges from captivity better than when he started. James Mulligan makes this common theme explicit in his autobiography: "If nothing else, I would come home a better man than when I entered there."[12] One has to ask whether Jeremiah Denton and John McCain would ever have reached Congress, whether Everett Alvarez would ever have achieved top positions in the Peace Corps and Veterans Administration, whether James Stockdale would have ever become the president of The Citadel or a candidate for vice-president without the impetus—political or otherwise—provided by a positive POW experience.

The implication is that the POW experience was positive, an asset to the victim. As Young says of the Holocaust narratives, the act of writing itself affirms the present self at the expense of the experience itself. A case in point might be the narrative accounts of those who resisted and died in captivity. No matter how hard the survivors try to inflate the image of those who died in captivity, their death, juxtaposed against the author's continuing life, as evidenced by the text, inadvertently claims an authority over the dead, privileging the living at the expense of the dead, who can never speak. This dynamic is an intimate part of pilot lore, Tom Wolfe's "right stuff." Dying in captivity, although ostensibly the exclusive fault of the North Vietnamese, was an out. The subtext of many accounts appears to be the same epitaph Wolfe finds in test pilot mentality: "How could he have been so stupid?"[13] The men who died were guilty of failing to properly estimate either the enemy of themselves. The implication is that the survivors did both correctly and received their lives as reward.

What makes many of the marginal narratives so difficult for the valorized military officer-captive to accept is that the very existence of these marginal subjects subverts the implicit "right stuff" of the POW-pilot. Few of the narratives admit the existence of Monika Schwinn in the Hanoi Hilton, because her very survival as a woman subverts the tale of male trial and triumph implied by many of the other texts. Similarly the mainstream myth dismisses figures like James Daly and George Smith because they apparently refused to play the deadly game of cat and mouse with the North Vietnamese. The Peace Committee as depicted in James Daly's *A Hero's Welcome* and Zalin Grant's *Survivors* contended that resistance was meaningless, a futile act to support an unjust war. Other narratives take the other position by justifying resistance, if not by political then by moral imperatives that should have been taken for granted. This is implicit in a title like Brace's *A Code to Keep*.

Testimony that made the Vietnam POW experience appear somehow arbitrary and needless in the context of the Vietnam War strips away the value and authority of survival. The overwhelming majority of POW stories work against such notions to reconstruct a positive history, a "usable past" from an otherwise debilitating experience.[14] This usable past highlights POW victories while eclipsing more troubling aspects of the war.

The usable past is a common imperative in POW literature. If there was no lesson, no point, why write about the experience at all? In the case of the autobiographies, as I have said, the authors most often attempt to see captivity as somehow productive, improving or confirming some aspect of the American self. This effort was made easier by attempts within the Nixon administration to use the media to amplify the image of the Vietnam POW, thus salvaging something positive from an otherwise disastrous war effort.[15] The political importance of the POW issue inflated the fame of the POWs to fantastic proportions. The most prominent POW figures (and I would contend the most "famous") were those authorized by the American President and sold by the American media. The most prominent POW figures, the authentic POWs, were those who were freed by the efforts of Henry Kissinger at the Paris peace talks. Others, those who escaped or were otherwise released (examples are George Smith, Dieter Dengler, Kate Webb, and Richard Dudman), did not have the qualities of fame accorded those who were repatriated as part of Operation Homecoming in February and March of 1973. Escape and other forms of release were inherently suspicious. In hindsight, the POW almost had to play a passive-victim role to be an authorized hero.

Leo Braudy defines the "desire for fame" as a "culturally adaptive trait by which the individual retailors traditional standards of distinctive personal nature into a costume by which he can succeed before his chosen audience."[16] For most POWs this "costume" was an integral part of Operation Homecoming. The POWs took that costume and tried to make sense of it. American culture took that costume and used it as billboard space.

To make sense of their past, POW autobiographers used a number of strategies and belief systems to structure their experience. Whether these strategies were at work in the original experience, changing the day-to-day struggle, or primarily at work after the fact is impossible to tell. I see no reason to focus on the time these interpretations took place. Rather, I would focus here on the belief systems themselves. This portion of my archeology focuses on the various structures that represented the POW story as a positive experience in the context of POW lives.

T he most prevalent belief system in the autobiographical texts is religion. Religious belief provided an apolitical and redeeming framework for the POW experience. Religion, to explain the POW experience as being *With God in a P.O.W. Camp,* sidestepped the difficult political contradictions of the Vietnam War.[17] The religious figuration of the POW experience begins with shootdown for James Mulligan: "First came the ooze of gray and the sound of a whispering movement of air as I felt that I was being transported from one state of nature to another, from the natural to the supernatural, a journey of my soul I imagined."[18] Mulligan relates his experience in religious terms many times during his narrative. At one point, in a politically unstable metaphor, he compares himself to a Christian in Rome: "I was the Christian that had been thrown to the lions. . . . I had nothing.

I had lost everything, even my self-respect. 'Lord forgive me. Please Lord, help me,' I cried as I dropped off into a sound sleep, the tears still running down my cheeks."[19] He eventually reveals what we already know: religion was the "main spring of my resistance."[20] He concludes his narrative with a statement in which he all but compares himself with Christ: "It was the Judgement Day and Day of Resurrection when I would be born again into a free world to be reunited with my wife and family, with my relatives and friends."[21] Here Mulligan conflates two separate events in religious doctrine and compares himself to Christ in a dubious metaphor. In attempting to express at once the triumph of his own faith and the ecstasy of release, he alludes to events in religious history that have little in common with the structure of his own experience.

A different integration of religion and experience occurs in Robinson Risner's *Passing of the Night*. A quotation on the cover of the first edition reads: "One man's unyielding faith in the mercy of God!" This quotation sets the tone for a very somber and humble description of the events of captivity. Risner makes no mention of the political mistakes or cultural divisions that might explain his captivity. He takes a didactic approach by describing the "lessons of life in a Vietnamese prison" in terms of his religious beliefs.[22] At one point another prisoner, Ron Storz, makes a claim similar to Mulligan's: "They took everything." Risner responds: "According to the Bible, we are sons of God. Everything out there in the courtyard, all the buildings and the whole shooting match belong to God. Since we are children of God, you might say that all belongs to us, too."[23] Another lesson was that the prison experience broke down inhibitions the POWs had about discussing religion: "I guess if there was any one thing that happened to many of us in prison, it was that we were no longer embarrassed talking about God or religion. We gained a lot of strength not only from our private prayers but also from sharing our feelings about God with each other."[24] Religion emerged as a benefit of the POW experience.

Isolated and tortured, Risner concludes that "praying was like talking on the telephone."[25] He offers what he calls the "four essentials" of survival as a prisoner. But we find that "none was more important than the fourth—faith in God." Risner sums up his fourth essential:

"4) I believed God would bring me out of prison—better for my stay."[26] He invests his experience as a prisoner in his religious beliefs and derives a positive outcome.

Eugene McDaniel also perceives his experience as essentially religious. Immediately after being shot down, he seeks meaning in his past religious education and upbringing: "But what did that all mean right now as I slapped at mosquitoes and tried to ignore the pain in my knee and my back, trying to get some sleep in the blackness of the jungle around me?"[27] His quest for meaning ends where his captivity ends. The final lines of McDaniel's text complete the frame for his entire experience:

> But, even more than that, I knew now what the apostle Paul meant when he said, "Who shall separate us from the love of Christ? Shall tribulation, or distress, or persecution, or famine, or nakedness, or peril, or sword?" These things are very real to me now. And Paul answers, "For I am persuaded that neither death, nor life, nor angels, nor principalities, nor powers, nor things present, nor things to come, nor height, nor depth, nor any other creature, shall be able to separate us from the love of God, which is in Jesus Christ our Lord" (Romans 8:35, 38–39). The darkness of loneliness and pain was worth it all to enter into the knowledge of that fantastic truth.[28]

I cannot emphasize the implications of the last line enough. McDaniel makes it explicit: it "was worth it all" to achieve what he sees as a "fantastic truth." He comes to see pain as productive: "Pain has a way of focusing for a man, giving him recall of what really matters."[29] For him it all begins to make sense: "It struck me that God must have led me here, let me get shot down, that I might now enter into the totality of what it was all about to be in him."[30] Again the experience in the religious frame appears to bring the prisoner into a closer relationship with God, allowing him to see some eternal truth that, at least implicitly, would have eluded him had he not been a POW.

Larry Chesley acknowledges how captivity influenced his beliefs: "There's nothing like prisoner-of-war life in a communist country to emphasize the importance of religion and patriotism in one's life, and we made love of God and our country the paramount theme."[31] Chesley equates America and Christianity without reservation. He says "this land [America] is blessed above all other lands even in a material sense" and that "under God's blessing the United States of America is the greatest country on the earth." He sees his consistent faith and patriotism as a result of his "deep gratitude to the American people and government who cared about us."[32] He replaces more specific, historical observations about his POW experience with testaments of faith. Although he was skeptical about "prisoners of war finding God in prison" and notes that "there are no atheists in hell holes,"[33] his logic remains locked in archetypical, hegemonic thinking best summed up as something like "war is hell but God is on our side."[34]

Ernest Brace uses a different structure to relate his captivity. A Korean war ace with an otherwise unblemished service record, Brace was court-martialed for misconduct after a crash on a training mission in 1961. Plagued by debt and his wife's infidelity, he took the opportunity to attempt a fresh start: "The notion came to me suddenly that I could walk off from here [the crash site], and people would think I was dead, that I had parachuted into the darkness into the river and drowned. I could leave my old life, a life that had grown unbearable, and somehow start again."[35] Brace was court-martialed by the Marine Corps for "conduct unbecoming" after his brief AWOL stint following the crash. He landed a job flying for a CIA operation in Thailand. As a civilian pilot on a mission over Laos, he was captured and spent what he claims was "the most extraordinary POW tenure served by an American in the war in Southeast Asia—especially considering that American was a civilian."[36] Brace's captivity is structured around his self-styled quest for redemption by the military institution. In *A Code to Keep* he ties his experience as prisoner to vindication of his failed career as a marine aviator. He focuses on his civilian status: "I wondered if civilians were bound by the Code of Conduct; somehow I knew in my heart that I was."[37] By framing his captivity in terms of this question, Brace provides himself with the narrative structure needed to make a coherent and redeeming story from an otherwise chaotic and "extraordinary" experience. Unlike many others, he explicitly rejects religious structures in favor of an almost existential self-reliance: "The only person in the world who could help me was the man who had stared back at me from the bathroom mirror in Chieng

Mai [his launch airfield in Thailand] on the morning before I was captured, two and a half years before."[38] The focus of Brace's struggle is not torture or the Vietnamese, but his own past. For him, as for many other POWs, the past assumes a heightened importance. In particular, Brace's bad conduct discharge from the marines provides the focus of his redeeming prisoner experience.

The POW experience provides a positive counterpoise to his earlier mistake as a marine aviator. In one passage he neatly juxtaposes the two experiences while highlighting the valence of both. In a chance contact while they were in adjacent cells, Brace and Lieutenant Commander John McCain exchange hopes and fears: "The wall was like a confessional booth. Both of us found ourselves telling each other things we would never say to anyone else. When John started to tell me what a great hero I would be when we went home, I felt compelled to tell him about my court-martial. It was probably one of the few times I felt sorry for myself."[39] Brace saw life as a prisoner as an opportunity to "start a new life." Unconsciously repeating the day he walked away from his crashed aircraft in peacetime, he saw the POW experience as an opportunity to walk away from his unsatisfying life as a dishonorably discharged marine.[40] As the title of his book implies, Brace structures his own experience on the Code of Conduct and recovering the position (officer-pilot) he sees as essential to his sense of self-worth. The POW experience allows him to recover his self-image and becomes a a "triumph" in the context of a miscarried military career.

John McGrath's *Prisoner of War* uses autobiographical narrative and pencil sketches to convey another captivity theme: American nationalism. McGrath's text focuses attention on the tools of torture. He makes his intent clear: "When we returned to the United States, we used the words shackles, stocks, manacles, and irons; yet many Americans could not picture what the words meant. I hope that this book will succeed in showing what these and other words meant."[41] McGrath creates a reciprocal structure of word and sketch that will "lift pain and its attributes out of [his] body and make them visible" by making us "recognize pain in the weapon" of torture.[42] His skillful integration of literature and art as testimony indicts his captors and attaches the pain and discomfort of his experience to the place where he experienced them: North Vietnam. He implicitly damns the North Vietnamese by attaching his bodily pain to their culture. He thus sets the scene for his concluding remarks: "Then I realized how great it was just to be alive, to be wanted and loved, and most of all, to be an American. As so many of my friends and comrades said, as they stepped from the giant Air Force C-141s to the land of the free, 'God Bless America!' "[43]

By juxtaposing the site of his pain (North Vietnam) with the site of his freedom (America) without explicit reference to the war, McGrath structures his presentation in terms of an unarguable binary opposition. This powerful rhetorical frame forces a choice: pain or freedom. For him, the experience of captivity should allow Americans to make the clearheaded choice that eluded them in the late 1960s and early 1970s:

> On only a few issues were the American people united. One of these was the emotion-charged issue of the POWs and MIAs (Prisoners of War and Missing in Action). After the peace treaties were signed and the POWs began arriving on American soil, the entire nation was stirred as the POWs spoke heartfelt words of praise, thanks and patriotism instead of words of cynicism and condemnation that so many citizens had become accustomed to hearing directed against their country.[44]

McGrath's words both define his narrative and predict the future of the POW story. When all was said and done, the POW experience provided a positive, essential impetus for American nationalism.

National and institutional validation are, similarly, at the heart of Jim and Sybil Stockdale's *In Love and War.* James Stockdale saw his captivity as a crusade against the injustice of the North Vietnamese and betrayal by uncertain politicians in Washington. He writes his narrative of captivity as a message to both the North Vietnamese and the political leaders of the United States. He sees his captivity in terms of leading his fellow prisoners toward survival and "proving the briefers wrong" by surviving the ordeal himself, thus proving the slip-stick civilian hierarchy wrong and parrying blame he sees unfairly placed on the military and the officer corps. His wife sums up his captivity:

Rear Admiral Stockdale resolved to make himself a symbol of resistance regardless of personal sacrifice. He deliberately inflicted a near-mortal wound to his person in order to convince his captors of his willingness to give up his life rather than capitulate. He was subsequently discovered and revived by the North Vietnamese who, convinced of his indomitable spirit, abated in their employment of excessive harassment and torture toward all the Prisoners of War. By his heroic action, at great peril to himself, he earned the everlasting gratitude of his fellow prisoners and of his country. Rear Admiral Stockdale's valiant leadership and extraordinary courage in a hostile environment sustain and enhance the finest traditions of the U.S. Naval Service.[45]

Stockdale's captivity, much like McGrath's, targets national values. In particular, the story of Stockdale's behavior during captivity emphasizes the importance of the military institutions that trained him: Annapolis and the United States Navy. His narrative bolsters military institutions he sees as being at risk in post-Vietnam America. Stockdale's overdetermined narrative, like McGrath's, becomes a positive and essential force in affirming a national military tradition.

Jim and Sybil Stockdale's narrative also affirms another American institution: the family. It is interesting to note that when Jeremiah Denton's narrative became the film *When Hell Was in Session*, Denton's wife came to share almost equal time. The Stockdale's book and television movie, *In Love and War*, focuses on the important roles played by both husband and wife in their survival of years of torture in Hanoi and betrayal in Washington. The television movie *Intimate Strangers* reaches past several provocative issues (the MIAs; feminine captivity) to focus on the healing power of family, the American family in particular.

Gerald Coffee recovers his POW experience in a number of ways. In his final chapter he juxtaposes his experience in post-Vietnam America with that of other veterans. He affirms the divisions that plagued America during the war and its aftermath but concludes that the war was a just and ultimately successful cause: "Although we were unable to fulfill our primary mission for the government and people of South Vietnam, millions of people in the other countries of Southeast Asia are thriving in relatively free and democratic societies today because of our ten years of holding action there." Coffee sees the Vietnam experience as positive: "So it wasn't all for naught. Every veteran, every American touched by that noble effort should take pride in the commitment, the effort, and what was accomplished." He sees his experience in terms of intense nationalism: "Just as the institutions of our society are microcosms of our country, our country is a macrocosm of each individual." His personal struggle is metonymic for America's struggle, and both are successful: "As we seek and change, we can simply do our best, sometimes stumbling but always growing and evolving toward the best within us. And so it is with our country. With that as our destination, we can do more than survive. We can go beyond survival to fulfill our vision of a world at peace."[46] He implies that America can never really be wrong. He struggles to see his experience as something more than mere "survival."

Coffee wants to replace the reality of a divisive war with his own struggle, which allows him to conclude: "We did not lose the Vietnam war." Earlier in his concluding chapter, however, he is more honest about the results of the war: "The return of the POWs had been perceived as the final chapter of a most painful volume of American history. After years of frustration and disappointment, it was experienced by most as the only positive event concerning Vietnam and it really symbolized the end of our involvement there."[47] Coffee admits here to what he earlier tries to deny. But whether or not we accept his argument attaching the POWs struggle to the outcome of the war, it is quite clear that he sees the POW experience as inherently "positive." The POW struggle was a battle for the self, a battle which America won.

Fred Cherry takes a metaphysical approach to organizing his experience. At one point he is near death from an untreated wound. His reaction is unique.

> I just would leave my body. I would go right through the wall. . . . Another time I left my body and went into town. Before then, when they moved you, it was in blindfolds. And if you could peek, you couldn't tell much 'cause it was at night. But the first time I was able to see anything in daylight in Hanoi, I recognized a stream, bridges, and other things I saw when I left my body.[48]

Elaine Scarry analyzes such a reaction in her analysis of strategies victims use in dealing with pain and torture. She shows "the human being's impulse to project himself out into a space beyond the boundaries of the body in acts of making, either physical or verbal, that once multiplied, collected, and shared are called civilization."[49] Cherry's efforts within his narrative and his own experience are one and the same: to escape the structures of crime and punishment in order to reach for future hope beyond his present reality. It is perhaps significant that the senior-ranking black POW uses this structure in his narrative and experience rather than some other abstraction such as religion, nationalism, or other belief system. Such ideas are much less comforting to Cherry than they are to white male Americans who have long profited from the exclusions inherent in such systems.

Cherry does, however, refer to his solidarity with a group: not pilots, not officers, not Americans, but "24 million black Americans."[50] Whatever structure you might see in Cherry's narrative, the results of captivity for Cherry were concrete. For him captivity authenticated his voice: "I speak across the country for the Tuskegee Airmen's Association—black fighter pilots of the last three wars—telling young black people to study engineering, science, and technology."[51] Cherry not only uses his experience as a positive force in his life, but also exhorts his audience to follow his footsteps; to repeat his "success" as a black American hero.

One member of the fraternity from the Hanoi Hilton is equivocal about his experience. John Dramesi attempts to frame his narrative in terms of religion, national values, and American culture, but he ultimately fails. His narrative is openly critical of fellow POWs who, at one point, convene a trial and convict him of attempting to escape (a radical act of resistance attempted by few other prisoners) without approval from senior-ranking POWs. His partner in one escape attempt is apparently tortured to death for his efforts. In the context of these events, Dramesi sees his captivity as a quest for Honor, an Honor that he, unlike the other POW narrators I have discussed, never finds. In a revealing passage, he dramatizes a conversation with another POW:

> Getting serious for a moment, I said, "I'm afraid your gadfly has not been too successful. I have failed on all accounts. It's pretty damned difficult to talk about resisting when people are unwilling to accept abstracts such as honor, respect, and pride."

"In another place and time," Dick said, "they would agree with you, but here it's just too difficult to make the effort."

"But don't you think we're all going to have to account for our actions while we're here, Dick? That's why we resist—that's why we try to keep our self-respect."

"John, let me tell you—when we get out of this place, you'll be surprised who the good soldiers are going to be. Everybody's going to be a good soldier. And everybody will be so tired of the Vietnam war and the P.O.W. issue that the question of resistance won't even be brought up. We'll all be part of one big group."

"Not if some of the people I know are still around. And if that happens the way you say it will, it won't be the military I'm familiar with. We can forgive and forget here, but out there it's a different world. If this whole situation isn't examined to determine the proper attitudes, then how in the world are we going to benefit from this experience? Somebody, some-where along the line has to determine whether you do attempt to escape or you don't—whether you try to resist and limit the enemy's psychological weapon or you don't."

"I'm afraid we're going to be in for quite a few surprises when we get back," Dick commented.

"Well, there may be changes when we get back," I said, "but there is one truth. If we as a nation find ourselves without the will to play the game right, we're really going to be in trouble."[52]

In this passage Dramesi struggles to make sense of his prison experi-ence. For him, the narrative structure is a struggle for how one plays the "game." He must "play the game right."

Dramesi's narrative highlights how narrative structure reveals the assumptions of experience. Dramesi asks, "Don't you think we're all going to have to account for our actions while we're here, Dick?" The answer is an emphatic yes, but not in the way Dramesi believes in this particular passage. He is hoping for some collective accounting. In-stead, as I have shown in examples from other narratives presented in this chapter, each individual accounts for his experience according to the needs he seeks to satisfy.

Dick's prophetic comments drive home some important points. When he says, "Everybody's going to be a good soldier," he is only partly right. Everybody who tells the right kind of story will be a "good soldier." Everyone who finds some form of redemption, some politically validating truth, becomes a "good soldier."

Dick says, "We'll all be part of one big group." This statement is also prophetic. He understands the political economy of a mass society. He sees that the POW experience will be reduced to an "issue," an image byte. The POWs will function as one group or cease to exist. The Eastern Pilots ad referred to in chapter 5 is a case in point.

Dramesi's frustration mounts as he questions Dick: "If this whole situation isn't examined to determine proper attitudes, then how in the world are we going to *benefit* from this experience?" (emphasis added). He is searching for what his narrative never achieves: a positive resolution of the POW experience. Dramesi fails to find a satisfying conclusion in lived experience. He comes to realize that the abstractions he refers to, "honor, respect, pride," have less to do with the actual experience than with the superstructure of ideology or belief.

But Dramesi does find answers. At the end of his narrative, he learns that his escape partner died in captivity. In the final lines of his text, he calls to his dead friend for help: "Were we right? Did we do the right thing? Have we been right all these years? Before I could answer my own questions, the gong rang."[53] By ending his text in the Hanoi Hilton instead of in front of cheering crowds or at a jubilant family reunion, Dramesi implies the answer. There was no happy ending. He comes to realize what few other POWs consciously acknowledge: that there is no objective frame for his story. As I have said, each narrative is constructed with certain needs in mind. Despite the fact that Dramesi was probably one of the most hard-core resisters during captivity, his narrative and image spin into obscurity largely because they fail to conclude, fail to satisfy, fail to construct a useful superstructure.

───────────

The first film to feature a Vietnam POW appeared in 1972. In *Welcome Home, Johnny Bristol* Captain Johnny Bristol (Martin Landau) survives as a prisoner of the Vietcong by reliving his happy childhood in Charles, Vermont. Bristol remembers his hometown so well that he saves another prisoner by buoying his spirit with gratifying and convincing tales of an America both prisoners hope to see again. The army rescues Bristol and sends him back to the United States to recover from his harrowing experience. Once he is well enough, a nurse is assigned to escort him back to the hometown he remembers so well. But there is no Charles, Vermont. Johnny Bristol had made it all up in captivity. His parents, his childhood, his hometown, and all the memories that sustained him in captivity were pure imagination. Johnny Bristol was really an orphan from a poor Philadelphia neighborhood on the corner of Charles and Vermont streets.

The film's rather direct irony does demonstrate how far we might stray from reality. Johnny Bristol and his fellow POW believed the story because they needed to. Charles, Vermont, was ideal America, the opposite of everything Bristol experienced in his bamboo cage, the perfect counterpoise to his experience in "hell." Johnny Bristol built Charles, Vermont, from hatred, deprivation, and torture. The logic was simple and compelling, but it ultimately led him nowhere. The idealizations constructed with such pain over so much time worked in one narrow context. Johnny had defined his world negatively, creating America from what was not. Once Bristol was lifted from the POW camp in Vietnam, the myth that had sustained him for so long stabbed him in the back.

Welcome Home, Johnny Bristol is, to be sure, a fiction itself, just another kind of Charles, Vermont. But it is not so much the story itself but how "historical memory, understanding, and meaning were constructed" by Johnny Bristol that is important.54 Charles, Vermont, did not have a physical reality, but it did have a functional reality. So it is with the structures we find in prisoner autobiographies: however convincing or limiting the reality of their conclusions may seem today, we cannot deny that they once may have been real enough to save lives.

11
The Consequences of Myth

During the 1980s and early 1990s former Vietnam POWs were frequent speakers on the lecture circuit. They drew consistently large if not sensational crowds to churches, school auditoriums, corporate training seminars, and political action group meetings. Gerald Coffee, a POW for six years in Hanoi, is still a regular speaker on the network. His talks have become so popular that his publisher is marketing an audio recording of a speech he makes to "the leading professional, business, and service organizations in America." Coffee tags the tape "Beyond Survival: The Next Chapter," presenting it as a sequel to his autobiography, *Beyond Survival.*

The introduction to the audio program explains that Captain Gerald Coffee is "a very special man" whom "we know you will consider one of our heroes." The narrator claims that Coffee "brings to the podium a testimonial to the power of the human spirit to survive and triumph in the most adverse circumstances." Coffee himself begins by describing the importance of the "lessons that can be drawn from such a unique experience." He hopes to make it clear that his experience "is so much more than my experience . . . but really every one of yours. Believe me, you were there with us every day. You were there giving us the strength and sustenance and the will to go on. . . . Believe me, I'm talking about our shared experience."

He beckons his audience to become part of the clan, to share in the power of the POW totem. His story appeals to Americans because it resonates with the important role captivity has played in American experience for hundreds of years. When he speaks to an audience about his captivity experience, he can say that we were all there because captivity is an accepted and tried ingredient of American character. The captivity paradigm is so powerful because it has united us as a nation again and again just as the POW "Homecoming" did in 1973, just as the hostages in Iran did in 1980. Since the Revolutionary War, when entire communities of the original colonies were surrounded and "imprisoned" by British soldiers, we have had a fear of captivity and a fascination with prisoners.

Coffee suggests that he has learned four essential lessons that might be of interest to his audiences. Such reducible codes occur in dozens of POW accounts. Many Vietnam POW autobiographies head-line in their titles usable paradigms for personal conduct: *Code of Conduct, Code of Honor, A Code to Keep, The Hanoi Commitment, Beyond Survival, Bouncing Back.* Such presentations participate in the en-semble of "TV, psychologistic 'counseling,' 'self-help' manuals, the 'human potential' regimens, and other self-perpetuating therapies ad-ministered to keep us on the job." We are seduced into internalizing a quick and easy set of rules because the rules will supposedly make us well; in reality they become most useful as a way for us to monitor ourselves for existing systems of power. These programs help us inter-nalize and supplement the "diffuse apparatus of surveillance built all around" us.[1] The simple codes of these self-help regimes seduce us into staying at work. By concentrating on our self-images and inscrib-ing political and social problems in the self, POW self-help advice diverts our attention from powerful social and political forces. Cof-fee's speech and autobiography, like many POW accounts, carefully avoid the political circumstances of his captivity to focus on the self, the same self that was imprisoned in Hanoi for over six years. Such schemes, in making us the subject of scrutiny, divert our attention from the authority that governs our lives.

Corporations don't engage POW speakers like Coffee just because their messages make people feel good; they endorse them because they help keep employees living and thinking in ways that make them "docile and useful" for those who need them at work. By at once uniting listeners and affirming authorized roles of individual action and strength, such speeches become synonymous with the confining interests of corporate and government authority. It should, therefore, not be surprising to find Coffee touting one of his "lessons," "unity over self," as "not a bad corporate motto." Ironically, for all that he teaches about years of successful resistance in Hoa Lo prison, his "lessons learned" finally make his audience prisoners of themselves.

Coffee's message is a co-optation of experience. He is a paid speaker for "the leading professional, business, and service organizations in American." He has recently added his POW authority to Tony Robbins's line of "Personal Power" self-help products. His presentation mimics the self-help themes promoted by Tony Robbins's other testimonials, narrated by a sensitive Fran Tarkenton. America buys such information at an alarming rate. In the 1980s, when Americans seemed to put less into primary and secondary education, they increased their spending on self-help products by almost one thousand percent.

Coffee was aware of the dangers of co-optation. He saw that by retelling his story, he would be changing it. Everett Alvarez reports in his second book, *Code of Conduct:* "Jerry Coffee claims that an honest man has only one speech."[2] But Coffee would go out and tell his story again and again. Everett Alvarez quoted what Coffee had to say, but nevertheless, "quickly learned how to tailor the testimony to the interests of the audience while keeping the essential shape of the message."[3] We must ask how the message of Alvarez's Philip Morris ad, his coauthored autobiography, *Chained Eagle,* and the appearance of Lieutenant Oliviero in *The Hanoi Hilton* is somehow essentially the same. Alvarez seems to believe he cannot be co-opted by his appearances. He thinks that he can "tailor" his message in spite of the way two coauthors, publishers, advertising executives, movie directors, and television producers might spin it.

Everett Alvarez is not a naive public figure. Early in *Code of Conduct,* a virtual excursus on his public life, he describes a speaking appearance: "I knew none of the people. I knew nothing about their organization or what it stood for." Later he realizes what had happened: "When I turned on the ten o'clock news, there I was endorsing an agenda I knew nothing about."[4] It would be interesting to know what agenda Alvarez saw at work in his appearances in the Philip Morris ad, *People* magazine, on *Prime Time Live,* or as an advisor for *The Hanoi Hilton.* But he does not mention his involvement with any of these projects in his second book. This becomes ironic when we find that Alvarez laments the "popular distortions of the veteran's image" when it came to the "strange sympathy—or suspicion—about our state of mind and body" he saw manifested in movies like *Platoon*.[5] Regardless of what he may have intended, what he says about *Code of Conduct* is equally true of his previous appearances in the more prominent venues of American culture: "It probably isn't hard to see how I cut the cloth of the story."[6]

Alvarez's appearance for Philip Morris, Coffee's speech and testimonial for Tony Robbins, and Arthur Ballard's endorsement of Harry Lorayne's "Memory Power System" on paid TV have not come by popular demand. We have been fed such stuff on television, in magazines, and in books because it works to keep us living in certain roles that seem to liberate our individual energies but ultimately leave us serving corporate, military, and government interests that want to hide from us. Easily consumed rules and codes are satisfying because they give us a simple pretext and justification for being and acting consistently within the existing order. Such structures are tremendously attractive because they simplify complex problems that seem to overwhelm us. The POW story was and is attractive, in part, because it simplifies the otherwise confusing terms of a war we have yet to understand.

In 1963 an episode of the popular television series "Outer Limits" featured a psychological drama about earthlings trapped as POWs on a distant planet, Ebon. In the "Nightmare" episode, two of nine POWs die from mental and physical stress while captive of the weird-looking Ebonites. The remaining men attempt to execute one of their fellow POWs when they convince themselves that he has betrayed them. But toward the end of the film we find out that the POW ordeal on Ebon is just a hoax perpetrated to train these future warriors for the rigors of other interplanetary wars. Earth is not really at war with Ebon. When the senior POW finds out that his men have been tortured and killed in a "training" exercise, he confronts the Earth general running the operation. The general explains with paternal firmness the justification for such brutality to his Ebonite host: "You don't know what happened in the Korean War. It was a disgrace." He goes on to list the statistics of death and betrayal among Korean War POWs. The creators of "Nightmare" wanted to show that the legacy of the Korean POW experience might haunt Americans far into the future. The episode suggests the need to do whatever is necessary to "train" soldiers to avoid embarrassing earthlings the way POWs in Korea embarrassed Americans.

The Vietnam POW stories that appear in popular culture seem to convey much the same message. Something horrible happened to the American character in Korea—we would not let it happen in Vietnam. "Nightmare" and Coffee's speech have an uncanny symmetry. They make us believe that the problem of captivity is not the POW predicament in the first place, but how we live it. The implicit message of the Coffee story answers the anxiety played out in the POW episode on Ebon. Americans can and should stay at work, even as POWs.

Americans were horrified when POWs appeared again on television during the Gulf War. Former POWs like Everett Alvarez and Gerald Coffee were shocked and dismayed: it was happening all over again. But it should not have come as such a surprise. The former POWs had trained Americans for it. They had proved Americans could face the POW tragedy yet again.

Those of us who were not POWs ourselves can only know the Vietnam POW experience through representations of it.[7] But however much we read, hear, or see, we can never know the Vietnam POW experience outside the representations that surround it. It is through these texts in contemporary popular culture that we have constructed the story of the American POW of the Vietnam War.

Just as the codes and beliefs of POWs in captivity had a powerful functional reality, so do representations of the POW story in American culture. POW Sam Johnson "sometimes wondered . . . if my mind had created a scene for me to savor in this desolate place. It didn't really matter, of course, but I still wondered."[8] But it did matter, not so much because ideas spawned in captivity were helpful for POW survival, but because those same ideas would survive captivity and be amplified by the powerful forces of the American culture industry. The religion, moral codes, intense patriotism, and satisfaction found in captivity are no more or less real than the racism, ethnocentrism, sexism, homophobia, and hatred. The autobiographies alone play the entire scale. All became a part of POW lore.

In film, the representations of the POW have taken on their own realities. Major Rane in *Rolling Thunder* may have proclaimed that he was a better man for his experience, but he lost his family, his career, and his life to the haunting memories of captivity. The better man Rane claimed to be became a vengeful killer and a sadist who "loved the rope." Corporal Eddie Keller, who began by asserting that he was "a better person, a better husband and a better father" in *Some Kind of Hero*, became a deserter and criminal. He traded his role as husband and father for life as sometime-friend of a well-to-do hooker.

Even though these two stories seem to work against the heroic qualities defined by the Vietnam POW autobiographies, the films define their own heroes by appropriating the base of POW experience. Major Rane uses the physical endurance and mental toughness built in captivity to avenge the murder of his estranged wife and child. Corporal Keller confronts the comic ironies of his return to "freedom" by rejecting the institutions he had trusted in captivity in order to find his own freedom. *Rolling Thunder* and *Some Kind of Hero* both take the POW experience and reinterpret it to create new heroes. The importance of these texts lies not in their authenticity but in the way they interpret experience.

Interpretation plays a crucial role in how we understand the POW experience. It is the shape of interpretation that ultimately drives how we use what we see and hear. We must critically read the patterns of interpretation in POW autobiography, film, and media in order to qualify the judgments and describe the consequences of the POW experience. It is difficult for anyone to control the "essential shape of the message" in the media jungle. This is the dream of political, advertising, and propaganda campaigns. Although such programs are geared for and sometimes achieve short-term success, few of their messages survive through the next fad or political term. In the early 1960s American anxiety about the American POWs in Korea manifested itself in odd plots like the "Outer Limits" episode. The earthlings in "Nightmare" interpret the Korean experience as justification

In *Rolling Thunder* Major Rane (William Devane), who claims to be "a better man" for his POW experience, goes on a killing spree to avenge the murder of his estranged wife and son. Rane acted out one of America's worst and most persistent fears after the Vietnam War: that mentally withdrawn, physically hardened, emotionally displaced POW veterans would be unable to recover from the rigors of captivity. Even though this paranoia would be central to a whole cycle of POW films, actual Vietnam POWs reacted differently. *Courtesy of the Museum of Modern Art/Film Stills Archive.* (1977, American International Pictures)

for brutal training regimes to select, refine, and assure the character of future soldiers. The Vietnam POW experience seems to have carried out exactly such a program, for real. Mock POW scenarios of recent movies like *Opposing Force* and *Kill Zone* continue to rejuvenate the imperatives of correct training and call our attention again to anxieties in the American self. They point to the Vietnam POW as touchstone, reassurance that there is such a thing as essential and durable American selfhood.

The popular conscience can never reach objective truth or essential experience. Few will ever meet the POWs themselves, let alone witness their testimony. Just reading the autobiographies instead of watching the movies or pausing on the tabloid ads does not get the experience more right.9 We can only accept the plurality of experience and representation that exists. Examining the entire spectrum of POW representation is a healthy enterprise that sometimes leaves us ashamed of our own assumptions—but this should not be surprising or daunting. By expanding the ways in which we might come to know the POW experience, we can dissipate uncritical beliefs in the kinds of knowledge we have of that experience.

Over the past twenty years the POW story has taken on the qualities of myth. Myth is a fabulous narrative that becomes operative when experience falls short of our needs. Myth is a kind of Godzilla, an ensemble of what we need and fear assembled to thrill and entertain us.10 The POW myth survives by devouring representations that fail to confirm authorized roles and behaviors. The story constantly mutates to satisfy our changing needs. As the mythology grows, it becomes radically ahistorical. It increasingly must do away with the clutter of diverse culture and the anomalies of experience in order to allow its icons to slip decal-style onto whatever particular product might fulfill our immediate needs.11 In the inevitable economic selection at work in the marketplace, the Godzillas that are myth almost always win. Americans see, know, and try to become the myths themselves.

In the 1980s the POW myth fueled a return to violent images conjured up to solve frustrating national and international problems. Today we watch criminologists endlessly puzzle over the incidence of murder, rape, and other violent crime in a nation whose most recent heroes are overmuscled male bodies bristling with an array of lethal weaponry.[12] We live in a nation that has been anesthetized by a continuous stream of violence, thereby fulfilling Theodore Adorno's fear that we might end up "wringing pleasure from the naked pain of the victims."[13] An America watching films like *The Hanoi Hilton, When Hell Was in Session, Rolling Thunder, In Love and War, Intimate Strangers, The Forgotten,* and *Welcome Home* appears to have realized Adorno's fears. These films provide vicarious scenarios of torture and deprivation for the entertainment of a gluttonous armchair audience who, in its discussion of these representations, is apt to juxtapose the agony of a POW with the trials and tribulations of a soap opera star.

The recursive structures of the POW story are not simply arbitrary patterns but echoes and responses to American captivity lore. Dominant narratives of the POW experience like *The Hanoi Hilton, Chained Eagle, In Love and War, Six Years in Hell, Scars and Stripes,* and *When Hell Was in Session* fail to convey something of their "relative status" with regard to the POW experience as a whole. These texts seem to ignore and to some extent deny their own "artfulness, construction, and . . . ideological premises."[14] Alvarez thought he could retain "the essential shape" of his "message" through his endless tour of speaking engagements. Perhaps he did. But his vastly more popular appearances in *People* magazine, in an ad for Philip Morris, on "Prime Time Live," on the "Larry King Show," in *The Hanoi Hilton,* and in his two coauthored books seemed to play differently. The majority of POW narratives and representations seem to ignore the fact that the figurative language they use "is never entirely innocent and is almost always complicit in the actions we take in the world."[15] They also make the "technologies of self" that aid their struggle somehow essential to all, an unarguable final vocabulary. By ignoring their own assumptions and perspectives, these texts fail to recognize their own complicity in compromising the very objectivity they seek.

The few texts that foreground their tenuous relation to some objective facticity or ideological righteousness are exactly those texts which become marginalized in the machine of popular culture. Michele Ray lamented the prospects for telling the story of her short captivity by the Vietcong: she was "afraid . . . that . . . [her] capture might become, after a while, almost legend and no longer the very real and very deep emotional experience it was."[16] Ray's story wouldn't become "legend": it was overshadowed by other stories that would assume the qualities of legend much less self-consciously. The prestige and authority of more popular POW texts make their stories myths. Such stories reject equally possible and valid accounts of captivity. Monika Schwinn, George Smith,[17] James Daly, Dieter Dengler, and John Dramesi do not get government jobs, advertising contracts, and television spots. Their texts slip from the cultural venue and fail to adhere to the surfaces of mass media particularly because they deny the privileged authority many of the other texts claim. In shrinking from describing their experience as some highway to heaven, furnace of natural selection, or scheme of self-improvement, the marginalized texts consciously shun the vestments of media fame. We cannot exist somehow outside of the poetics used to express the experience, so we must be self-conscious enough to avoid claiming that the story can be otherwise: that we can somehow escape the plight of participant-observer in telling and retelling experience.

Some of these belief systems and myths allowed POWs to survive a tragic and terrible experience. But these same systems may not always be abstracted and applied to other contexts; they may not be taken as models for others' behavior, as they sometimes are. Malcolm McConnell's *Into the Mouth of the Cat* is explicit about his intent to provide a model for today's young people: "Without question, their stories [the POW Medal of Honor winners Sijan, Stockdale, Day, and Norris] would provide inspirational models for the nation, especially the country's young people."[18]

The metaphors and structures appropriated to relate the POW experience are not essentially wrong; the conclusions are not lies. But the stories and conclusions do become unstable when we abstract them from experience, strip them away from their history. POW stories that have always had a place in United States history became most prominent when they amplified existing ideologies and delivered a victory in a lost war. In this way the dominant POW stories have thematized their own place in our culture.[19]

E ugene McDaniel described his six years as a POW in Hanoi in terms of a binary opposition. "If I lost, then I was reduced to what the VC said all Americans, even Christian Americans, had come to in the end: disillusionment with God, country, and the image of self, all of which led to hopelessness and despair."[20] Mc-Daniel structures his experience in terms of a life-or-death struggle for the American self. His words express an anxiety that could have come out of the mouth of the general on Ebon in "Outer Limits." McDaniel's structuring implies both a real fear that the Vietnamese may be right and an imperative to resist. Ironically, with or without the North Vietnamese, the "disillusionment" McDaniel contemplated during captivity was happening in the America he left behind. While McDaniel underwent rigorous sessions of torture to leave the institutions of his American self unquestioned, back in America everyone else was renegotiating those same institutions.

McDaniel puts himself in a double bind. By seeing his struggle as strictly a win-or-lose proposition, he reifies the American self, whose flexibility and adaptability have made it so appealing and persistent. By reifying his self-concept, he destroys the very characteristics that made concepts of American selfhood so remarkable. By figuring his captivity as the struggle for the American self he at once puts his own ego in jeopardy and dooms himself to the terrible struggle he endures.

Although many of the POWs saw their captivity as just such a struggle, we might ask if all this was really necessary. In a way the POWs who saw their struggle in these terms from the very beginning played right into the hands of the North Vietnamese by betting the American self in a game they may not have even had to play. In some ways the POWs themselves put their religion, self-conception, or patriotism at stake when it might have been better not to have anted up at all. It would be interesting to explore the possibility of telling future prospective POWs that their captivity was no test, no struggle, in fact required no resistance at all. What if we just announced that any statement a POW might make would be discounted out of hand?

Would abuse and torture for propaganda statements still be imminent for future American POWs?

For McDaniel the very struggle became the focus of survival. Mc-Daniel eventually hedges his bets, concedes that his imprisonment is not a win-or-lose situation: "It's not a win you're after; a draw might do. . . . But I couldn't turn it off that easily. I had to hang on to winning, I had to compete, or I was dead in this place. . . . And yet I knew, too, as Grantland Rice put it, 'He marks—not that you won or lost—but how you played the game.'"[21] But if it wasn't about winning, if it wasn't a struggle to save God, country, or the American self, why play this game of excruciating torture, starvation, self-mutilation, and death? If it was just how you "play the game," then we can not help but remember with a chill that paranoid training scheme on Ebon. Like Gerald Coffee's "inspirational" speech and the "Outer Limits" episode "Nightmare," McDaniel wants to divert attention from the predicament of captivity and focus on the self, the struggle.

Over a decade later McDaniel would displace his struggle as a POW in North Vietnam to his ordeal facing the very bureaucracy he had served: "The flak I've taken since I got into this battle here for the POWs [those still unaccounted for] is much worse than the torture and isolation I endured in the Hanoi Hilton."[22] McDaniel undercuts the sanctity of the POW struggle with this comparison. If we are involved in just such struggles here in the United States, how has McDaniel's POW experience become so important? Although he was, to be sure, speaking in loose metaphorical terms, Dorothy McDaniel makes the irony of her husband's postcaptivity struggle explicit: "The Vietnamese Communists had not been able to break his spirit. The ultimate tragedy would be for his own countrymen to do what his enemy in Vietnam could not."[23] She quotes her husband as saying: "I can't figure out who the enemy is."[24] For the McDaniels the struggle they both fought so hard to support during the Vietnam War collapses into a metaphor for their life in 1980s America. The structure of "enemy" that seemed to function so well in the context of the war and a POW camp dissolves when the race, ideology, and sexuality of the enemy cannot be objectified and reduced in useful ways. Can the structures of power in America be as damaging as the physical torture meted out by the North Vietnamese? Can we give the bureaucrats in

Washington derogatory nicknames and dismiss their personal habits as somehow inimical to human character? Eugene McDaniel's comparison and the irony Dorothy McDaniel sees reveal how the North Vietnamese are somehow essentially enemy, easily identified and destroyed in the context of a holy struggle. While sitting in church listening to her husband speak, Dorothy McDaniel remembers thinking, "God, your shadow did reach all the way to Vietnam."[25] The distance between God and North Vietnam couldn't have been greater. Such a statement emphasizes the ethnocentricism of religious assumptions. The North Vietnamese appear as a race of godless heathens struggling in a spiritual outland far removed from the concerns of a Christian God. When the struggle was in America the enemy became "unseen" and the rhetoric became less religious. Eugene McDaniel's comparison unmasks the superstructure America has erected on the corpus of POW experience.

———

During his gratifying experience on the lecture circuit as an air force pilot and POW-hero, Fred Cherry voiced his hopes for the future: "Maybe one of those young black lads that hears me will walk across a field one day, look up at an airplane, like I did so long, long ago, and say, 'I'm going to fly. I'm going to be a fighter pilot.'"[26] In this passage Cherry appears to be appealing to minority members to take charge of their own lives and succeed. The use of his dreadful experience as authority to advise and motivate "young black lads" seems to be a great idea.

But what Cherry implies is not so great. Cherry would hold himself up to the youth of America as a success story. His confessed hope is that young blacks will follow his footsteps and become officers in the military. Perhaps they might even become POWs and then, if they are lucky, they might achieve the status and authority to "speak across the country" for affirmative action. But it would be a crime, a travesty, to suggest that anyone endure what Cherry was forced to endure as a prisoner. His long and difficult career as a pilot became nationally significant only when he became a POW. I would suggest there are other ways of authorizing a black voice and achieving success for minorities in America. What Fred Cherry implies is that he wants some youngster to repeat his success, follow his bloody, deforming trail from frustrated teenager to POW-hero.

Myth accrues its force through repetition. Are we doomed to repeat the POW experience as Fred Cherry unconsciously exhorts his young listeners to do? The positive conclusions of the valorized POW story is a form of reinforcement, a reward we might seek for duplicating the experience. Of course, the road to authority was inadvertently achieved by Fred Cherry and his fellow POWs. We should, at this point, consider the obvious: that the experience, the difficult captivity endured by Fred Cherry and virtually all of the other POWs, is not the best way to gain authority, to achieve prominence in America. If the pain in John McGrath's sketches, James Stockdale's self-mutilation, Fred Cherry's lost family and deformed body, and the lives lost mean anything, they surely mean that we should never again ask people to endure such atrocities.[27]

The cultural logic of the POW myth has become a model, a rule for future action, a possibility for achieving all the things that some of the POWs see at the end of their struggle. But is it all worth it? Does this economy work? Should we become captives? The overarching implication of the POW story is that we should, that being a POW is a good thing, a means toward a positive end. If we are to believe Eugene McDaniel, "The darkness of loneliness and pain was worth it all to enter into the knowledge of that [religious belief in the love of God] fantastic truth."[28]

No POW would say that he wants anyone to repeat his terrible experiences, yet that is exactly what most POW stories imply. The POWs' triumph as heroes presents their experiences, however twisted and arbitrary they may be, as the highway to some positive outcome; they represent their adjustment to captivity as religious, moral, or social self-help education.[29] Albert Biderman commented on the process at work in the POW narratives of the Korean War: "From the accounts of the experiences of any small sample of repatriated prisoners, one would be able to fashion a story illustrating almost any kind of moral regarding human behavior in the face of adversity—heroism or cowardice, loyalty or disloyalty, altruism or selfishness."[30] The force of cultural representation, not some essence of experience, is what drives the myth. If we accept the most redeeming conclusions of the POW story uncritically, we are repressing the pain and attempting to win the war vicariously through representation.[31] If we accept the logic of the Lazarus-like experience and the authority of the POW uncritically, the "means of correct training" becomes locking people away in small rooms, starving them, and beating them occasionally so they may too learn the "lessons" of captivity.

When prisoners entered captivity, many of them began by jettisoning the myths of previous captivities, which left them totally unprepared for their own experience.[32] However bankrupt these previous myths might have appeared to them, the POWs of the Vietnam War fail to see that their own stories participate in the same myth-making process. Their narratives, however different, are creating a new fiction of captivity that will inform the conceptions and myths the next generation of American POWs carries into captivity. What is perhaps most troubling about these new myths is that they continue to recover the captivity experience in positive terms. The positive results of endured horror sanctify captivity as a holy quest. Most of the authors implicitly insist upon making themselves into heroes and their narratives into legends.

R obinson Risner's autobiography begins with an explicit statement of his authorial intent:

Someone asked me why I was writing this book and my honest answer is this: I believe that today's young people are searching for a dragon to slay. I want to help them find the right dragon. I want our young people to be proud of the things that count. I want to show that the smartest and the bravest rely on their faith in God and our way of life. I hope to show how that faith has been tried by fire—and never failed. I would like to say, "Don't ever be ashamed of your faith, nor of your wonderful heritage. Be proud of those things which made America great and which can, with our help, be even greater."[33]

This passage points directly to the important role myth plays in figuring Col. Risner's autobiographical account. First, he believes there is some essential myth out there that has direct bearing on what "our young people" do. What's more, this is a particular kind of myth: it is a quest to "search" and slay some particular kind of "dragon."[34] It professes a faith that the dragon can be identified and slain. Such thinking is powerfully seductive, but ultimately delusive. Our problems are never quite so simple.

Risner's authority springs from an experience he figures as hell itself. He and his "faith . . . [have] been tried by fire." He implicitly places himself and the other POWs in a group of the "smartest and the bravest," those with the right stuff. His hero status authorizes him to bring back the amazing story he is about to tell. That story attaches his survival to "God and our way of life." But his narrative describes little about "our way of life." His story is about his horrible struggle in North Vietnam. If we accept his story as a portrait of American life, it is yet another negative definition based on the binary opposite of his prison experience in Hanoi.

When he exhorts us, "Never be ashamed," and at the same time tells us America is "great," he asserts the cultural and religious hegemony of the American "way of life" over all others. Through his experience, Risner has come to know the things "that count." Those things, interestingly enough, have nothing to do with the war or Vietnam. He instead asserts a transcendent self that embodies God and America. His statement directs our gaze away from the political realities of the war and stretches to recover the religion and patriotism found lacking in the America of the early 1970s. His call in 1974 prefigures the array of self-help regimes that became the rage of the 1980s. The problem with America was us, every one of us, and not a government struggling to shape another nation in its own image or Cold War ideologies chewing up a distant nation at the tip of God's shadow.

If we believe Risner, he found the way to "the things that count," which have "been tried by fire—and never failed." Such a life must be an example, a map for our own "search." If we are really going to find that "dragon" for sure, we had better follow Risner's trail: first through his narrative and then by repeating his divine quest. Only then are we sure to find the Holy Grail.

Risner was and is, no doubt, a tremendous human being. But there is trouble in his story. He didn't have such a good time. His quest was more like a set of tragic accidents than a divine quest.

There is another tale to tell here. In that tale some men got caught doing their job. That job was their duty. They were captured and tortured by other people from a very different culture who did not see things the same way. The prisoners did what they had to do to survive. Many of them were starved and tortured; some even mutilated their own bodies to keep from making political statements.

But their struggle ended only when enough people got angry about American participation in the very war they fought. The POWs came home after some tough negotiations about withdrawal, money, and a massive campaign of aerial bombardment. The return of the POWs had less to do with the greatness of America than with the admission of a mistake, a miscarried effort. The American "way of life" only became threatened when the majority of Americans began to realize great soldiers like Risner were suffering for nothing.

Risner resorts to the superstructure of God and country to help him close the gap between his POW experience and what he sees in postrelease America. He must compensate himself and his intended audience with some redeeming kernel of faith, salvage a moral lesson from all the pain and suffering he endured. It has become difficult to believe that Risner protected or proved anything by enduring what he did. His sacrifices and those of countless others were very real but now appear almost pointless in the context of an America that welcomed another group of American POW heroes who, by their own admission, willingly made the kind of statements Risner fought so hard to resist.

———

The POW stories are, to be sure, well intentioned, if unavailing. Jay Jensen's hopes for his autobiography are exemplary: "My story can help others to realize their inner strengths; to appreciate their blessings, freedom, liberty, and free agency; and to gain personal strength from sharing my experiences."[35] Jensen's hope for benevolent self-enlightenment is dashed by wide-screen images of vengeful superheroes who use their captivity as a pretext for vengeance. The array of POW representations deepens rather than reconciles the most troubling problems of the captivity drama. The struggle continues.

What most Americans get of the Vietnam POW story through mass media has more to do with selling self-help tapes, cigarettes, and influence than with relating a tragedy in the American experience.[36] It is wonderful to see great men like Jeremiah Denton, Gerald Coffee, Eugene McDaniel, Everett Alvarez, and John McCain recover from a terrible experience and succeed. There is a justice in thinking of these men living comfortable lives after their years of prison poverty. But it is less reassuring to see their compelling stories, their deforming injuries, their broken families eclipsed by appearances on "Prime Time Live" and paid television programming, or in deceptive media advertising. America has built an image, cultivated an episode of POW fame that has slipped out of control. The POW has moved from the unified sign of icon to the slapstick but sad improvisation of circus clown. If we believe that the ultimate triumph of the American POWs in Vietnam was to retain their identity,[37] then it is doubly tragic that the returned POWs seem to lose that very identity, not to their Vietnamese captors but to the America they fought so hard to protect.

Go to your nearest video mart and check the shelf. There you will find the current cycle of films that appropriate POW images to authenticate a wide array of rabid characters. Take a look at *No Dead Heroes, Kill Zone, The Forgotten, Nightforce, Night Wars, High Velocity, Covert Action, POW Deathcamp, Fireback, Rolling Thunder, The Firing Line,* the Rambo series, and the Braddock series. These representations of captivity have little to do with lived experience, but instead seem to tell stories that reinforce suspicious and violent ideologies. They capitalize on the positive value of the POW image to sell us superheroes who can resist all torture and save the day with just the right touch of violence. Captivity in these films titillates the audience while empowering the POW for his imminent rescue, escape, or triumphant return. How many times must a story be told to become truth?

But no one believes this stuff, do they? If they do not, we are in no danger: books, film, and television are great places to try new roles, negotiate a place where our cultural assumptions can be safely criticized (even though some forms of media leave little or no space for such criticism).

But what if people do believe? We have to ask what our new prospective POWs have learned from the Vietnam POW experience. The answer could be as short as the romantic titles of the POW narratives themselves: *Code of Conduct, Code of Honor, In Love and War, A Code to Keep, The Hanoi Commitment, Beyond Survival, Chained Eagle, Bouncing Back, With God in a P.O.W. Camp, Captive Warriors,* or *Love and Duty.*

————

M y five-year-old daughter plays Cowboys and Indians. She often plays the captive. She enjoys the thrill of the role, the exclusivity, the excitement, the suspense, the thrill and satisfaction of release.[38] But such imaginative identifications are ultimately destructive. It is no fun being a captive: at best it is boring, at worst it means death. After all is said and done, how do I tell my daughter it's no good playing captive?

Those who read the POW stories should know what is at stake and how the stories were produced. The distortions in the stories must be made visible and negotiable. We should make more of the overall story known before the next human being marches into captivity armed with the Code of Conduct and a myth. Ultimately, I would like us to think about why we have prisoners at all.

12
The History of the Present

On the evening of 16 January 1991, retired Navy Vice Admiral William Lawrence stepped up to the podium in the Eisenhower Hall auditorium at West Point. Lawrence had been asked to address the Corps of Cadets. His authority for such a task was unarguable. He had had an impressive service career: he was the first man to fly at twice the speed of sound, he had been superintendent of the United States Naval Academy, and he had served as Deputy Chief of Naval Operations. But his introduction to the Corps of Cadets highlighted his other distinction: he had spent six years as a POW in Hanoi. The officer who introduced Lawrence quoted an army colonel and fellow POW to confirm Lawrence's authority.

Although Lawrence said nothing about captivity during his forty-minute speech on the "Emerging World Order," the first two questions from eager cadets were about his POW experience. The cadets jumped through his other career accomplishments and the subject of his speech to mine his crucial experience as a Vietnam POW. They wanted to know how Admiral Lawrence had survived; what he had learned about religion, the family, America, the Code of Conduct, literature, and the self while sitting in a closet-sized cell in Hanoi. On the same night that Lawrence was describing his POW experience to an eager audience, more Americans were becoming POWs in Iraq. West Point, it seemed, would be assured an ample supply of guest speakers for years to come.

Initial speculation about the POWs of the Gulf War made headlines when Iraqi Television released film footage of captured pilots. The media distributed and read these images in a variety of ways. Most often the images were shown as justification for the war. A host of POW experts, including Charles Plumb, Fred Cherry, John McCain, and Jim Stockdale, saw the signs of physical torture on the faces of the despondent POWs: positive evidence of Iraqi mistreatment of American POWs. President Bush, a former navy aviator who had been shot down himself, vowed that Saddam would never get away with it. The interpretations of these initial images drew heavily on our memory of the Vietnam POWs, whose forced confession and years of torture at the hands of a demonic, inscrutable, and racially distinct enemy had become legend.

Unlike their predecessors, however, the Americans held in Iraq seemed to be making statements against the war effort, statements that went beyond the routine giving of name, rank, date of birth, and serial number described in the Code of Conduct. In fact, the POWs were answering all the questions their captors asked on the tape. Surely, after hearing the stories of POWs who resisted debilitating episodes of torture to keep from making such statements during the Vietnam War, Americans had to believe that these POWs had been coerced in some horrible way.

Former POWs had been quite explicit about how Americans should interpret propaganda concerning future POWs. Just describing such a confession made former Vietnam POW Ralph Gaither ill: "Even now, my heart screams out in protest and my insides churn in anger. My ears ring with humiliation and my mind almost overwhelms me." He makes the lesson explicit for his readers: "When other wars are fought, when other men are prisoners, when other statements like this one [confessions of criminality, admissions that the war was wrong] come out of prison camps, to know, to know, to know, never to forget, that those statements are brought about by the worst kind of torture."[1] The apparent distress and physical condition of the captured men on the screen confirmed our worst fears. The cover of the

4 February 1991 issue of *Newsweek* featured an unusually large full-face close-up of Jeffrey Zaun. The headline read, "The POWs: Torture and Torment."

———

Aㅤfter he greeted the first returned POWs, General H. Norman Schwarzkopf told the media: "They're all heroes." Because Schwarzkopf probably had little detailed information about POW treatment or conduct at the time, his statement seemed a little premature. Few in the media questioned this stance, however. His statement was reproduced along with the rest of the Gulf War news provided by the military, perhaps another example of the "proleptic and prophylactic censorship" that characterized much of the Gulf War news coverage.[2]

After the POWs returned to the United States the Pentagon arranged a highly structured press conference. Panels of POWs from two of the services made statements and answered questions from the media. Their answers undercut most speculation concerning their treatment. Although there certainly was abuse, the Iraqis apparently had not systematically tortured POWs as the Vietnamese had. Torture appeared almost unnecessary: the POWs played along with their captors and made the statements that Iraqi Television broadcast. The POWs justified their behavior by saying that they expected their statements damning the United States government and the President to be discredited (a contention possibly informed by the Vietnam experience) and that they saw their statements as more helpful to than disruptive of the United Nations' war effort. The broadcast of their images could and did function to confirm their status as POWs.

Jeffrey Zaun, the navy POW who appeared on the cover of *Newsweek*, admitted that ninety percent of his facial injuries were caused by ejection from his plane. But Zaun had learned from previous experiences: "I hit myself in the nose and the face as hard as I could stand it when I knew they were taking me to a TV station." Disfiguring himself prevented a second visit to the TV station. Zaun was on his way to

Feb. 4, 1991

Newswee

February 4, 1991 : $2.50

INSIDE
PULLOUT MAP OF
THE WAR ZONE

HARD DAYS AHEAD

A Brutal War on the Ground?

The POWs: Torture and Torment

Saddam's Environmental Terror

The first images of American POWs during the Gulf War came via Iraqi Television. Jeffrey Zaun became "the face" of war. Speculation concerning his injuries started a lively public debate, which evaporated once the POWs were home. When Zaun returned home, he explained that most of the injuries obvious in this picture occurred when he ejected from his aircraft.

becoming a Gulf War hero in the tradition of Vietnam POWs who had disfigured themselves, gargled with lye, and feigned mental illness to avoid enemy propaganda efforts.

━━━━━━━━━━

T he public reaction to the POW experience was remarkably mute. Except for the initial headlines prompted by Iraqi TV and the welcoming ceremonies, little was heard from the POWs. Zaun's newspaper interview in the 8 June 1991 issue of the *Lahontan Valley News* (in Fallon, Nevada) was all but a media footnote. He did little rabble-rousing: "I don't ever want to kill anybody again. This country didn't get to see the cost of the war. I did." Zaun went on to collapse any demonology that others might read into his experience: "All in all, I didn't feel they were the bloodthirsty, amoral people we had heard they were." His statement worked against the assumptions we had made about his captivity and the ideology of the war.

Unlike the Nixon administration's "Operation Homecoming," which included focused media attention and a gala banquet at the White House, the Gulf War POWs received neither a concentrated publicity campaign nor a presidential homecoming event in their honor. Nor have we heard much from the military. Four Medals of Honor, the highest U.S. military award, were presented to Vietnam POWs. Nothing of the sort was awarded to the most recent former POWs.

Our latest experience with the image of American POWs seems to leave us with a number of contradictions and unanswered questions. If the POWs were "all heroes," why not reward them as such? What does the conduct of these POWs say about our expectations of American POWs from the Korean and Vietnam wars? The news hype of early February 1991 made a great story: Would they cave in? Were they tortured? What about the women? Unlike the Vietnam POWs, however, the Gulf War POWs faded into the context of the hundreds of yellow ribbon parades for all Gulf War veterans. We won. Few were interested in pursuing the POW sideshow. And, after all, the story did not turn out to be as good as we thought. We expected brutal torture at the hands of shadowy captors. We expected George Bush to fulfill his promise to bring the Iraqi demons to court. But all we got was Jeffrey Zaun, the sensational face of captivity, telling us he did not want to kill anyone again. His story failed to fit our expectations; we could not fit his story into the myth. Zaun would not be a hero after all.

More than a year after the Gulf War, Rhonda Cornum broke her silence on the POW issue. Before a presidential commission on women in the military Cornum revealed the details of her POW experience. The *New York Times* reported that members of the panel were "stunned" by her testimony, which included descriptions of mistreatment and "indecent assaults" that had gone otherwise unreported in the media. Cornum also revealed that many of the POWs, both men and women, were mistreated when they were held captive.

Cornum's testimony came not in postcaptivity news conferences or Pentagon reports on the conduct of the war, but in the context of hearings on women in the armed forces where her tales of sexual abuse and mistreatment could be used and interpreted to limit combat roles for women—exactly the agenda Cornum herself was working against. The article that detailed her testimony mentioned in the next-to-last paragraph Cornum's fears: "Major Cornum expressed concern that her mistreatment had been blown out of proportion and would be used by those who want to keep women out of combat." Ironically, the article that reported Cornum's concern had spent part of the front page and three columns of a succeeding page doing exactly that.

Cornum's testimony before the commission and her book, *She Went to War: The Rhonda Cornum Story,* have not been used by the media or the government to make her a hero, but instead to highlight certain consequences of women serving on the front lines. Immediately after the war Cornum did not make the "Yellow Ribbon" issue of *People* magazine reserved for heroes, but a year later her testimony of sexual assault merited a two-page story in *People.* Her painful experiences as a captive have been reduced and appropriated for their usefulness in a national political debate a year after captivity. It appears that the administration has rigorously censored reports of POW mistreatment in much the same way that it has sanitized other aspects of the Gulf

War in order to promote the immaculate victory many Americans once celebrated.

It is important to note that the incidence of sexual abuse is only foregrounded for female captives. Film, autobiography, and popular patriotic lore rarely discuss sexual activity as an issue of male captivity except when it becomes useful in X-rated movies that exploit the Vietnam POW theme like *Bimbo: Hot Blood* (1985) or *Ramb-ohh: The Force Is in You* (1986). Most certainly male POWs as well as women POWs have been molested or raped in captivity, but the overwhelming assumption of POW stories is that captivity is somehow asexual (or pleasurably sexual as in pornography) for the male and explicitly sexual (and disqualifying) for the female. The marque event of female captivity stories is always the sexual violation of the captive. In contrast, male captivity stories scrupulously avoid such fare. Nothing could make an inherent bias of American lore and cultural production more obvious.

Americans might also examine the truth quotient associated with women's testimony of sexual abuse and harassment. When women have come forward with allegations of abuse by friendly soldiers in the Gulf War or when they claim molestation at a fraternal event like the Tailhook Association, the media treats the issue much differently than when women testify to abuse by an enemy, particularly a racially different enemy. In many ways popular captivity lore prepares us for and leads us to expect the abuse of women in enemy captivity, whereas it seldom foregrounds American "Top Guns" who gang-rape or a "Major Dad" who commits incest. Cornum's testimony is accepted unconditionally while Anita Hill's becomes problematic.

━━━━━━━━━━━━━━━

On her television show "Real Life" Jane Pauley praised Cornum. Her comment also appears on the cover of Cornum's book: "Challenge is what Rhonda Cornum is all about—it's obvious she has the right stuff." Perhaps no statement could resonate better with masculine mythology than conjuring the "right stuff" to describe a woman, a doctor, a mother, a wife, and a soldier like Cornum. Pauley had reduced the complexity of Cornum's experience to yet another popular masculine stereotype in one neat sound byte—another episode of the way cultural myth might asphyxiate experience.

T he first two chapters of this book described the historical disruption and continuities between Vietnam War captivity narratives and earlier American captivity stories from Korea, World War II, the frontier experience, and early America. The disruptions helped make American assumptions about captivity more visible. They showed how changing expectations fueled a persistent mythology. The new disruption between Vietnam and Gulf War experiences provides the immanent boundary that the first part of this book implies. These new disruptions are useful in making the contradictions of the existing order visible. They violate the established and comforting assumption that past, present, and future should somehow be consistent. It may seem that Vietnam POWs have little in common with the new generation of POWs, but, as will become obvious, the Gulf War POW has been and will be controlled and deployed in American culture in much the same way previous war prisoners have been. It is difficult to avoid the conclusion that, for instance, Cornum's testimony was not strategically scheduled and authorized to preempt revelations of her book and to absorb the impact of such discussions in the context of a forum serving a conservative agenda.

The latest POW experience has slipped more quickly from the representational venue than might have been expected. The American POW of Desert Storm has testified to the unreliability of assumptions, however well informed by precedent. Few who speculated on the possibility of Iraqi torture are eager to return and examine the POW issue. The media and the administration have dampened interest in such a story to downplay the possible consequences. The POWs have not received media attention because their plight has ceased to be an issue. The administration finished the war short of Baghdad. Prosecution of Iraqis for mistreating prisoners of war as promised by President Bush is not a possibility. The mistreatment of the POW is, therefore, nothing the present administration wishes to pursue. Even if it were, such prosecutions would invite scrutiny of prisoner conduct, which few in the military or the administration are eager to execute. Such scrutiny would be an unnecessary complication of what has been hailed as a landmark victory in the Gulf War.

The issue of female captivity, however titillating to the media, has also failed to capture much concerted attention. The two female Gulf War POWs received some press, but most of it was topical and of the tabloid variety. Major Rhonda Corman spoke during the national broadcast of the Army-Navy game. Melissa Rathbun-Nealy (now Coleman), when she was expecting a child in late 1991, appeared in the media not for the knowledge she gained during captivity or lessons learned about American life but for the racist hate mail she received (she is married to an African-American, Michael Coleman). When Cornum revealed that Rathbun had also been molested, Rathbun refused to comment.

The Top Gun image of the military pilot validated in countless popular films had done quite well without mentioning the POW. The highly publicized efficiency of the air campaign would be undermined by a focus on the Gulf War POW. We could not watch Tom Cruise disfigure his handsome face to avoid interrogations. Why even suggest it?

And, of course, at this writing, no one on the outside knows what prohibitions or restrictions have been put in place by the services to shape the "story" that can be told. It will be important to watch how America listens to and interprets the POW stories that will eventually emerge. It will also be important to compare the structure and reception of male versus female POW stories, a developing process in which Rhonda Cornum's revelations are only a start.

Perhaps the most recent experience does nothing so much as mark the slippage of the POW issue to what Richard Garrett calls the "uncivil face of war," a part of war we shrink from acknowledging unless it serves to recover victory from an otherwise lost war or as a pretext for a one-sided prosecution of the enemy for its share of the crimes of war.

As Margot Norris has pointed out, the Gulf War may have "reinstated the acceptability of modern warfare once shaken by the nuclear terrors" of the Cold War and the "uncontrollability of Vietnam."[3] Hostages and POWs, unless undeniably heroic, would not fit into the flash of images that makes the acceptability of the Gulf War plausible.

The POW of Desert Storm has become almost an antihero in this respect. She is a part of the war Americans want to forget. He seems to tarnish our notion of how Americans should make war by the apparent ease with which he made statements damning his nation. Her plight, if she was tortured or otherwise mistreated, demands an immediate justice still beyond the reach of prosecution. The victors, despite their tremendous military might, again seem impotent. As in Korea and Vietnam, and unlike the two World Wars, Panama, and Grenada, the United States has not been able to prosecute the enemy. The POW "face of war" is a messy business, the business of capture an arbitrary and somewhat embarrassing side effect that will never be put under the control of laser designators and real-time imagery.

The most recent American POW experience did prove encouraging in some small way. Americans apparently were not systematically tortured. Their difficult captivity experience, like the war, could be counted in weeks, not years. Their images were used but then quickly withdrawn from the propaganda show. Unlike the Vietnam War, where the positive fallout from a jubilant homecoming worked to occlude our flagging efforts to "save" South Vietnam and the lies of a President, the tragedy of captivity, which was far briefer in the Gulf War, was not appropriated to divert attention from savings-and-loan failures or the plight of the Kurds.

It was also encouraging and troubling to watch weaker but persistent reaction to the Cornum testimony. Cornum herself described a letter from other women assaulted during the Gulf War—not by the Iraqis but by American soldiers. Jacqueline Ortiz also went public with her story of sexual assault by a U.S. Army sergeant. These stories were given short but prominent media coverage; however, neither incident received the top billing afforded Cornum's story of mistreatment by Iraqis.

In the months after the war I expected to see the Gulf War POW emerge in magazine articles, book promotions, and other prominent spaces in American culture. As I watched, I saw a POW image emerge, but it was not the one I expected. It was the Vietnam POW who reemerged after the Gulf War, not only in the various pathetic and useful resurrections of the POW/MIA issue, but as a heroic image in and of itself. The Vietnam POW seems to be the preferred referent for our culture. We seem to be reaching back across the Gulf War to recover the Vietnam POW just as we preferred the image of the World War II POW to that of the Korean POW. American culture is programmed to give its consumers what they want. Troubling or unsatisfying images do not excite an audience as much as properly endorsed heroes. Images that problematize something we could better dismiss as success do not last long. It is more comforting for Americans to think of a stalwart Vietnam POW such as Lance Sijan, who resisted to the death, than to think about Jeffrey Zaun and other Gulf War POWs who did less and lived.[4] We want POW heroes to conform to certain preexisting notions of conduct, sexuality, and image. We want pure POW heroes at center stage—no matter what.

———

All prisoners, hostages, and POWs have something in common. Terry Anderson, a hostage in Lebanon for seven years, reflected on his captivity in an article for the Associated Press. He talked about the Bible, solidarity with other prisoners, and, most of all, the refuge he had found in the love of his fiancée and daughter. People listen closely to tales of captivity. They capture attention, particularly in America, because they define a crucial political and social term: freedom. The Freedom Forum trumpeted a cash award of $245,500 in a full page ad in the *New York Times*. The "Free Spirit Award" was presented to Anderson because he had "through word and deed, . . . contributed greatly toward a better understanding of the established goals of The Freedom Forum: free press, free speech, free spirit."[5] Such attention illustrates how Americans use and define freedom negatively. It is always simpler and more comforting to point

Opposite: Terry Anderson, like countless American captives before him, supposedly had "a better understanding" of freedom after living in captivity.

to something that is not rather than what is. Americans use the ideology of freedom as an incentive in our economy, for punishment in our penal system, and as a key axiom in our political rhetoric. Hostages and prisoners define freedom for America. They reassure us that our lives are indeed free by comparison. They make us feel better. It is no coincidence that the plight of the POW/prisoner adheres so well to self-help programs. What better way to make people instantly self-satisfied than by having them contemplate a captivity not happening to them: they could always have it worse.

But such a mentality only perpetuates the cult of captivity. Prisoners and hostages will continue to be a reality as long as we continue to value them, as long as we continue to need them. The challenge of the prisoner's dilemma is not in reaping our gratification from their predicament, but in understanding why we have prisoners. No matter how many times political leaders deny that they are willing to deal for hostages, their efforts will always be in vain: American culture is doing just the opposite. Prisoners seem to deserve and always get our undivided attention. We look for some jewel of knowledge from the compression of their situation, but, instead, we should examine the reasons we find their stories so compelling.

The appeal of captivity stories is legend in American culture. Stories of hostages held by a demonic foreign oppressor work for both press and government. These stories provide media and political interests with eager audiences without the complexity and controversy that domestic news stories might generate. The POW/hostage saga distracts us from immediate issues that might otherwise divide the electorate/market. They galvanize audiences with the pathos of the story, an ever ready Cold War paradigm. The story seems uncomplicated: Americans and the hostages are good, they and the captors are bad. Publicity allows audiences to share in the rescue, pretends to contribute to the eventual release of the POW/hostage. But captivity stories are often useful for everything except helping the subjects.

Hostages and POWs provide a ready political lever. Nothing makes this dynamic more evident than John Lawrence's recent study of POW/hostage episodes. Since the lavish welcome afforded Vietnam POWs by President Nixon, White House welcome-home ceremonies have become ritual for hostages. Recent examples include the return of the hostages from Iran, medical students from Grenada, Navy Lieutenant Robert O. Goodman from Lebanon, passengers of TWA Flight 847, and hostages from Lebanon. Lawrence has made a convincing case that the past five administrations have shown symptoms of being a "captive presidency," ham-handedly focusing attention on POW/hostage crises while, in reality, doing very little to solve them effectively.[6] However credible such conclusions might be, there is no question that hostage and POW crises continue to be useful and expedient issues for the press and politicians alike.

The political expediency of the hostage scenario for Americans is not hard to explain. Captivities and "carnivals of return" constitute some of our first indigenous literature. The captives, absolved of any complicity in their unfortunate situations, become generic, blameless Americans, who can be exploited as metonyms for larger and more complex political situations. The hostages are also carefully identified with us through their innocence and the pretensions of moral greatness confirmed by their survival. As with Vietnam POWs, hostages are presented as symbolic of all Americans; they suffered for and represented us. Nothing made this more explicit than a statement by Ronald Reagan when he received the TWA hostages at the White House: "None of you were held prisoner because of personal wrong you had done to anyone; you were held simply because you are Americans. In the minds of your captors, you represented us."[7] The resultant innocence sets up the inevitable rescue, however symbolic, by the President. The ritualistic ceremonies at the White House allow the President to become the rescuer, asserting both American moral superiority through the survival of captives during their trial and American political and military supremacy for bringing them home.

It is almost irrelevant whether we negotiated with the captors: the political strategy and results were essentially the same, if, perhaps technically, less criminal. The MIA of the Vietnam War seems a tragedy aching for our attention. Sensational media stories have done nothing to solve the issue, yet persistent interest in such a story provides a sure pretext for continuing sanctions against a struggling former enemy and a convenient attention-getter for a panhandling Russian president. Media and political interests converge so neatly on few other issues.

Terry Anderson, despite the joy of his return and new-found freedom, concluded: "Their [his captors'] logic was impossible to grasp. Our differences went beyond culture or religion or language. Their minds were just different from ours. Two and two made not four but six, or 16 or 60 or whatever it might be fantasized to."[8] It was just this irreconcilability that had made Anderson a hostage, and it will be such differences that make more Americans hostages and prisoners again. Anderson's remarks echo the feelings of countless other captives in other narratives. We cannot help but recall Steve Ross explaining the "corkscrew mentalities" of the Japanese in *First Yank into Tokyo* or Everett Alvarez describing the "strange quirks" of his Vietnamese captors in *Chained Eagle*.

Anderson could not fathom his situation from behind the blindfold. It would be incredible to think that he could, but that seems to be exactly what we expect. We expect POWs and hostages to solve the prisoner's dilemma with some transcendental understanding gained during captivity. We hear their stories and feel quite satisfied. Meanwhile the real prisoner market continues to rally. More human beings languish in America's prisons than anywhere else in the world. While we ignore them, we wait for the next group of POWs to appear on our television screen. But they might also divert our attention from the more immediate issues of the next war.

━━━━━━━━━━━━━

One of the first captivity narratives to emerge from the Gulf War was not from a POW but instead from an American journalist, Bob Simon. His narrative follows a tradition of captivity lore that includes the narratives of journalists captured during the Vietnam War: Richard Dudman, Michele Ray, and Kate Webb. In fact, the title of Simon's *Forty Days* closely resembles the title of Dudman's *Forty Days with the Enemy*.

Even though twenty years separated these two narratives, the ironic dilemma of the journalist-prisoner had changed little. Simon had reported and spun the stories of countless other human beings for years: now it would be his turn to face war alone, without his press pass and camera crew.

> My notebook, my jacket, my pen had been taken from me. I had lost my distance, my observer status. I had become the story; not in the sense of "TV Correspondent Held Hostage," but in a far more basic, a far more dangerous way. I wasn't the storyteller anymore. I was a character, a participant, like any soldier or refugee. I was involved in the war, entrapped by it. The cops had taken me away from the keyhole. They wouldn't let me be a voyeur anymore. I thought back on my enthusiasm at the beginning of the buildup . . . with more than a little shame.[9]

Simon declared that eventually he would "capture the experience, deal the last blow," but it would be the experience and media fame that would capture Simon. His terrifying captivity experience would be followed by a year of frustration dealing with media surrounding his own story. Despite Simon's best efforts, his image, like that of countless other captives, would slip beyond his control.

B y the time Simon was captured by Iraqi soldiers during the Gulf War, POW "lore" had, to his mind, become "axiomatic,"[10] Simon could not help but compare his plight as roving newsman and then Iraqi hostage to the "army deskmen" who doled out information to other, less aggressive members of the press corps. Simon, who had spent a career reporting war and aggression to the American public, found his capture experience "strangely cinematic."[11] But the "movie sense" of his experience soon became "unremittingly grade B."[12] He was surprised to find that he and his captors had "the same cultural references." His Iraqi captors asked him: "Did you dream you were Rambo?"[13]

Despite his awareness and knowledge of world events, Simon believed in the cultural myths found in POW lore. He writes of being "part of the crowd, POWs just like them" and of the "chances of a rescue operation." He recalls hoping for his life to imitate a scene from a "grade-B movie": "First we'd hear the sirens, then the bombs, then the helicopters, and then the voices shouting, 'Any Americans here?' "[14] Unfortunately, he failed to remember the dismal record of rescue operations in POW/hostage espisodes during the four decades since World War II. He also forgot that American POWs were ruthlessly segregated during much of the Vietnam War. His hopes of "being part of the crowd" as a POW had more to do with POW lore than with recent history. He had met the error of his own expectations.

Simon's story endorses the conclusions found in countless earlier captivity narratives: the discovery of the true, essential self. Simon reflects on his physical and metaphysical discovery: "My thinning frame was revealing the outline of a hard core I never knew was inside me before because it had been concealed by layers of comfort. It was a round metal disc, or so I pictured it, and it was nothing but an implacable will to survive."[15] His captivity thus has a positive result; it was very much a trial in which he was able to find something he would have found nowhere else. Although conscious of a "nostalgia creeping in" to his apprehension of his own experience, he could not resist the "revisionism" that he was "worried" about.[16] He takes the advice of Robert Polhill and "nurses" his anger by admonishing the KGB, CIA, and Mossad: "One fascist with a mustache is making monkeys of you all. Take him out. Do it. Justify your existence."[17] Simon fails to see that those clandestine organizations he counts on may be making a monkey of him: they may have never wanted to get rid of Saddam Hussein in the first place.

In the acknowledgments to *Forty Days,* Simon explains the "intensity and breadth of the campaign" that led to his release. Unfortunately, he decides that "to explain it all would be another book, and an uplifting one." Simons writes instead the story of this captivity from the inside, at least partly because his wife assured him "that reliving the pain would produce something worthwhile."[18] In one way this advice was quite correct. The story proved marketable to and entertaining for an American audience. It adhered to the persistent and voluminous body of captivity lore that already existed in American culture and consciousness. On the other hand, we might ask just how useful such a story might be. Would it have been better for Simon to write that "other" book, which might have explained how to resolve the captivity dilemma? Or was it more important for him to cater to the traditional autobiographical plot of capture, trial, and redemption? The question comes down to whether Simon has really told us anything new about captivity. Has he expanded our understanding of the atrocity of war, the arbitrariness of capture, the pointlessness of confinement, or the politics of release?

Simon claims that "the special irony of our situation—how the makers of stories were becoming the subjects of a story—was never lost on us."[19] But such consciousness did little to change how the story was told. Despite Simon's equivocations, his narrative apes the trajectory of previous captivity stories—his narrative, however revealing, cannot escape the centripetal forces and the inevitable tropes of captivity lore. His other book will probably never come out; his unique observations will fall into the shadow of the structures that make his story so marketable. At one point Simon claims "to understand the process of mythmaking. I could see how, when the need is great enough, a series of random events becomes infused with meaning; how, in retrospect, days which were ruled by coincidence and chaos become coherent stages in a voyage of discovery."[20] This knowledge seems not to have helped him avoid the quicksand of tradition. At least partly unaware and unprepared for the crushing force of captivity lore, Simon had, to put it in his own words, "unwittingly become a symbol."[21] More than that, he had become a captive of that symbol, the image he understood so well.

O ur understanding of how we came to know the Vietnam POW experience should inform the ways we read what we are about to see. Perhaps now that America has a "victory" in the Gulf War to place between itself and the Vietnam War, Americans are better equipped to deal with the legacy of our longest war. Perhaps they will move toward a composite narrative of the war without so many of their immediate hopes and fears. Perhaps once removed from that conflict America will begin to see itself and that war more clearly. Perhaps we can finally know how the myth, triumph, and tragedy of the POW experience have become the history of our present.

Almost twenty years after he returned from Hoa Lo Prison in North Vietnam, Sam Johnson reflected on his experience in his POW autobiography, *Captive Warriors*. In a passage echoing the sentiments of James Stockdale quoted in the introduction to this book, he recalls the vicious propaganda efforts of the North Vietnamese: "He [Ho Chi Minh] applied his most creative energies to employing unwilling and injured American POWs to tell his story. He danced us across the stage of world opinion and presented the world with the best orchestrated propaganda show this century has beheld."[22] With all that we have seen representing the POW in America for the past twenty years, it is hard to agree with Johnson. There was more than one "orchestrated propaganda show" featuring the Vietnam POW, and the "best" one opened and continues to appear right here in America.

Notes

INTRODUCTION

1. Todd Gitlin, "Television's Screens: Hegemony in Transition," in *American Media and Mass Culture,* ed. Donald Lazere (Berkeley: University of California Press, 1987), 240.

2. James E. Young, *Writing and Rewriting the Holocaust: Narrative and the Consequences of Interpretation* (Bloomington and Indianapolis: Indiana University Press, 1988), 80.

3. James B. Stockdale, foreword to *Prisoner of War: Six Years in Hanoi,* by John McGrath (Annapolis: Naval Institute Press, 1975), vi.

4. Albert D. Biderman, *March to Calumny: The Story of American POWs in the Korean War* (New York: Macmillan, 1963), 3.

1. A HISTORY OF THE POW IMAGE

1. The escape theme was romanced in other POW films, such as *Grand Illusion* (1937), *First Yank into Tokyo* (1945), *Stalag 17* (1953), *The Secret War of Harry Frigg* (1968), *Von Ryan's Express* (1965), *Escape to Athena* (1979), and *Victory* (1981).

2. Larry Guarino, *A P.O.W.'s Story: 2801 Days in Hanoi* (New York: Ivy Books, 1990), 17.

3. Michael Paul Rogin, *Ronald Reagan, the Movie and Other Episodes in Political Demonology* (Berkeley: University of California Press, 1989), 39.

4. Here I am using Joseph Campbell's term for those agents of myth who carry the core values of a culture.

5. The image of the event was so powerful that twenty-three years later, captive journalist Bob Simon feared that his Iraqi captors would take him "downtown on flatbed trucks bearing floats, a parody of the Macy's Thanksgiving Day parade. The pilots would be sitting in mock cardboard bombers. I would be chained to a distorted CBS eye over my head. People would throw

bags of urine and stones" (Bob Simon, *Forty Days* [New York: G. P. Putnam's Sons, 1992], 146).

6. Scott Blakey dramatizes Dorothy Stratton's experience in the Strattons' biography, *Prisoner at War: The Survival of Commander Richard A. Stratton* (New York: Penguin, 1979), 213–226.

7. Jim and Sybil Stockdale, *In Love and War* (New York: Bantam Books, 1985), 296–297.

8. Sybil Stockdale appears to have learned much from these books. Among the things that may have caught her eye was Albert Biderman's assessment of the "POW myth" of the Korean War. At one point in *March to Calumny* Biderman does an empirical analysis of positive and negative images of the POW experience in the *New York Times Index* for the years 1951 to 1956. Biderman concluded that the negative image of the Korean POW resulted from "propaganda by Americans, about Americans, directed to Americans."

9. Her own testament of how the POW issue became a national concern is her autobiographical account, *In Love and War* (coauthored with her ex-POW husband).

10. Stockdale, *In Love and War*, 227.

11. Ibid., 231.

12. Ibid., 297.

13. Ibid., 302.

14. Ibid., 311.

15. The *New York Times* ran a long article about POW mistreatment on 31 July 1969.

16. The administration went public at a news conference by Secretary Laird condemning the North Vietnamese for lacking "even the most fundamental standards" of human decency. September 1969 saw the POW issue become the subject of cabinet-level White House concern, congressional resolution, and a national media blitz. Stockdale organized and launched a delegation from her League of Families to the Paris peace talks. On 12 December 1969 President Nixon met with representatives of the League of Families and held a press conference with Sybil Stockdale.

17. I am borrowing the phrase "evil versus evil" from John Colabro's "Stories of War and the End of Warfare," *Transaktie* 20, no. 3 (1991): 205.

18. As Sybil Stockdale put it: "It was a real shot in the arm to know our government was trying to do something to help our men" (Stockdale, *In Love and War*, 382).

19. James Stockdale, a POW for seven and a half years, describes the effect the raid had on the Hanoi Hilton: "A yelp of joy went up all over Las Vegas [a particular cellblock in the camp]. The racket the other night, the sounds of

construction, the new guards—all of it started to fit together. America had raided a POW camp someplace near Hanoi" (Ibid., 382).

20. Former POW and later Congressman Sam Johnson poses just such a question in his autobiographical account: "It is possible intelligence knew the camp had been emptied but was ordered to carry out the mission anyway, using the operation as a politically expedient tool to build support for an unpopular president?" (Sam Johnson and Jan Winebrenner, *Captive Warriors: A Vietnams POW's Story* [College Station, Tex.: Texas A & M University Press, 1992], 240).

21. Benjamin F. Schemmer, *The Raid* (New York: Harper & Row, 1976), 6.

22. Schemmer reported that there had been "more than 60 POW raids in South Vietnam and Cambodia—the net result of which had been to recover exactly one American POW, who died two weeks later of wounds inflicted by his captors as the rescue was under way" (Ibid., 229).

23. Johnson, *Captive Warriors*, 260.

24. Everett Alvarez, Jr., with Samuel A. Schreiner, Jr., *Code of Conduct* (New York: Donald Fine, 1991), 10.

25. Tom Morganthau and Kim Willenson, "We're Still Prisoners of War," *Newsweek*, 15 April 1985, 34–37.

26. The films that recover the POW/MIA issue are too numerous to list definitively here but include: *First Blood; Rambo: First Blood Part II; Rolling Thunder; Uncommon Valor; Death without Honor; Missing in Action; Missing in Action 2: The Beginning; Welcome Home; Fireback; Kill Zone; No Dead Heroes; Private War; Strike Commando; Intimate Strangers; The Forgotten; Operation Nam;* and *Some Kind of Hero.*

27. The American Ex-POW Association's MedSearch study claims: "Morbidity studies have shown that former prisoners of war have a higher incidence rate of illness and disease in all body systems" (*The American Ex-Prisoners of War* [Paducah, Ky.: Turner Publishing Company, 1988], 50).

2. MYTH AND TRAGEDY ON THE NEW FRONTIER

1. Much of my discussion of the early captivities comes directly from the defining article on the subject: Greg Sieminski, "The Puritan Captivity Narrative and the Politics of the American Revolution," *American Quarterly* 42 (March 1990): 35–37.

2. Henry Louis Gates, Jr., found this quote in the February 1853 issue of *Graham's Illustrated Magazine of Literature.* In his explanation of the popularity of slave narratives, he quite rightly sees the elements of autobiography and

the picaresque, but goes too far when he asserts that slave narratives took advantage of what he calls a "bipolar moment." As I have shown, captivity was another popular literary convention that created the appeal of slave narrative. For Gates's discussion see *Figures in Black: Words, Signs, and the "Racial" Self* (New York: Oxford University Press, 1987), 80–84.

3. Here I use the term "archeology" to mean an "analysis of local discursivities." The aim of archeology in this context is to "emancipate historical knowledges from subjection" in order to "struggle against the coercion of a theoretical, unitary, formal, and scientific discourse" (Michel Foucault, *Power/Knowledge: Selected Interviews & Other Writings 1972–1977*, ed. Colin Gordon [New York: Pantheon, 1980], 85).

4. Richard Slotkin, *Regeneration Through Violence: The Mythology of the American Frontier, 1600–1860* (Middletown, Conn.: Wesleyan University Press, 1973), 8.

5. Ibid., 10.

6. A list of POW texts that exhibit the archetypal structure I describe would include: *Chained Eagle; Five Years to Freedom; Prisoner of War; Beyond Survival; The Hanoi Commitment; When Hell was in Session; Before Honor; A Code to Keep; Prisoner at War; In Love and War; the Passing of the Night; They Wouldn't Let Us Die; Code of Honor; i'm no hero;* and *A P.O.W.'s Story.*

7. Johnson, *Captive Warriors*, 188.

8. Geoffrey Norman describes the pilot's relationship to justification for the war in this way: "For that matter, most pilots—including Stafford—held no deep convictions one way or the other about the war. That was a component of their professionalism" (*Bouncing Back: How a Heroic Band of POWs Survived Vietnam* [Boston: Houghton Mifflin, 1990], 12).

9. Charles Plumb makes this analogy: "Instead we were 350 men cut off from the world like astronauts on the dark side of the moon" (*i'm no hero* [Independence, Mo.: Independence Press, 1973], 280).

10. Slotkin, *Regeneration*, 103.

11. Norman, *Bouncing Back*, 45.

12. Johnson, *Captive Warriors*, 141.

13. Slotkin, *Regeneration*, 107.

14. Norman, *Bouncing Back*, 44–45. This is identical to the "purification ritual" described by Slotkin in *Regeneration*, 527.

15. Plumb, *i'm no hero*, 281.

16. Jay R. Jensen, *Six Years in Hell* (1974; Orcutt, Calif.: Publications of Worth, 1989), xi.

17. McDaniel apparently discounts the fact that someone raised in the "jungle" might describe Manhattan on a gray day in much the same way (Eugene

McDaniel and James J. Johnson, *Before Honor: One Man's Spiritual Journey through the Darkness of a Communist Prison* [New York: A. J. Holman, 1975], 25).
18. The majority of POW texts use the word "hell" to describe Hoa Lo Prison. Jeremiah Denton and Ed Brandt's *When Hell Was in Session* (Clover, S.C.: Commission Press, 1976), and Jensen's *Six Years in Hell* foreground this metaphor. Jensen makes the religious implications of his comparison explicit: "It truly was 'Six Years in Hell'! A physical, mental, emotional and spiritual 'HELL.' But the Lord delivered me from that hell" (xi). One text does just the opposite. James Daly describes his move from a jungle camp to the Hanoi Hilton: "The only way I could ever describe how different the Plantation Gardens was from all those POW camps in the south would be to say that it was like going from hell to heaven" (Daly and Lee Bergman, *A Hero's Welcome* [Indianapolis: Bobbs-Merrill, 1975], 174). Of course, Daly's text, partly because he was associated with a group called the "Peace Committee' in captivity, does not participate in the formation of the Vietnam captivity myth.
19. This mirrors the component of the myth that Richard Slotkin describes in Puritan narratives: "Once in the wilderness condition, the captive is figuratively in hell" (Slotkin, *Regeneration*, 109).
20. "Thoreau's American epic is the epic of the captive, in which the adventuring impulse turns inward and becomes a moral and psychological struggle against the forces that imprison the body and against the torpor of mind and spirit that bind the soul to Satan or (to use a term more appropriate to Thoreau) to death and 'deadness' " (Ibid., 538).
21. Norman, *Bouncing Back*, 45.
22. It should come as no surprise that many POW autobiographies dedicate themselves in title to the codes, the structures which sustained the pilots during captivity. Examples include *A Code to Keep, Code of Honor, With God in a P.O.W. Camp, In Love and War,* and *Bouncing Back.*
23. Sam Johnson, speaking of fellow POW Jim Stockdale, made this point explicit: "He had defeated the North Vietnamese at their own game, but the cost had been great" (*Captive Warriors*, 235).
24. Carolyn Porter defines "ahistoricism" this way: "I mean, then, a set of assumptions about the American romantic tradition which are related, on the one hand, to the theory of American exceptionalism, and on the other, to an emphasis on Adamic innocence, and which, taken together, yield a reading of that tradition in which an 'end to the memory of history,' along with a faith in the transcended sovereignty of the individual, are seen as definitive" (Porter, *Seeing and Being: The Plight of the Participant Observer in Emerson, James, Adams, and Faulkner* [Middletown, Conn.: Wesleyan University Press, 1981], xiii). Porter's definition might explain much about the POW myth in that it predicts

how the POW story at once worked to end the memory of the Vietnam War by substituting the "transcended sovereignty of the individual" in the guise of the POW for that war.

25. An example of this logic comes from James Mulligan: "There might be a lot of things wrong with the U.S. war in Vietnam but for the POW part of it, ours was an honest effort in a basically just cause." (*The Hanoi Commitment* [Virginia Beach, Va.: RIF Marketing, 1981], 260).

26. Ernest Brace, *A Code to Keep* (New York: St. Martin's Press, 1988), 147. For the opposite position see my discussion of McDaniel in chapter 10. McDaniel concludes that God did get him shot down and eventually returned him to America to spread the word.

27. Ibid., 150.

28. Paul Eakin discusses this effect in "Malcolm X and Autobiography," in *Autobiography: Essays Theoretical and Critical,* ed. James Olney (Princeton: Princeton University Press, 1980), 183.

29. Slotkin, *Regeneration,* 20.

30. Ibid., 112.

31. Guarino, *A P.O.W.'s Story,* 328. James Mulligan puts it this way: during captivity, "the past, in fact, replaced the present and the near past" (Mulligan, *The Hanoi: Commitment,* 181). Howard Rutledge points explicitly to "Rip Van Winkle" (Howard and Phyllis Rutledge, with Mel and Lyle White, *In the Presence of Mine Enemies* [Old Tappan, N.J.: Fleming H. Revell, 1973], 94).

32. Norman, *Bouncing Back,* 238.

33. Jensen, *Six Years in Hell,* xi.

34. Slotkin, *Regeneration,* 368.

35. Contemporary critics of American culture, including Richard Slotkin, H. Bruce Franklin, Keith Scott Christianson, and Greg Sieminski, have concluded that captivity is somehow essential to American experience and identity.

3. AUTOBIOGRAPHY AND THE POW EXPERIENCE

1. Alvarez with Schreiner, *Code of Conduct,* 26.

2. Ibid., 36–37.

3. Robert F. Sayre, "Autobiography and the Making of America," in Olney, *Autobiography,* 147.

4. Here I am borrowing from Sayre's discussion of Benjamin Franklin's *Autobiography* (Ibid., 158).

5. Ibid., 168.

6. Robinson Risner, *The Passing of the Night: My Seven Years as a Prisoner of the North Vietnamese* (New York: Ballantine, 1975), vi–vii.

7. Roger Rosenblatt, "Black Autobiography," in Olney, *Autobiography*, 176.

8. Mulligan, *The Hanoi Commitment*, 14.

9. Philippe Lejeune, *On Autobiography*, trans. Katherine Leary (Minneapolis: University of Minnesota Press, 1989), 22–24. This dynamic is what Lejeune calls the "autobiographical pact," but this bond is more like a prison sentence than a "pact." It is unlike any pact I am familiar with because it entails one party (the author) confessing his most personal experience in exchange for absolutely no commitment from a faceless other who will read and do with this confession as he pleases. Although Lejeune works hard at defining the fine lines between various textual categories of autobiographical and fictional texts, his formalistic categories are often "whitened out" (to borrow from Derrida) as the critical frame expands from the written text itself to the venues of popular culture such as film, television, and popular magazine. James Young works in a broader context of representations from written text to architecture in his study of the Holocaust. He portrays this "pact" as a process of "memorialization" in movement between events, icons, and ourselves and takes into account the dimensions of fame and cultural media, which Lejeune fails to examine (Young, *Writing and Rewriting the Holocaust,* 189).

10. Richard Slotkin points out that "American myths—tales of heroes in particular—frequently turn out to be the work of literary hacks or of promoters seeking to sell American real estate" (*Regeneration*, 6).

11. James Young observes the problems of the autobiographer in his study of Holocaust narratives. "But when he left Auschwitz, it became clear that his mind—his meaning-making capacity—was still interned. The camp and its realities became his new tradition, his new mythos; he was reborn in the world with a new set of expectations" (Young, *Writing and Rewriting the Holocaust,* 106).

12. Phil Beidler, "Bad Business: Vietnam and Recent Mass-Market Fiction," *College English* 54, no. 1 (January 1992): 64–75.

13. James N. Rowe, *Five Years to Freedom* (New York: Ballantine, 1971), 463.

14. Elaine Scarry describes the experience of pain in terms of "the making and unmaking of the world" in *The Body in Pain: The Making and Unmaking of the World* (New York: Oxford University Press, 1985).

15. Rowe, *Five Years to Freedom*, 81.

16. Ibid., 450.

17. Ibid., 453.

18. John McGrath, *Prisoner of War* (Annapolis: Naval Institute Press, 1975), ix.

19. Rowe, *Five Years to Freedom*, 459.

20. Michel Foucault, *The History of Sexuality, Volume 1*, trans. Robert Hurley (New York: Random House, 1978), 62.

21. Leo Braudy puts it this way: "Through the media of sound, sight, and print individuals can aspire to a dream of ubiquity in which fame seems unbounded by time or space: constantly present, constantly recognizable, and therefore constantly existing" (*The Frenzy of Renown: Fame and Its History* [New York: Oxford University Press, 1986], 553).

22. Ibid., 557.

23. Baudrillard puts it this way: "As soon as this scene is no longer haunted by its actors and their fantasies, as soon as behavior is crystallized on certain screens and operational terminals, what's left appears only as a large useless body, deserted and condemned. The real itself appears as a large useless body" ("The Ecstasy of Communication," in *The Anti-Aesthetic: Essays on Postmodern Culture*, ed. Hal Foster [Port Townsend, Wash.: Bay Press, 1983], 129).

24. Fredric Jameson, "Postmodernism and Consumer Society," in *Postmodernism and its Discontents: Theories, Practices*, ed. E. Ann Kaplan (New York: Verso, 1988), 28.

25. Braudy, *The Frenzy of Renown*, 577.

26. Porter, *Seeing and Being*, xiii.

27. Michel Foucault, *Discipline and Punish: The Birth of the Prison*, trans. Alan Sheridan (New York: Random House, 1977), 239.

28. Philippe Lejeune describes the widening "gap" in terms of its "internalization" by the individual in his struggle to construct a self in works of autobiography. Lejeune sees that this internalization may be "pleasant" or it may "be tragic and . . . reveal the explosion of an identity." Many of the POW narratives exhibit the qualities that Lejeune describes. If, however, we accept Lejeune's polarization of these effects on the individual and my critical appraisal of the "positive" narratives that emerge from the experience, all the POWs end up in a double bind with no hope of reconstructing their lives (Lejeune, *On Autobiography*, 212). Georges Gusdorf points to the obvious "doubling" that occurs with any self-examination: "After self-examination a man is no longer the man he was before" ("The Conditions and Limits of Autobiography," in Olney, *Autobiography*, 47). Many POW narratives display "the widening of that chasm between seeing and being as well as the compensatory strategies designed to overcome it" (Porter, *Seeing and Being*, xii).

29. Braudy, *The Frenzy of Renown*, 579.

30. Risner reduces his experience to "four essentials" that hinge on his belief

in a transcendent and dominant American ideology (Risner, *The Passing of the Night*, 169).

31. Slotkin, *Regeneration*, 6.

32. Russell Reising, *The Unusable Past: Theory and the Study of American Literature* (New York: Methuen, 1986), 265.

33. The potential of the "fortunate fall" is described by R. W. B. Lewis in *The American Adam: Innocence, Tragedy, and Tradition in the Nineteenth Century* (Chicago: University of Chicago Press, 1955): "As a metaphor in the area of human psychology, the notion of the fortunate fall has an immense potential. It points to the necessary transforming shocks and sufferings, the experiments and errors—in short, the experience—through which maturity and identity may be arrived at" (61). But two falls occur in the POW experience. The first occurs when the captive faces his situation in contrast with the given myths, as I describe in chapter 6. The fall I discuss here is the second one, where the identity derived from the first fall must inject itself back into the context of the American culture to which the POW must return after a violent and prolonged absence.

34. Michael J. Fischer, "Ethnicity and the Arts of Memory," in *Writing Culture*, ed. James Clifford and George E. Marcus (Berkeley: University of California Press, 1986), 198.

35. Foucault, *Discipline and Punish*, 305.

36. Robert Sayre points out the dangers of reification that come with autobiographical form, particularly in America: "Autobiography in America is not only a genre with significant origins and distinguished classics [a canon], it is also an industry, a sometimes handmade, sometimes machinemade common commodity" ("Autobiography and the Making of America," in Olney, *Autobiography*, 149).

37. I have borrowed Fredric Jameson's term, "cultural asphyxiation" from *Signatures of the Visible* (New York: Routledge, 1990), 87.

4. HISTORY AND *THE HANOI HILTON*

1. Young, *Writing and Rewriting the Holocaust*, 10.

2. Ibid., 11.

3. Some of the narratives may be attempts to prosecute vicariously the case against dissident POWs who cooperated with the North Vietnamese in ways some found unacceptable and in conflict with the Code of Conduct. Many of the narratives, including *In Love and War* and *A Hero's Welcome*, partially focus on the miscarried hearings concerning POW misconduct.

4. Plumb and DeWerf, *i'm no hero,* 283.

5. Former POW Sam Johnson describes the incident in his account, Johnson, *Captive Warriors,* 160.

6. Mulligan, *The Hanoi Commitment,* 17.

7. Everett Alvarez, Jr., and Anthony S. Pitch, *Chained Eagle* (New York: Donald Fine, 1989), 184.

8. Ibid., 187.

9. John Dramesi, *Code of Honor* (New York: W. W. Norton, 1975), 235.

10. The other POW, Edwin Atterbury, was apparently tortured to death for his attempt to escape.

11. The POWs had been successful in protesting treatment of individual prisoners before this incident. When others were singled out for punishment, the POWs openly protested. This incident was apparently a strange exception.

12. Dramesi, *Code of Honor,* 239.

13. Young, *Writing and Rewriting the Holocaust,* 40.

14. Ibid., 157.

15. "The myth is articulated by individual artists and has its effect on the mind of each individual participant, but its function is to reconcile and unite these individualities to a collective identity" (Slotkin, *Regeneration,* 8).

16. Alvarez with Schreiner, *Code of Conduct,* 168.

17. James Clifford, introduction, Clifford and Marcus, *Writing Culture,* 24.

18. In "The Subject and Power," Foucault describes how the Enlightenment motivated a conflation of absolute sovereignty and democratization that produced a specific mode of individualization. The subject could be individual, but only in ways authorized by the state. This is the function of normalization. (Hubert L. Dreyfus and Paul Rabinow, *Michel Foucault: Beyond Structuralism and Hermeneutics* [Chicago: University of Chicago Press, 1982], 208–226).

19. I have borrowed this line from Young's critique of the Hasidic structure in Holocaust survivors' narratives (Young, *Writing and Rewriting the Holocaust,* 41).

20. Ibid., 42.

21. Kate Webb, *On the Other Side: 23 Days with the Viet Cong* (New York: Quadrangle Books, 1972), 101.

5. SELLING AND THE POW

1. This Philip Morris advertisement appeared in a variety of publications in 1990. Here I am reading the advertisement that appeared in *Off Duty America,* July/August 1990, 5.

2. David Grogan, "Eight Years a POW in North Vietnam," *People,* 19 February 1990, 25–28.

3. My reading of Alvarez's *People* spot draws ideas from Foucault's discussion of confession in *The History of Sexuality,* 1:58–71.

4. Alvarez with Schreiner, *Code of Conduct,* 11.

5. "The Meaning of Thanksgiving," "Prime Time Live," ABC, 23 November 1989.

6. *New York Times,* 1 June 1989.

7. Many accounts call the latter period of captivity, after the unsuccessful Son Tay raid, "camp unity." Robinson Risner uses these words to title one of his chapters (Risner, *The Passing of the Night,* 192).

8. Advertisements often present ideas that are attractive to and accepted by a target audience. Corporations present these ideas in conjunction with their corporate logo or a particular product that has little or no relation to the idea, but the ad image works to persuade the audience otherwise (Richard Ohmann, "Doublespeak and Ideology in Ads: A Kit for Teachers," in *American Media and Mass Culture: Left Perspectives,* ed. Donald Lazere [Berkeley: University of California Press, 1987], 106–115).

9. William Meyers devotes an entire chapter to Philip Morris in his study of "power and persuasion on Madison Avenue." His critique refers to Philip Morris's rise to corporate dominance in these terms (*The Image-Makers: Power and Persuasion on Madison Avenue* [New York: New York Times Books, 1972], 64–65).

10. Alvarez with Schreiner, *Code of Conduct,* 19.

11. Braudy, *The Frenzy of Renown: Fame and Its History,* title.

12. Ibid., 598.

13. I use this term to describe those POWs who were freed in February and March as a result of the Paris peace accords. I call these the authorized POWs because of the authority lent to them by the Nixon administration and the media attention orchestrated for their release.

6. ERRORS AND EXPECTATIONS

1. Risner, *The Passing of the Night,* 17.

2. Ibid., 27.

3. I discuss Risner's "new" conception in chapter 9.

4. Stockdale, *In Love and War,* 157.

5. James Stockdale, making an indirect reference to criminals in American film, at one point in his narrative calls George Coker "our 'Jimmy Cagney,' our

escape artist." Using an image from film, Stockdale reaches for a celluloid character to describe a fellow prisoner, but hesitates to go further and thus associate his experience with the context within which that character functions (Stockdale, *In Love and War,* 405). See H. Bruce Franklin, *Prison Literature in America: The Victim as Criminal and Artist* (New York: Oxford University Press, 1978).

6. Webb, *On the Other Side,* 99.

7. Rowe, *Five Years to Freedom,* 461.

8. See my discussion of Rowe's reaction to the question of mistreatment in chapter 3. The passage in the Rowe text appears on page 44.

9. Young, *Writing and Rewriting the Holocaust,* 99.

10. George Smith, *P.O.W.: Two Years with the Vietcong* (Berkeley, Calif.: Ramparts Press, 1971), 131. See also 37, 235.

11. Monika Schwinn and Bernhard Diehl, *We Came to Help,* trans. Jan van Heurck (New York: Harcourt Brace Jovanovich, 1973), 11–12.

12. Ibid., 244.

13. Ibid., 254.

14. Dieter Dengler, *Escape From Laos* (San Rafael, Calif.: Presidio Press, 1979), 138.

15. Dramesi, *Code of Honor,* 87.

16. Rowe, *Five Years to Freedom,* 457.

17. Richard Slotkin describes the process this way: "We continually strive to resolve the inherent contradictions between present circumstances and received wisdom, by testing remembered facts against present difficulties" ("Myth and the Production of History," in *Ideology and Classic American Literature,* ed. Sacvan Bercovitch and Myra Jehlen [New York: Cambridge University Press, 1986], 75).

18. Here I am accepting Daniel Boorstin's idea as it is explained in *The Image: or What Happened to the American Dream* (New York: Kingsport Press, 1962). The quote comes from Lazere, *American Media and Mass Culture,* 101.

19. Guarino, *A P.O.W.'s Story,* 166.

7. "Young Men, Husbands, Sons"

1. Julian Smith points to the Pentagon's reluctance but doesn't speculate about why the Pentagon found *Limbo* so troubling beyond its propaganda value for the North Vietnamese. Smith discusses Robson's problems with *Limbo*'s production in *Looking Away: Hollywood and Vietnam* (New York: Scribner's, 1975), 19n.

2. The POW autobiographies echo the "psychological enclosure" and "claus-

trophobia" frequently found in female autobiographies that describe feminine experience as a "prison of the self." Mary C. Manson points to the metaphor of imprisonment in "women's writing from Charlotte Perkins Gilman's autobiography to the story of Sylvia Plath" in "Autobiographies of Women Writers," in Olney, *Autobiography*, 234.

3. Dorothy McDaniel, *After the Hero's Welcome: A POW Wife's Story of the Battle Against a New Enemy* (Chicago: Bonus Books, 1991), 207.

4. Ibid., 38.

5. Sam Johnson explains with apparent relief that although he "had no fears that Shirley [his wife] would get tired of waiting for me and give up . . . many wives of American POWs did just that, and the Vietnamese delighted in delivering such bad news from home to already suffering prisoners" (Johnson, *Captive Warriors*, 261).

6. John G. Hubbell, *P.O.W.: A Definitive History of the American Prisoner-of-War Experience in Vietnam, 1964–1973* (New York: Reader's Digest Press, 1976), xi.

7. D. McDaniel, *After the Hero's Welcome*, 87.

8. Ibid.

9. Ibid., 190.

10. Ibid., 194.

11. Dorothy McDaniel refers to her husband's physical and emotional scars on the first page of her book and many times in the final chapter, "God Sees the Scars." At the beginning of this chapter she quotes the words she heard in church: "When the eyes of God examine a man's heart, they look for his scars, the scars from his battles for justice and righteousness" (Ibid., 191–192).

12. Ibid., vii.

13. Stockdale, *In Love and War*, 34.

14. Ibid., 386.

15. Ibid., 447.

16. Mulligan, *The Hanoi Commitment*, 53.

17. Ibid., 102.

18. Ibid., 173.

19. Dramesi, *Code of Honor*, 53.

20. Alvarez and Pitch, *Chained Eagle*, 282.

21. Mulligan, *The Hanoi Commitment*, 265.

22. Alvarez and Pitch, *Chained Eagle*, 302.

23. Charlie Plumb's account shares many issues with Alvarez. Ironically, Plumb recalls giving his "good friend Ev Alvarez" mail to carry back to his wife, Anne. Unfortunately, Plumb found that "Anne was no longer interested in my letters . . . or my love." The chronological narrative of *i'm no hero* ends with Plumb's brief conversation with his wife when he returned. Plumb's last

words to Anne emphasize her betrayal in contrast to the many "vows" Plumb
has had to keep during a difficult captivity: "You broke your vow" (Plumb and
DeWerf, *i'm no hero*, 277–279). Ernest Brace echoes this sense of betrayal in *A
Code to Keep*. When Brace returned to the United States, he found that his wife
had remarried twice during his absence. He put his reaction to this situation
in the context of his POW experience this way: "Through all the years of
harassment, the leg irons, the beatings with bamboo rods, the rope burns, and
the efforts they had made to demoralize us, neither of us [Brace and a fellow
POW whose wife had remarried] could remember crying. Steve and I cried in
front of each other in that quiet room" (252).

24. Jeremiah Denton's *When Hell Was in Session* works directly against the
betrayal theme of the Alvarez account. Denton points to a discussion with Jim
Stockdale: "I gave him a message for Jane in case he got home. I wanted her
to get married again. My love for her was so great that I could even love the
man she married" (Denton and Brandt, *When Hell Was in Session*, 84). This
appears to be an attempt to reduce the significance and notoriety of errant
wives like Tangee Alvarez.

25. Alvarez and Pitch, *Chained Eagle*, 203.

26. Ibid., 205.

27. Ibid., 204.

28. Ibid., 198.

29. Here I am referring to those texts that "rewrite" the POW experience from
historical or journalistic perspectives. Examples include Hubbell, *P.O.W.*, and
the POW biographies that emerged after the POW release in 1973.

30. Alvarez and Pitch, *Chained Eagle*, 119.

31. Plumb and DeWerf, *i'm no hero*, 99.

32. Ibid., 100.

33. Denton, *When Hell Was in Session*, 34.

34. Ibid., 35.

35. Ibid., 39.

36. Guarino, *A P.O.W.'s Story*, 89.

37. Mulligan, *The Hanoi Commitment*, 226.

38. Ibid., 227.

39. Denton, *When Hell Was in Session*, 136.

40. Ibid., 135.

41. Dramesi, *Code of Honor*, 185.

42. Ibid., 143.

43. Denton, *When Hell Was in Session*, 136.

44. Despite Denton's professed devotion, his narrative, *When Hell Was in Session*, mentions little about his wife. This contrasts dramatically with the televi-

sion movie that was produced from the same experience. The movie, unlike the book, juxtaposes the experiences of Denton's wife at home with Denton's prison experience, a structure very similar to the textual structure of Jim and Sybil Stockdale's book and television movie, *In Love and War.*

45. Ibid., 136.

46. Ibid., 137.

8. ANOTHER TALE TO TELL

The chapter title is borrowed from Fred Pfeil, *Another Tale to Tell: Politics and Narrative in Postmodern Culture* (New York: Verso, 1990).

1. Michele Ray, *The Two Shores of Hell,* trans. Elisabeth Abbott (New York: David McKay, 1968), 139.

2. Ibid., 209.

3. Alvarez and Pitch, *Chained Eagle,* 72.

4. Ibid., 117.

5. Ibid., 36.

6. Guarino, *A P.O.W.'s Story,* 272.

7. Richard Dudman, *forty days with the enemy* (New York: Liveright, 1971), 14.

8. Ibid., 18.

9. A good example of such an incident comes from late in Webb's captivity: " 'Do you realize,' said the old man in civilian clothes, 'that you are a prisoner of war, and that one shot through the head could finish you just like that?' " (Webb, *On the Other Side,* 109).

10. Schwinn and Diehl, *We Came to Help,* x–xi.

11. Webb, *On the Other Side,* 3.

12. Ibid., 8.

13. Ibid., 10.

14. Ibid., 14.

15. Ibid., 17.

16. Examples of such incidents include the following passages: "I am led to an underground hole, big enough for one person to lie in. The others are together in another" (21). "The soldiers noticed the men's arms pulling the vines and wires so tight they bit. The veins stood out on their hands, and they bowed forward trying to ease the strain. My ropes were left alone" (19). "Suzuki and the others were motioned off. . . . As night fell dark, the mosquitoes bit, and I reconciled myself that the others were gone for good" (19).

17. Ibid., 23.

18. Ibid., 27.

19. Ibid., 25.
20. Ibid., 103.
21. Ibid., 82.
22. Ibid., 136.
23. Ibid., 116.
24. Ibid., 109.
25. Schwinn realizes that she and Diehl, the other surviving nurse, were not on any "list" at the end of their captivity. "The peace agreement had stipulated that women were to be released first; yet Bernhard and I had not been freed. The Hanoi Hilton would soon be empty. Had Bernhard and I not been included on the prisoners' list?" (Schwinn and Diehl, *We Came to Help,* 248).
26. Ibid., 47.
27. Ibid., 40.
28. Ibid., 54.
29. Ibid., 67.
30. Ibid., 87.
31. Ibid.
32. Ibid., 126.
33. Daly and Bergman, *A Hero's Welcome,* 147.

9. THE USES OF DIFFERENCE

1. Webb, *On the Other Side,* 18.
2. Plumb and DeWerf, *i'm no hero,* 92.
3. See my discussion of the rhetoric used in the Eastern Pilots Association advertisement. Plumb points to the Communist rhetoric explicitly used by POWs to characterize at least one successful American capitalist, Frank Lorenzo (Plumb and DeWerf, *i'm no hero,* 14).
4. Ibid., 16–17.
5. Ibid., 93.
6. Ibid., 93–94.
7. Ibid., 104–105.
8. Ibid., 102.
9. Ibid., 113.
10. Ibid., 117.
11. Ibid.
12. "The MacNeil Lehrer Newshour" broadcast on 21 January 1991 featured Plumb as one of four "experts" discussing the POW situation in Iraq.

13. Mulligan, *The Hanoi Commitment,* 21.

14. Ibid., 22.

15. Ibid., 229.

16. Webb, *On the Other Side,* 26–27.

17. I use this term, borrowed from Joseph Campbell, in order to foreshadow my later arguments, which will show how the male-officer-pilot narrative compels us to repeat the ordeal of the POW (see chapter 10).

18. Risner, *The Passing of the Night,* 30.

19. Ibid., 17.

20. Webb, *On the Other Side,* 44.

21. Stockdale, *In Love and War,* 112.

22. Ben and Anne Purcell, *Love and Duty* (New York: St. Martin's Press, 1992), 222.

23. G. Smith, *P.O.W.,* 270.

24. Ibid., 270–271.

25. Ibid., 271.

26. Brace, *A Code to Keep,* 247.

27. Michel Foucault examines the similarities between the prison and the military in his work, *Discipline and Punish.* The comparison is also implicit in Scarry, *The Body in Pain.*

28. Daly and Bergman, *A Hero's Welcome,* 14.

29. Ibid., 15.

30. Ibid., 140.

31. Ibid., 65.

32. Ibid., 165.

33. Ibid., 145.

34. Ibid., 147.

35. Ibid., 190.

36. Ibid., 15.

37. Fred V. Cherry, "Fighter Pilot," in Wallace Terry, *Bloods* (New York: Random House, 1984), 291.

38. Daly and Bergman, *A Hero's Welcome,* 211.

39. Schwinn and Diehl, *We Came to Help,* 214.

40. Webb, *On the Other Side,* 44.

41. Schwinn, *We Came to Help,* 215.

42. A similar but perhaps more aggressive statement occurs in Daly's narrative. Daly reflects the same realization that reciprocity is at the heart of the struggle (Daly and Bergman, *A Hero's Welcome,* 15).

43. Alvarez with Schreiner, *Code of Conduct,* 223–225.

10. STOP MAKING SENSE

For the title of this chapter I have borrowed the Talking Heads' album title, *Stop Making Sense.* The title suggests what I would have us do with the POW experience.

1. John Hellmann, *American Myth and the Legacy of Vietnam* (New York: Columbia University Press, 1986), 182.

2. Jensen, *Six Years in Hell,* xi.

3. Ibid., xi.

4. Hellmann, *American Myth,* ix–x.

5. Young, *Writing and Rewriting the Holocaust,* 36.

6. Risner, *The Passing of the Night,* v.

7. E. McDaniel and Johnson, *Before Honor,* 39.

8. Michel Foucault coined this term. He defines it this way: "Technologies of self . . . permit individuals to effect by their own means or with the help of others a certain number of operations on their own bodies and souls, thoughts, conduct, and way of being, so as to transform themselves in order to attain a certain state of happiness, purity, wisdom, perfection, or immortality" (*Technologies of Self,* ed. Luther H. Martin, Huck Gutman, and Patrick Hutton [Amherst: University of Massachusetts Press, 1988], 18).

9. Young, *Writing and Rewriting the Holocaust,* 37.

10. In his critique of Mendel Mann, Young writes: "He fears the Derridean suggestion that 'things come into existence and lose existence by being named,' but he finds solace in the Hegelian corollary that there is 'simultaneous sacrifice of existence to the word and consecration of existence by the word' " (Ibid., 38).

11. Although Smith does eventually conclude that there is a certain pleasure in denial ("You could never appreciate it unless it had been denied you") and subscribe to the Lazarus-like figuration of rebirth ("It was like the end of one life and the beginning of another"), he also concludes that his entire experience was more like *Catch-22* than a heroic epic (G. Smith, *P.O.W.,* 275 and 279).

12. Mulligan, *The Hanoi Commitment,* 279.

13. Tom Wolfe, "The Right Stuff," in *In Depth: Essayists for our Time,* ed. Chris Anderson, Rebecca Faery, and Carl Klaus (New York: Harcourt Brace Jovanovich, 1990), 779.

14. I am troping on the title of Russell Reising's *The Unusable Past: Theory and the Study of American Literature* (New York: Methuen, 1986).

15. Ironically, the North Vietnamese prophetically suggested this political imperative for the Nixon administration when they assured James Daly, while

he was still in captivity, that he would not be prosecuted for cooperating after release. "Nixon is using the POWs to gain support. . . . None of you will be put into prison" (Daly and Bergman, *A Hero's Welcome,* 235). Donald Duncan makes this issue clear in the "Introduction" he writes to George Smith's *P.O.W.:* "The Nixon administration persists in offering the issue of the POWs as a justification for continuing the war. Hysterical charges of torture and cruelty are still being voiced to excuse the latest decision to prolong the war, to stall the Paris talks another week, month or year; and the grief of separated families is still being exploited to renew the old stereotype of the inhuman enemy" (15).

16. Braudy, *The Frenzy of Renown,* 598.

17. This is the title of Ralph Gaither's autobiographical account of his POW experience.

18. Mulligan, *The Hanoi Commitment,* 9.

19. Ibid., 37.

20. Ibid., 48.

21. Ibid., 292. Norman A. McDaniel in his autobiography, *Yet Another Voice* titles chapter 3 "Resurrection."

22. Risner, *The Passing of the Night,* 27.

23. Ibid., 67.

24. Ibid., 103.

25. Ibid., 103.

26. Ibid., 172.

27. E. McDaniel and Johnson, *Before Honor,* 30.

28. Ibid., 173.

29. Ibid., 114.

30. Ibid., 120.

31. Larry Chesley, *Seven Years in Hell: A POW Tells His Story* (Salt Lake City: Bookcraft, 1973), 21.

32. Ibid., 155–158.

33. Ibid., 82.

34. Linda Dittmar and Gene Michaud, eds., *From Hanoi to Hollywood: The Vietnam War in American Film* (New Brunswick, N.J.: Rutgers University Press, 1990), 10.

35. Brace, *A Code to Keep,* 51.

36. Ibid., 6.

37. Ibid., 54.

38. Ibid., 147. On the same page he says, "I felt like praying, but months before I had rationalized that God hadn't put me here and God wasn't going to get me out." Brace reiterates this conviction throughout his text: "I was

convinced, now more than ever, that no one was going to extract me from my misery but myself" (150).

39. Ibid., 175.

40. Brace's captivity ends up as a positive experience: "Citing my behavior in the prison camps, President Gerald Ford granted me full and unconditional pardon for my Marine court-martial conviction, and I received an honorable discharge. It was quietly done, unlike my ouster from the Marines, which had led to trumpeting headlines about the war hero tossed out of the Corps. But for me, the return of my self-respect was a triumph" (Ibid., 258).

41. McGrath, *Prisoner of War,* ix.

42. Scarry, *The Body in Pain,* 16.

43. McGrath, *Prisoner of War,* 108–109.

44. Ibid., viii.

45. Stockdale, *In Love and War,* 450.

46. Gerald Coffee, *Beyond Survival: Building on the Hard Times—a POW's Inspiring Story* (New York: G. P. Putnam's Sons, 1990), 285.

47. Ibid., 280.

48. Fred Cherry, "Fighter Pilot," 285–286.

49. Scarry, *The Body in Pain,* 39.

50. Cherry, "Fighter Pilot," 291.

51. Ibid., 300.

52. Dramesi, *Code of Honor,* 258.

53. Ibid., 271.

54. Young, *Writing and Rewriting the Holocaust,* vii.

11. THE CONSEQUENCES OF MYTH

1. Mark Crispin Miller, *Boxed In* (Evanston, Ill.: Northwestern University Press, 1988), 329.

2. Alvarez with Schreiner, *Code of Conduct,* 200.

3. Ibid., 200.

4. Ibid., 26.

5. Ibid., 168–169.

6. Ibid., 200.

7. James Young in his extensive work on Holocaust narratives eventually realized that "none of us coming to the Holocaust afterwards can know these events outside the ways they are passed down to us." The same is true of the story of the American POW experience of the Vietnam war (*Writing and Rewriting the Holocaust,* vii).

8. Johnson, *Captive Warriors*, 138.

9. Young discusses the consequences of such testimony in detail in his first chapter. "For even though a survivor's testimony is 'privileged' insofar as it is authentic, the factuality of his literary testimony is not necessarily so privileged" (*Writing and Rewriting the Holocaust*, 22). As Young later points out, the pretended "factuality" of narrative eventually displaces the facts themselves.

10. Richard Slotkin begins his study of myth and narrative in early American literature by pointing out the dangers of myth. He quite rightly challenges us to avoid the "failure of writers and critics to recognize and deal with the real mythological heritage of their time." Slotkin sees "that myths reach out of the past to cripple, incapacitate, or stike down the living." His history explains the situation that allowed prevailing cultural myths to overcome the "antimythologists" of the "rational republic" in early America when the "Jeffersonian republic was overcome by the Jacksonian Democracy of the western man-on-the-make . . . when racist irrationalism and a falsely conceived economics prolonged and intensified slavery in the teeth of American democratic idealism; and when men like Davy Crockett became national heroes by defining national aspiration in terms of so many bears destroyed, so much land preempted, so many trees hacked down, so many Indians and Mexicans dead in the dust." It should come as no surprise that Slotkin's comments, written in the early 1970s, are at once historical and prophetic. The previous passage might easily stand for the Reagan U.S. of the 1980s, with its free-market ideology, veneer morality, and imperialist assumptions about its role in world affairs. It is in this political climate that the POW myth found its home. See Slotkin, *Regeneration*, 4–5.

11. Slotkin alludes to such effects: "But mythological narrative does not admit a multiplicity of perspectives, and is not arranged to encourage questions—as a modern work of fiction or history does—about the values that shape history" (in "Myth and the Production of History," *Ideology and Classic American Literature*, ed. Bercovitch and Jehlen, 83).

12. Here I am talking about the Sylvester Stallone/Chuck Norris genre of POW rescue films, as well as the whole ensemble of resurgent superheroes from Superman to Teenage Mutant Ninja Turtles. For critiques of these figures see Susan Jeffords, *The Remasculinization of America: Gender and the Vietnam War* (Indianopolis: Indiana University Press, 1989), or Thomas Andrae, "From Menace to Messiah: The History and Historicity of Superman," in *American Media and Mass Culture*, ed. Lazere.

13. Young, *Writing and Rewriting the Holocaust*, 62.

14. I have borrowed this examination of the "rhetoric of fact" from Young's

chapter entitled "Documentary Theater, Ideology, and the Rhetoric of Fact" (Ibid., 79).

15. Ibid., 84.

16. Ray, *The Two Shores of Hell*, 213.

17. George Smith wrote and published his book about the POW experience while James Daly remained in captivity. Apparently the North Vietnamese felt Smith's text was a good representation of the captivity story; they gave Daly a copy of it. I say this partly because my study otherwise ignores texts that give the perspective of the Vietnamese. See Daly, *A Hero's Welcome*, 211.

18. Malcolm McConnell, *Into the Mouth of the Cat: The Story of Lance Sijan, Hero of Vietnam* (New York: Signet, 1985), 247.

19. Stephen Greenblatt, "Culture," in *Critical Terms for Literary Study*. ed. Frank Lentricchia and Thomas McLaughlin (Chicago: University of Chicago Press, 1990), 229.

20. E. McDaniel and Johnson, *Before Honor*, 63. John Dramesi describes his struggle in very similar terms: "I could think of only three principal reasons why the North Vietnamese tortured: initially to extract military information; to achieve a propaganda gain, a "confession," or a tape recording; and to strip us of our individuality, our self-respect, our American identity, to break the American spirit" (*Code of Honor*, 83).

21. E. McDaniel and Johnson, *Before Honor*, 112. Dramesi and Brace echo McDaniel on this point: "Resistance was the essence of our existence" (*Code of Honor*, 187). "If I stopped resisting and accepted the conditions of my confinement, I would never survive" (*A Code to Keep*, 122).

22. D. McDaniel, *After the Hero's Welcome*, 194.

23. Ibid., 191.

24. Ibid., 153.

25. Ibid., 106.

26. Fred Cherry, "Fighter Pilot," 300.

27. Here I am referring to deaths due to torture, neglect, and suicide. Suicide itself was viewed as one way of dealing with the captivity experience. Some attempted this form of escape, which, as Foucault tells us, is the ultimate act of resistance in that it attempts to "usurp the power of death" from the captor (*The History of Sexuality*, 138).

28. E. McDaniel and Johnson, *Before Honor*, 173.

29. This process is nothing new in the history of the American captivity myth. Richard Slotkin warns about the consequences of accepting myth uncritically: "A people unaware of its myths is likely to continue living by them, though the world around that people may change and demand changes in their psychology" (*Regeneration*, 5).

30. Biderman, *March to Calumny,* 190.

31. Rick Berg, "Losing Vietnam," in Dittmar and Michaud, eds., *From Hanoi to Hollywood,* 65

32. See my discussion of pre-Vietnam captivity myths as discussed by the POWs themselves, chapter 6.

33. Risner, *The Passing of the Night,* vi–vii.

34. One dated but nevertheless relevant study of the "dragon" figure occurs in G. Elliot Smith, *The Evolution of the Dragon* (New York: Longmans, Green, 1919).

35. Jensen, *Six Years in Hell,* xi.

36. Malcolm McConnell, who pieced together the story of Lance Sijan in *Into the Mouth of the Cat,* ironically chastises antiwar activists Jane Fonda and Tom Hayden for becoming "born again capitalists, beneficiaries of America's short memory and overdeveloped popular culture industry" (283). In hindsight it is ironic that some POWs seem to be the ones nibbling at the fringes of the "overdeveloped popular culture industry" at the expense of their own terrible experience, long after Hayden and Fonda have apologized for any suffering they caused American POWs.

37. An example of such a claim comes from Dramesi, *Code of Honor:* "Others before him had accepted certain privileges and had fulfilled the requirements demanded by their captors, but by refusing to abandon his ideals, principles, and strengths John McCain had retained his identity" (203).

38. Richard Slotkin explains one motivation for this game: "The language of the Cowboy and Indians 'game' was one way to get a handle on experiences too terrible, too upsetting to be morally acceptable" ("Myth and the Production of History," 71).

12. THE HISTORY OF THE PRESENT

1. Gaither, *With God in a P.O.W. Camp,* 72–73.

2. Here I borrow a phrase from Morgot Norris, "Military Censorship and the Body Count in the Persian Gulf War," *Cultural Critique* 19 (Fall 1991): 230.

3. Ibid., 223.

4. Sijan's story has appeared in numerous publications as recently 1992. Sijan received the Congressional Medal of Honor posthumously for his efforts. Malcolm McConnell has reconstructed an extensive account of Sijan's experience in *Into the Mouth of the Cat.*

5. See the *New York Times,* 4 May 1992, C18.

6. John Shelton Lawrence, "The Captive Presidency," unpublished article, 1988.

7. "Transcript of World Airlines Hijacking Incident," *Weekly Compilation of Presidential Documents*, 21, no. 27 (2 July 1985): 286.

8. Terry Anderson, "Loved ones more important than anything," *Middletown Sunday Record*, 15 March 1992, 77.

9. Simon, *Forty Days*, 151–152.

10. Ibid., 24.

11. Ibid., 21.

12. Ibid., 35, 43.

13. Ibid., 45.

14. Ibid., 119.

15. Ibid., 121.

16. Ibid., 264–265.

17. Ibid., 121.

18. Ibid., 9.

19. Ibid., 78.

20. Ibid., 53.

21. Ibid., 249.

22. Johnson, *Captive Warriors*, 8.

Bibliography and Filmography

AUTOBIOGRAPHICAL ACCOUNTS OF VIETNAM CAPTIVITY

Alvarez, Everett, Jr., and Anthony S. Pitch. *Chained Eagle.* New York: Donald Fine, 1989.

Alvarez, Everett, Jr., with Samuel A. Schreiner, Jr. *Code of Conduct.* New York: Donald Fine, 1991.

Brace, Ernest C. *A Code to Keep.* New York: St. Martin's Press, 1988.

Cherry, Fred V. "Fighter Pilot." In *Bloods,* compiled by Wallace Terry. New York: Random House, 1984.

Chesley, Larry. *Seven Years in Hanoi: A POW Tells His Story.* Salt Lake City: Bookcraft, 1973.

Coffee, Gerald. *Beyond Survival: Building on the Hard Times—A POW's Inspiring Story.* New York: G. P. Putnam's Sons, 1990.

———. *Beyond Survival, The Next Chapter.* Audiotape. Chicago, Illinois: Nightingale-Conant Audio, 1990.

Daly, James, and Lee Bergman. *A Hero's Welcome.* Indianapolis: Bobbs-Merrill, 1975.

Dengler, Dieter. *Escape from Laos.* San Rafael, Calif.: Presidio Press, 1979.

Denton, Jeremiah, and Ed Brandt. *When Hell Was in Session.* Clover, S.C.: Commission Press, 1976.

Dramesi, John. *Code of Honor.* New York: W. W. Norton, 1975.

Dudman, Richard. *forty days with the enemy.* New York: Liveright, 1971.

Gaither, Ralph, as told to Steve Henry. *With God in a P.O.W. Camp.* Nashville, Tenn.: Broadman Press, 1973.

Guarino, Larry. *A P.O.W.'s Story: 2801 Days in Hanoi.* New York: Ivy Books, 1990.

Heslop, J. M., and Dell R. Van Orden. *From the Shadow of Death.* Salt Lake City: Deseret Book Company, 1973.

Jensen, Jay R. *Six Years in Hell.* 1974. Reprint. Orcutt, Calif.: Publications of Worth, 1989.

Johnson, Sam, and Jan Winebrenner. *Captive Warriors: A Vietnam POW's Story.* College Station, Tex.: Texas A&M University Press, 1992.

Lawrence, William. "POW." In *Everything We Had,* compiled by Al Santoli. New York: Ballantine Books, 1981.

McDaniel, Eugene, and James L. Johnson. *Before Honor: One Man's Spiritual Journey through the Darkness of a Communist Prison.* New York: A. J. Holman, 1975.

McDaniel, Norman A. *Yet Another Voice.* New York: Hawthorn Books, 1975.

McGrath, John M. *Prisoner of War: Six Years in Hanoi.* Annapolis: Naval Institute Press, 1975.

Miller, Carolyn Paine. *Captured!.* New York: Christian Herald Books, 1977.

Mulligan, James A. *The Hanoi Commitment.* Virginia Beach, Va.: RIF Marketing, 1981.

Nasmyth, Spike. *2355 Days: A POW's Story.* New York: Orion, 1991.

Plumb, Charlie, and Glen H. DeWerf. *i'm no hero.* Independence, Mo.: Independence Press, 1973.

Purcell, Ben and Anne. *Love and Duty.* New York: St. Martin's Press, 1992.

Ray, Michele. *The Two Shores of Hell.* Trans. Elisabeth Abbott. New York: David McKay, 1968.

Risner, Colonel Robinson. *The Passing of the Night: My Seven Years as a Prisoner of the North Vietnamese.* New York: Ballantine, 1975.

Rowe, James N. *Five Years to Freedom.* 1971. New York: Ballantine, 1984.

Rutledge, Howard and Phyllis, with Mel and Lyla White. *In the Presence of Mine Enemies.* Old Tappan, N.J.: Fleming H. Revell, 1973.

Schwinn, Monika, and Bernhard Diehl. *We Came to Help.* Trans. Jan van Heurck. New York: Harcourt Brace Jovanovich, 1973.

Smith, George. *P.O.W.: Two Years with the Vietcong.* Berkeley, Calif.: Ramparts Press, 1971.

Smith, Philip E., and Peggy Herz. *Journey Into Darkness.* New York: Pocket Books, 1992.

Stockdale, Jim and Sybil. *In Love and War.* New York: Bantam Books, 1985.

Webb, Kate. *On the Other Side: 23 Days with the Viet Cong.* New York: Quadrangle Books, 1972.

SECONDARY SOURCES AND FICTION ABOUT THE VIETNAM POWS

Blakey Scott. *Prisoner at War: The Survival of Commander Richard R. Stratton.* New York: Penguin, 1979.

Carpenter, William Lee. "A Literature Survey of Selected Aspects of the Psychological Reactions to the Stresses of Imprisonment and Repatriation Upon United States' Vietnam Prisoners of War." Master's thesis, Montana State University, 1973.

Clarke, Douglas. *The Missing Man: Politics and the MIA*. Washington, D.C.: National Defense University, 1979.

Colvin, Rod. *First Heroes: The POWs Left Behind in Vietnam*. New York: Irvington, 1987.

Doan Van Toai, and David Chanoff. *The Vietnamese Gulag*. Trans. Françoise Simon-Miller. New York: Simon and Schuster, 1986.

Dunn, Joe P. "The POW Chronicles: A Bibliographic Review." *Armed Forces and Society* 9 (Spring 1983): 495–514.

———. "The Vietnam War POW/MIAs: An Annotated Bibliography." *Bulletin of Bibliography* 45 (2 June 1988): 152–157.

Franklin, H. Bruce. *M.I.A. or Mythmaking in America*. Brooklyn, N.Y.: Lawrence Hill Books.

Garrett, Richard. *P.O.W.: The Uncivil Face of War*. Wiltshire, Great Britain: David & Charles, 1981.

Grant, Zalin. *Survivors: American POWs in Vietnam*. New York: Berkley Books, 1975.

Groom, Winston, and Duncan Spencer. *Conversations with the Enemy: The Controversial Story of Vietnam P.O.W. Bobby Garwood*. New York: Putnam, 1983.

Hubbell, John G. *P.O.W.: A Definitive History of the American Prisoner-of-War Experience in Vietnam, 1964–1973*. New York: Reader's Digest Press, 1976.

Kim, Samuel. *The American POWs*. Boston: Branden, 1979.

Kimball, William R. *Vietnam: The Other Side of Glory*. New York: Ballantine, 1987.

McConnell, Malcolm. *Into the Mouth of the Cat: The Story of Lance Sijan, Hero of Vietnam*. New York: Signet, 1985.

McDaniel, Dorothy. *After the Hero's Welcome: A POW Wife's Story of the Battle Against a New Enemy*. New York: Bonus Books, 1991.

Norman, Geoffrey. *Bouncing Back: How a Heroic Band of POWs Survived Vietnam*. Boston: Houghton Mifflin, 1990.

Patterson, Charles J., and G. Lee Tippin. *The Heroes Who Fell from Grace*. Canton, Ohio: Daring Books, 1985.

Rowan, Stephen. *They Wouldn't Let Us Die*. New York: Jonathan David, 1973.

Schemmer, Benjamin F. *The Raid*. New York: Harper & Row, 1976.

Wyatt, Barbara Powers, ed. *We Came Home*. Toluca Lake, Calif.: P.O.W. Publications, 1977.

SOURCES ON THE POW EXPERIENCE IN OTHER WARS

Biderman, Albert D. *March to Calumny: The Story of American POW's in the Korean War.* New York: Macmillan, 1963.

Brown, Wallace. *The Endless Hours: My Two and a Half Years as a Prisoner of the Chinese Communists.* New York: Norton, 1961.

Cornum, Rhonda, as told to Peter Copeland. *She Went to War: The Rhonda Cornum Story.* Novato, Calif.: Presidio, 1992.

Deane, Philip [Philippe Deane Gigantes]. *I Should Have Died.* New York: Atheneum, 1977.

Dennett, Carl P. *Prisoners of the Great War: Authoritative Statement of Conditions in the Prison Camps of Germany.* New York: Houghton Mifflin, 1919.

Hatch, Gardner, ed. *The American Ex-Prisoners of War.* Paducah, Ky.: Turner Publishing Company, 1988.

Keith, Agnes Newton. *Three Came Home.* Boston: Little, Brown, 1947.

Kenny, Catherine. *Captives: Australian Army Nurses in Japanese Prison Camps.* St. Lucia, Australia: University of Queensland Press, 1986.

Kinkead, Eugene. *In Every War But One.* New York: W. W. Norton, 1959.

Knightly, Phillip. *The First Casualty.* New York: Harcourt Brace Jovanovich, 1975.

Millar, Ward M. *Valley of the Shadow.* New York: David McKay, 1955.

Simon, Bob. *Forty Days.* New York: G. P. Putnam's Sons, 1992.

Snyder, Don J. *A Soldier's Disgrace.* Dublin, N.H.: Yankee Books, 1987.

White, William Lindsay. *The Captives of Korea: An Unofficial White Paper on the Treatment of War Prisoners.* New York: Charles Scribner's Sons, 1957.

CRITICISM AND THEORY

Adair, Albert. *Vietnam on Film: From the Green Berets to Apocalypse Now.* New York: Proteus, 1981.

Altieri, Charles. *Canons and Consequences: Reflections on the Ethical Force of Imaginative Ideas.* Evanston, Ill.: Northwestern University Press, 1990.

Beidler, Phil. "Bad Business: Vietnam and Recent Mass-Market Fiction." *College English* 54, no. 1 (January 1992) 64–75.

Bercovitch, Sacvan, and Myra Jehlen, eds. *Ideology and Classic American Literature.* New York: Cambridge University Press, 1986.

Boorstin, Daniel J. *The Image: or What Happened to the American Dream.* New York: Kingsport Press, 1962.

Braudy, Leo. *The Frenzy of Renown: Fame and Its History*. New York: Oxford University Press, 1986.

Campbell, Joseph, with Bill Moyers. *The Power of Myth*. Edited by Betty Sue Flowers. New York: Doubleday, 1988.

Christianson, Keith Scott. "The American Experience of Imprisonment, 1607–1776." Ph.D. dissertation, State University of New York at Albany, 1981.

Clifford, James, and George E. Marcus, eds. *Writing Culture: The Poetics and Politics of Ethnography*. Berkeley: University of California Press, 1986.

Colabro, John. "Stories of War and the End of Warfare." *Transaktie* 20, no. 3 (1991) 205.

Dittmar, Linda, and Gene Michaud, eds. *From Hanoi to Hollywood: The Vietnam War in American Film*. New Brunswick, N.J.: Rutgers University Press, 1990.

Foster, Hall, ed. *The Anti-Aesthetic: Essays on Postmodern Culture*. Port Townsend, Wash.: Bay Press, 1983.

Foucault, Michel. *Discipline and Punish: The Birth of the Prison*. Trans. Alan Sheridan. New York: Vintage Books, 1977.

———. *The History of Sexuality, Volume 1*. Trans. Robert Hurley. New York: Random House, 1978.

———. *Power/Knowledge: Selected Interviews & Other Writings, 1972–1977*. Edited by Colin Gordon. New York: Pantheon, 1980.

Freud, Sigmund. *Beyond the Pleasure Principle*. Trans. and edited by James Strachey. New York: W. W. Norton, 1961.

Franklin, H. Bruce. *Prison Literature in America: The Victim as Criminal and Artist*. New York: Oxford University Press, 1978.

Garland, Brock. *War Movies*. New York: Facts on File, 1987.

Gates, Henry Louis, Jr. *Figures in Black: Words, Signs, and the "Racial" Self*. New York: Oxford University Press, 1987.

Hellmann, John. *American Myth and the Legacy of Vietnam*. New York: Columbia University Press, 1986.

Jeffords, Susan. *The Remasculinization of America: Gender and the Vietnam War*. Bloomington and Indianapolis: Indiana University Press, 1989.

Kaplan, E. Ann, ed. *Postmodernism and Its Discontents: Theories, Practices*. New York: Verso, 1988.

Krystal, Henry. *Massive Psychic Trauma*. New York: International Universities Press, 1968.

Lazere, Donald, ed. *American Media and Mass Culture: Left Perspectives*. Berkeley: University of California Press, 1987.

Lejeune, Philippe. *On Autobiography.* Trans. Katherine Leary. Minneapolis: University of Minnesota Press, 1989.

Martin, Luther H., Huck Gutman, and Patrick H. Hutton, eds. *Technologies of the Self: A Seminar with Michel Foucault.* Amherst: University of Massachusetts Press, 1988.

Meyers, William. *The Image Makers: Power and Persuasion on Madison Avenue.* New York: New York Times Books, 1972.

Michaels, Walter Benn. *The Gold Standard and the Logic of Naturalism.* Berkeley: University of California Press, 1987.

Miller, Mark Crispin. *Boxed In: The Culture of TV.* Evanston, Ill.: Northwestern University Press, 1988.

Norris, Margot. "Military Censorship and the Body Count in the Persian Gulf War." *Cultural Critique* 19 (Fall 1991): 223–245.

Olney, James, ed. *Autobiography: Essays Theoretical and Critical.* Princeton: Princeton University Press, 1980.

Pease, Donald. *Visionary Compacts: American Renaissance Writings in Cultural Contexts.* Madison, Wis.: University of Wisconsin Press, 1987.

Pfeil, Fred. *Another Tale to Tell: Politics and Narrative in Postmodern Culture.* New York: Verso, 1990.

Porter, Carolyn. *Seeing and Being: The Plight of the Participant Observer in Emerson, James, Adams, and Faulkner.* Middletown, Conn.: Wesleyan University Press, 1981.

Reising, Russell. *The Unusable Past: Theory and the Study of American Literature.* New York: Methuen, 1986.

Rogin, Michael Paul. *Ronald Reagan, the Movie and Other Episodes in Political Demonology.* Berkeley: University of California Press, 1989.

Rowe, John Carlos. "From Documentary to Docudrama: Vietnam on Television in the 1980's." *Genre* 21, no. 4 (Winter 1988): 451–477.

Scarry, Elaine. *The Body in Pain: The Making and Unmaking of the World.* New York: Oxford University Press, 1985.

Sieminski, Greg. "The Puritan Captivity Narrative and the Politics of the American Revolution." *American Quarterly* 42 (March 1990): 35–56.

Slotkin, Richard. *Regeneration Through Violence: The Mythology of the American Frontier, 1600–1860.* Middletown, Conn.: Wesleyan University Press, 1973.

Smith, Julian. *Looking Away: Hollywood and Vietnam.* New York: Scribner's, 1975.

Taylor, Gordon O. "American Personal Narratives of the War in Vietnam." *American Literature* 52, no. 2 (May 1980): 294–308.

Wolfe, Tom. "The Right Stuff." In *In Depth: Essayists for our Time,* edited by

Chris Anderson, Rebecca Faery, and Karl Klaus. New York: Harcourt Brace Jovanovich, 1990.

Young, James E. *Writing and Rewriting the Holocaust: Narrative and the Consequences of Interpretation.* Bloomington and Indianapolis: Indiana University Press, 1988.

PRISONER-OF-WAR FILMOGRAPHY

American Commandos. Dir. Bobby A. Suarez. With Christopher Mitchum. Speigelman, 1985.

The Bamboo Prison (a.k.a. *I Was A Prisoner in Korea*). Dir. Bryan Foy. With Robert Francis and Dianne Foster. Columbia, 1954.

Behind Enemy Lines. Dir. Cirio H. Santiago. With Robert Patrick and William Steis. Eastern Film, 1988.

Bimbo: Hot Blood. Dir. J. Angel Martini. With Barbie Dahl and Linda Chu. Red Light, 1985.

Black Sunday. Dir. John Frankenheimer. With Bruce Dern and Marthe Keller. Paramount, 1977.

The Bridge on the River Kwai. Dir. David Lean. With William Holden and Alec Guinness. Great Britain, 1957.

Brushfire. Dir. Jack Warner, Jr. With John Ireland and Everett Sloane. Paramount, 1962.

The Camp on Blood Island. Dir. Val Guest. With Andre Morell and Edward Underdown. Hammer, 1958.

The Captive Heart. Dir. Basil Dearden. With Michael Redgrave and Basil Radford. Great Britain, 1946.

The Clay Pigeon. Dir. Richard Fleischer. With Bill Williams and Barbara Hale. RKO, 1949.

The Colditz Story. Dir. Guy Hamilton. With John Mills and Eric Portman. Great Britain, 1957.

Covert Action. Dir. J. Christian Ingvordson. With Rick Washburn and John Christian. Cinema Sciences, 1988.

The Deer Hunter. Dir. Michael Cimino. With Robert DeNiro and Christopher Walken. Universal, 1978.

Dog Tags. Dir. Romano Scavolini. With Clive Wood and Mike Monty. Cinevast (British Television), 1985.

Empire of the Sun. Dir. Steven Speilberg. With Christian Bale and John Malkovich. Universal, 1987.

Escape to Athena. Dir. George Pan Cosmatos. With Roger Moore and David Niven. Great Britain, 1979.

Fireback. Dir. Teddy Page. With Richard Harrison and Bruce Baron. Silver Star, 1986.

The Firing Line. Dir. John Gale. With Reb Brown and Shannon Tweed. Silver Star, 1991.

First Yank into Tokyo. Dir. Gordon Douglas. With Tom Neal and Barbara Hale. RKO, 1945.

Five Gates to Hell. Dir. James Clavell. With Neville Brand and Delores Michaels. Twentieth Century-Fox, 1959.

The Forgotten. Dir. James Keach. With Keith Carradine and Stacy Keach. Wilshire Court, 1989.

Grand Illusion. Dir. Jean Renoir. With Jean Gabin and Erich von Stroheim, France, 1937.

The Great Escape. Dir. John Sturges. With James Garner and Steve McQueen. United Artists, 1963.

The Hanoi Hilton. Dir. Lionel Chetwynd. With Michael Moriarty and Jeffrey Jones. Cannon, 1987.

High Velocity. Dir. Remi Kramer. With Ben Gazzara and Paul Winfield. First Asia Films, 1977.

The Hook. Dir. George Seaton. With Kirk Douglas and Robert Walker. MGM, 1963.

House. Dir. Steve Miner. With William Katt and George Wendt. New World, 1985.

House of 1000 Women (a.k.a. *2000 Women*). With Phyllis Calvert. 1944.

In Love and War. Dir. Paul Aaron. With James Woods and Jane Alexander. ABC, 1987.

Intimate Strangers. Dir. Robert Ellis Miller. With Teri Garr and Stacy Keach. Nederlander TV and CBS, 1986.

The Iron Triangle. Dir. Eric Weston. With Beau Bridges and Liem Whatley. Scotti Brothers, 1988.

Kill Zone. Dir. David A. Prior. With Fritz Matthews and Ted Prior. Spartan Films, 1985.

King Rat. Dir. Bryan Forbes. With George Segal and Tom Courtenay. Columbia, 1965.

Limbo. Dir. Mark Robson. With Kate Jackson and Kathleen Nolan. Universal, 1972.

The Long Journey Home. Dir. Rod Holcomb. With Meredith Baxter Birney and David Birney. Lorimar, 1987.

The Losers. Dir. Jack Starret. With William Smith and Bernie Hamilton. Fanfare, 1970.

McBain. Dir. James Glickenhaus. With Christopher Walken and Maria Conchita Alonso. Shapiro-Glickenhaus Entertainment, 1991.

The McKenzie Break. Dir. Lamont Johnson. With Brian Keith and Helmut Griem. United Artists, 1970.

Merry Christmas, Mr. Lawrence. Dir. Nagisa Oskima. With David Bowie and Tom Conti. Universal, 1983.

Missing in Action. Dir. Joseph Zito. With Chuck Norris and M. Emmet Walsh. Cannon, 1984.

Missing in Action 2: The Beginning. Dir. Lance Hool. With Chuck Norris and Steven Williams. Cannon, 1985.

Nighforce. Dir. Lawrence D. Folds. With Linda Blair and Richard Lynch. Vestron, 1986.

Night Wars. Dir. David A. Prior. With Brian O'Connor and Dan Haggerty. Action International Pictures, 1982.

No Dead Heroes. Dir. J. C. Miller. With John Dresden and Max Thayer. Cineventures, 1987.

Operation Nam. Dir. Larry Ludman. With Oliver Tobias and Christopher Conelly. Fulvia International, 1987.

Opposing Force. Dir. Eric Karson. With Tom Skerritt and Lisa Eichhorn. Orion Pictures, 1986.

The P.O.W. Dir. Philip H. Dossick. With Howard Jahre. Dossick, 1973.

POW Deathcamp. Dir. Jett C. Espirtu. With Charles Black and Bill Balbridge. Atlas Entertainment, 1989.

P.O.W.: The Escape. Dir. Gideon Amir. With David Carradine and Charles R. Floyd. Cannon, 1986.

Prisoner of War. Dir. Andrew Marton. With Ronald Reagan and Steve Forrest. MGM, 1954.

Prisoners of the Sun. Dir. Stephen Wallace. With Bryan Brown and George Takei. Skouras, 1991.

Prison Ship. Dir. Arthur Dreifuss. With Nina Foch and Robert Lowery. Columbia, 1945.

Private War. Dir. Frank DePalma. With Martin Hewitt and Joe Dallesandro. Smart Egg Pictures, 1988.

The Purple Heart. Dir. Lewis Milestone. With Dana Andrews and Richard Conte. Twentieth Century-Fox, 1944.

The Rack. Dir. Arnold Laven. With Paul Newman and Wendell Corey. MGM, 1956.

Rambo: First Blood Part II. Dir. George P. Cosmatos. With Sylvester Stallone and Richard Crenna. Tri-Star, 1985.

Ramb-ohh: The Force Is in You. Dir. Ron Vogel. With Peter North and Pauline Pepper. Sheer Essence, 1986.

The Red Spider. Dir. Jerry Jameson. With James Farentino and Amy Steel. CBS, 1988.

The Rescue. Dir. Ferdinand Fairfax. With Marc Price and Charles Haid. Touchstone, 1988.

Rolling Thunder. Dir. John Flynn. With William Devane and Tommy Lee Jones. American International, 1977.

Savage Justice. Dir. Joey Romero. With Julia Montgomery and Steven Memel. Eastern Film Management, 1987.

The Secret of Blood Island (a.k.a. *Prisoners of War*). Dir. Quentin Lawrence. With Barbara Shelley. Hammer, 1964.

The Secret War of Harry Frigg. Dir. Jack Smight. With Paul Newman and Sylva Koscina. Universal, 1968.

Seven Women from Hell. Dir. Robert Webb. With Patricia Owens and Denise Darcel. Twentieth Century-Fox, 1962.

Slaughterhouse Five. Dir. George Roy Hill. With Michael Sacks and Valerie Perrine. Univeral, 1972.

Some Kind of Hero. Dir. Michael Pressman. With Richard Pryor. Paramount, 1982.

Stalag 17. Dir. Billy Wilder. With William Holden and Don Taylor. Paramount, 1953.

Strike Commando. Dir. Vincent Dawn (Bruno Mattei). With Reb Brown and Chrisopher Connelly. Flora, 1987.

Three Came Home. Dir. Jean Negulesco. With Claudette Colbert and Florence Desmond. Twentieth Century-Fox, 1950.

Tiger Joe. Dir. Anthony M. Dawson. With David Warbeck. Flora, 1986.

Time Limit. Dir. Karl Malden. With Richard Widmark and Richard Basehart. United Artists, 1957.

Tornado. Dir. Anthony Dawson. With Timothy Brent. Gico, 1983.

Torpedo Run. Dir. Joseph Pirney. With Glenn Ford and Ernest Borgnine. MGM, 1958.

Uncommon Valor. Dir. Ted Kotcheff. With Gene Hackman and Fred Ward. Paramount, 1983.

Victory. Dir. John Huston. With Sylvester Stallone and Michael Caine. Paramount, 1981.

Von Ryan's Express. Dir. Mark Robson. With Frank Sinatra and Trevor Howard. Twentieth Century-Fox, 1965.

Welcome Home. Dir. Franklin J. Schaffner. With Kris Kristofferson and JoBeth Williams. Columbia, 1989.

Welcome Home, Johnny Bristol. Dir. George McGowan. With Martin Landau and Jane Alexander. CBS, 1972.

When Hell Was in Session. Dir. Paul Krasny. With Hal Holbrook and Eva Marie Saint. Aubrey-Hammer, 1979.

White Ghost. Dir. B. J. Davis. With William Katt and Wayne Crawford. Gibraltar, 1988.

The Wolf. Dir. Charlie Ordonez. With Ron Marchini. Romarc, 1986.

Women of Valor. Dir. Buzz Kulik. With Susan Sarandon and Kristy McNichol. CBS, 1986.

The Wooden Horse. Dir. Jack Lee. With Leo Genn and David Tomlinson. Great Britain, 1951.

A Yank in Indo-China (a.k.a. *Hidden Secret*). Dir. Wallace A. Grissell. With John Archer and Douglas Dick. Columbia, 1952.

A Yank in Viet-Nam (a.k.a. *Year of the Tiger*). Dir. Marshall Thompson. With Marshall Thompson and Enrique Magalona. United Artists, 1964.

Index

Page numbers for illustrations are in italics